EDDY JOKOVICH +
DAVID LEWIS

THE SHADOW OVER PALESTINE

AUSTRALIAN PERSPECTIVES OF THE GENOCIDE IN GAZA

The Shadow Over Palestine: Australian perspectives of the genocide in Gaza
ISBN (paperback): 978-1-7635701-5-3

December 2025.
Published by New Politics, an imprint of ARMEDIA Pty. Ltd.

New Politics
PO Box 1265, Darlinghurst NSW 1300
www.newpolitics.com.au
Email: info@newpolitics.com.au

Production: ARMEDIA

Published and produced on the lands of the Wangal and Gadigal people.

EDITORIAL NOTE ON THE USE OF AI TECHNOLOGY

We employ artificial intelligence tools in the editing process of our articles. These tools assisted with transcriptions of audio recordings, grammar correction, refinement and formatting.

A catalogue record for this work is available from the National Library of Australia

CONTENTS

CONCLUSION

ABOUT THE AUTHORS

EDDY JOKOVICH is editor of *New Politics*, and co-presenter of the New Politics Australia podcast. He has worked as a journalist, publisher, author, political analyst, campaigner, war correspondent, and lecturer in media studies at the University of Technology, Sydney and the University of Sydney; has a wide range of experience working in editorial and media production work and is Director of ARMEDIA, an independent publishing and communications company specialising in public interest media.

DAVID LEWIS is co-presenter of the New Politics Australia podcast, historian, musicologist, musician and political scientist based in Sydney. His lecturing and research interests include roots music, popular music, Australian, U.K. and U.S. politics and crime fiction. He has published in *Music Forum Australia*, *Eureka Street*, *Quadrant*, *Crikey* and has edited several books.

NEW POLITICS AUSTRALIA is a weekly podcast, providing analysis and opinions on Australian and international politics. It can be found at Apple and Google podcasts, Amazon Audible and Spotify. The articles contained here are based on the conversations, analysis and discussions from the podcast from October 2023 onwards, up until the end of 2025.

INTRODUCTION

THE AGE OF WITNESS AND DENIAL

Israel's assault on Gaza that commenced on 7 October 2023 wasn't a sudden eruption of violence but just another part of the continuum of occupation and dispossession of Palestinian people that began all the way back in 1948. This latest chapter of Israel's aggression might have been in response to the attack by Hamas that killed over a thousand Israelis but what has followed has been an unprecedented state-sanctioned brutality that has destroyed much of Gaza, killed tens of thousands of civilians and redefined what the word genocide means for a new generation of people. Over a two-year period, the Gaza Strip—an area that's just 365 square kilometres and was home for over two million Palestinians—has become the most heavily bombed and largest killing field on the planet.

Entire neighbourhoods, hospitals, universities, schools and refugee camps have been destroyed and reduced to rubble. The Israeli government, under Prime Minister Benjamin Netanyahu, might have commenced what he claims was a "war of self-defence," but many others around the world, including the United Nations, human rights groups and international legal experts, are increasingly describing Israel's actions as a campaign of collective punishment, ethnic cleansing and genocide.

Facing corruption charges and desperate to hold on to his fragile right-wing coalition, Netanyahu found his familiar political refuge of strength in the fog of war. Israeli intelligence had even received prior warnings of a possible Hamas attack, raising many questions about how—or whether—the tragedy was allowed to unfold for political advantage. While the attacks by Hamas were indefensible, Israel responded by implementing a genocide: within months, the death toll in Gaza had reached 30,000 and most of those were women and children. Israel deliberately targeted journalists, hospitals, aid convoys and food kitchens, in its inhumane campaign to quickly erase the existence of Palestinian life and culture in Gaza.

The global response revealed the moral fracturing and dysfunction of the international order: the United Nations voted overwhelmingly for a ceasefire, yet the United States, Israel and a handful of dependent allies—including Australia—refused to support it. Western leaders repeated the familiar phrase that "Israel has a right to defend itself," and news anchors would always preface their interviews with anyone remotely connected to the cause of Palestine with "but do you condemn Hamas", even as the evidence of Israel's war crimes were becoming more apparent. Humanitarian agencies such as UNRWA were crippled by funding cancellations, media outlets censored words such as "genocide" and "apartheid," and the information war and promotion of Israel's *hasbara* became as critical as the military one.

In Australia, the response reflected the broader Western pattern of political cowardice and media bias, with government and opposition leaders treating the crisis as another opportunity for partisan attack rather than moral leadership. Those who called for a ceasefire—such as Senator Fatima Payman, Labor's Ed Husic and many Greens MPs—were vilified and ridiculed. The Labor government's abstention at these early stages at the UN became a symbol of moral equivocation, revealing just how deeply Australian foreign policy remains tied to the agendas of the United States.

The brutal conflict in Gaza is also a war on truth and on those who want to hold power to account. Mainstream media outlets, shaped by decades of Israeli government "re-education" trips and the influence of the Zionist lobby, will mainly adopt and adapt Israeli government talking points. Yet there was an alternative system of independent reporting through social media platforms such as TikTok and X/Twitter—before those were neutered by algorithmic interference or forced sales to pro-Israel moguls—or citizen journalism and other avenues such as Substack—which bypassed all of those traditional gatekeepers of the news and revealed the true scale of Israel's role in the destruction and genocide in Gaza.

This has become more than just a regional tragedy in Western Asia—this was a moral test for Western civilisation itself, which it has easily failed; it's almost as though it didn't even bother turning up for the exam. The ease with which democratic governments excused mass slaughter exposed the shallow nature of their own human-rights rhetoric. The double standards were obvious: Russia's war on Ukraine was condemned as *barbaric*—which of course, it is—Israel's war on Gaza was explained away as *self-defence*. Western democracies that once claimed moral leadership were revealed as complicit liars and enablers of atrocity, resorting to basic talking points or showing *concern* of varying levels, as if they were the schoolmarm dealing with unruly children, instead of a horrific genocide that's being livestreamed all around the world. In Australia, as was the case in many other countries, these double-standards fueled public disillusionment with the political system and the mainstream media. The blatant suppression of the voices supporting Palestine—and the amplification and support of the narratives from Israel—has led to the public demanding honesty and accountability, and has exposed the corrosive influence of the Israel lobby, an issue which is now being openly debated for the first time in decades.

Towards the end of 2025, Israel's devastation of Gaza is complete. Much of Gaza has been destroyed, and over 70,000 Palestinians have been killed—although according to the United Nations, this number could be as high as 680,000—and hundreds of thousands have been displaced. Despite the international recognition of the genocide in Gaza—which now includes the United Nations and the International Criminal Court—Israel continues to receive unchallenged diplomatic and military support from the United States and its allies. The Netanyahu government is largely isolated but still remains defiant and will continue to do so, for as long as it receives this allied support. The Israeli left had all but collapsed, while internal dissent from Jewish communities in other countries—particularly in the United States, Britain and Australia—is rising sharply, as are the calls for boycotts, sanctions and trials for war-crimes. Yet Western leaders continued to hide behind the language of *complexity* and *security*, even as the moral clarity of Gaza's suffering burned away the last remnants of their credibility.

The war on the people of Gaza from 2023 onwards is not just a tragedy of numbers but of humanity's conscience. It has forced the world to confront what it means to look away—and what it means to speak up. As compromised governments equivocated and institutions failed, it was the Palestinian doctors, journalists, aid workers and activists—many of whom have been murdered by Israel—who became the true witnesses of the genocide.

The remaining ruins of Gaza are not just a symbol of this humanitarian disaster, but a mirror that reflects the political and moral decay of this era, as it was in the earlier parts of the twentieth century.

This book explores the narratives, the propaganda and the political cowardice that fueled the destruction of Gaza, and looks at the emerging movements that are following the path of truth and resistance. This war and brutal assault has not ended, despite what the U.S. President Donald Trump claimed in early October 2025. But the question that will define the coming decades will still remain: how did the world allow this to happen, yet again?

***

2023

THE NEW WAR ON GAZA:
A HISTORICAL CONTEXT

14 October 2023

The Israel–Palestine conflict has long been a source of tension and violence in the Middle East and recent events, such as the attacks by Hamas militants and Israeli military retaliation, have reignited this long-standing conflict. These events, which have garnered condemnation from various parts of the Western world, particularly in Australia, highlight the urgency of addressing this issue.

The actions of Hamas, the central Palestinian political organisation with a history of militancy, where their attacks resulted in the deaths of 1,195 people just on the other side of the border of the Gaza Strip, sparked outrage and condemnation. In response, the Israeli military launched a counteroffensive into Gaza, leading to even more casualties, almost 2,000. This cycle of violence has been a recurring theme in the Israeli–Palestinian conflict, with each side blaming the other for initiating hostilities, which then leads to other attacks and counter-offenses.

The timing of these events, as observed in previous conflicts, is often linked to political events and developments in Israel. Previous wars in 2008, 2014, and 2021 coincided with general elections and other key political events within the country, which had nothing to do with Palestine, but were primarily used by prime ministers such as Ehud Olmert and Benjamin Netanyahu to show their "tough-on-Palestine" credentials, a proven vote-winner in Israeli elections. In this instance, the push for a coalition government by Netanyahu that included "annexation and dispossession" plans for the Gaza strip only added to the tensions. The Israeli military had actually received a warning from Egyptian intelligence about an imminent attack on 7 October, emphasising the complex intelligence and political dynamics at play—the state of Israel possesses the most sophisticated missile alert systems in the world, and comprehensive surveillance over Gaza and, at this stage, it is quite unclear how Hamas managed to bypass this complex network and break its barriers.

Did Netanyahu want this attack to occur? It certainly helped achieve his political goals, as the coalition that he had been desperately trying to form since November 2022, was finally agreed to and signed, several days after the Hamas attacks.

A notable aspect of this ongoing conflict is the disproportionate casualty figures between the two sides, which is rarely featured within the western media. From 2008 up until September 2023, 6,407 Palestinians have been killed and over 152,000 injured, while 308 Israelis were killed and 6,307 injured, resulting in a ratio of approximately 20 to 1. This imbalance in casualties highlights the humanitarian crisis and the need for a balanced approach to resolving the conflict.

It is essential to recognise that the Israeli–Palestinian conflict is deeply rooted in historical, political, and territorial issues, making it a multifaceted challenge, along with the interference and influence over many years by large external powers: Britain, United States, the Soviet Union, and the manipulation of vassal states in the region. The perpetuation of this conflict is closely tied to political interests in all these countries and the manipulation of these events for political gain and international efforts have often exacerbated and prolonged conflict and deterred any potential for achieving a lasting resolution.

It is crucial to distinguish criticism of governments and movements from prejudice against people but this distinction is rarely applied within western media outlets. Criticising the actions of Hamas or the Israeli government should not imply a sweeping condemnation of the entire Palestinian or Israeli population. The conflict is not a black-and-white issue, and understanding its nuances is crucial for any meaningful resolution. The recent escalation highlights the urgency of addressing this long-standing and intractable conflict.

INTERNATIONAL RESPONSES AND THE PLIGHT OF PALESTINIANS

Australia, like many other countries, has historically shown solidarity with nations facing crises and attacks, and while it's not unexpected, the federal government has expressed support for Israel's "right to defend itself", as it has done in previous conflicts but this stance does not adequately address the complex realities on the ground, and largely ignores the experiences from the Palestinian perspective.

The statement by Australian Foreign Minister Senator Penny Wong highlights the predictable nature of the government's position: She recognises the apparent nature of the attacks and the security challenges Israel faces; there is a clear acknowledgment of the devastating loss of life and the attacks on civilians, reflecting the grim reality of the situation; the government's call for the release of hostages and its support for Israel's right to self-defence. These are all consistent with past positions taken by the federal government.

However, the concern lies in the double standard in Australia's foreign policy. While Australia has swiftly expressed solidarity with Israel during times of crisis, the same level of support or sympathy is rarely extended to the people of Palestine. Public buildings, including the Sydney Opera House, have been floodlit with the colours of Ukraine; of France; and now the blue and white of Israel, to show solidarity with the suffering of those countries. But why do we never see the black, white, green and red of the Palestinian flag when their peoples suffer the consequences of terror attacks and indiscriminate wars governed by corrupted Israeli prime ministers?

The Australian government's approach to this conflict lacks balance. When Israel initiates or responds to attacks with military force, the prevailing narrative often emphasises its "right to self-defence". However, such leniency is not typically extended to Palestinians, especially those living in Gaza, which is often described as the largest open-air prison in the world.

Gaza, a densely populated area of 365 square kilometres, is home to over two million people, who are facing severe restrictions on their movement due to Israeli naval and land blockades. This situation is classified as an "occupied territory" by the United Nations, and the collective punishment by the Israeli military—a clear war crime according to Common Article 33 of the Geneva Conventions—has exacerbated the humanitarian crisis.

The international community, including Australia, must consider the long-term consequences of this approach. Continuing to subject the people of Gaza to such dire living conditions only serves to deepen the roots of the conflict and fosters a sense of desperation and hopelessness among the population, which can contribute to further radicalisation and violence.

In the interest of achieving a peaceful resolution, Australia and the broader international community should certainly advocate for restraint on both sides and the protection of civilian lives. While recognising Israel's right to self-defence is important—as it is for any country—it should be equally vital to advocate for a fair and just resolution to the Israeli–Palestinian conflict. This entails addressing the legitimate aspirations of the Palestinian people, scaling back the incursions of Palestinian lands by Israeli settlers in the West Bank, and acknowledging the historical context and complexities of the conflict.

MEDIA REPRESENTATION AND ADVOCACY FOR A BALANCED VIEW

The media's role in shaping public perceptions of the Israeli–Palestinian conflict cannot be underestimated. The way news is framed, the narratives that are emphasised, and the voices that are heard all have a profound impact on how the public understands this complex and protracted conflict. It is essential to critically assess how media coverage and advocacy shape the discourse and influence public opinion.

One notable aspect of media representation is the difference in attention given to humanising the suffering on both sides. The spotlight often falls on Israeli victims, their names, and stories, while Palestinian casualties rarely receive the same level of coverage. *Israeli victims have names: Palestinian victims remain anonymous.* It's the basic rule of warfare—dehumanising the enemy makes it easier to eliminate them—and the western media has chosen who the enemy is, and quite clearly.

The exchange between the Australian Broadcasting Corporation's Sarah Ferguson and Mustafa Barghouti, the Secretary General of the Palestinian national initiative, highlights this issue:

Sarah Ferguson: "No one is disputing that all lives are of equal value, and we understand where you are coming from. But I would like your human response to the events that we have seen over the past few days that have been reported by media the world over."

Mustafa Barghouti: "I totally do not accept, and I refuse taking any child hostage. Do you want me to name to you, the 140 children who were killed in Gaza by Israeli airstrikes? Do you want me to tell you—let me answer—do you want me to tell you that I was shot by a sniper while I was treating an injured person with two gunshots and I'm still carrying these gunshots in my back. I am not going to talk about this ... let's look at the causes of this. The main cause of everything horrible that is happening to Palestinians and Israelis is the continuation of illegal Israeli occupation of Palestinian land."

When asked for a "human response", it is usually Palestinians who are expected to provide it, while the same empathy is rarely sought from Israeli officials. *No one is disputing that all lives are of equal value.* Yes, they are. Every western media outlet questions this value and always places the value of Israeli lives far above Palestinian lives. It's been obvious for many years.

This imbalance in media portrayal not only perpetuates a one-sided perspective but also fuels resentment and frustration among Palestinians. Such disparities in the portrayal of suffering can deepen the divide between the two communities and hinder the prospects for peace.

Another concerning aspect is the selective reporting of extremist rhetoric. While the media highlighted offensive chants by some Palestinian protestors at the steps of the Sydney Opera House, it is essential to acknowledge that extreme views can be found on all sides of the conflict, including on the Israeli side. The failure to consistently address inflammatory statements made by Israeli individuals or politicians leads to a skewed perception of the situation.

In addition, the lack of scrutiny when extremist statements are made by Israeli officials perpetuates an environment where moderation and balanced dialogue are stifled. The Israeli Defense Minister's reference to Palestinians as "animals" is one such example. The failure to challenge such rhetoric can contribute to the dehumanisation of Palestinians, making it easier to justify harsh and punitive actions against them.

Critics often accuse those who highlight these disparities of engaging in "whataboutism" and of simplifying the complexities of the conflict. However, this criticism can be seen as a way to avoid addressing these issues directly. Instead, it is crucial to acknowledge the ongoing humanitarian crisis, disproportionate casualty figures, and the long-standing issues that underpin this conflict. The mistreatment of any population and the suppression of human rights should be a cause for concern, irrespective of the geopolitical context.

The media plays a significant role in shaping public perceptions of the Israeli–Palestinian conflict and the coverage should aim for a balanced and nuanced view, which includes the humanisation of all victims and holds all parties accountable for their actions and rhetoric. A more comprehensive and fair portrayal of the conflict is essential for fostering understanding and, ultimately, for finding a just and lasting solution to this protracted and deeply entrenched issue.

THE ROLE OF POLITICAL COMMENTARY AND DIPLOMACY

The Australian political landscape, like those of other nations, has witnessed a spectrum of opinions regarding the Israeli–Palestinian conflict and such a multifaceted and deeply entrenched issue demands a nuanced approach from politicians and political commentators. However, recent statements from Australian political figures have drawn criticism for potentially exacerbating tensions and oversimplifying the situation.

Former Prime Minister John Howard's assertion that the Labor government "did not do enough to condemn" Hamas attacks and comments from Deputy Liberal Party leader Sussan Ley regarding the need for the government "to do more"—without ever articulating what this could be— exemplify the challenge of discussing a highly sensitive and multifaceted issue. The political point-scoring during a crisis can undermine diplomatic efforts and hinder Australia's role in the international community.

Liberal Party leader Peter Dutton's suggestion that Prime Minister Anthony Albanese was "condoning anti-Semitism" and calls for the release of national security details add another layer of complexity to the discourse, which were purely designed to undermine the Australian government. Why do conservative political figures always seek politicisation of national security and foreign policy issues? Foreign policy should be approached with seriousness and sensitivity, avoiding the politicisation of intelligence briefings and diplomatic matters.

The Australian political system generally adheres to the convention that opposition parties should refrain from overt criticism of foreign policy, particularly during international crises. Foreign policy decisions are often based on intricate international relationships, treaties, and strategic interests, which are not readily influenced by domestic political posturing. Instead, a bipartisan approach that puts national interests ahead of political advantage is essential in foreign policy matters.

If there is going to a push that "now is not the time for whataboutism" and to provide more balance perspectives— which essentially is another way of shutting down debate—it should also be acknowledged that now is also not the time for political point-scoring by conservative opportunists such as Dutton and Ley. Opposition parties have a role to play in holding the government to account, but during foreign policy crises, their approach should prioritise national interests and international diplomacy over partisan politics.

The Israeli–Palestinian conflict remains a highly complex and contentious issue with deep historical roots. International responses, including media representation, diplomatic engagement, and political commentary, play a significant role in shaping perceptions of the conflict and influencing potential pathways to peace.

While the conflict persists, it is imperative for all parties, including the international community and foreign governments, to exercise restraint and to support efforts for a just and lasting resolution. The delicate nature of this conflict requires careful and balanced diplomacy, and any political commentary should prioritise national interests and the wellbeing of all affected communities. A thorough understanding of the complexities and nuances of this conflict is essential for charting a path toward a peaceful and equitable resolution.

***

WHO SPEAKS UP FOR THE PALESTINIAN PEOPLE?

28 October 2023

Amidst the relentless cycle of violence and destruction that has gripped the Palestinian territories, the latest eruption of hostilities in the Gaza Strip has once again cast a grim shadow over the prospects for peace in the region. The conflict, though rooted in decades of historical animosities, has recently taken a turn for the worse, leaving both Palestinian and Israeli populations grappling with the consequences of a crisis that shows no signs of abating.

The predictability of this grim pattern is one of the most disheartening aspects of the ongoing conflict. As the latest round of hostilities escalates, observers have come to expect the same series of events to unfold. Israel, in response to perceived threats, launches harsh retaliatory measures, often involving airstrikes and military incursions into Gaza. These actions invariably result in the loss of innocent Palestinian lives, with civilians bearing the brunt of the violence. Meanwhile, the international community, represented by the United Nations and most Western governments, responds with strongly worded statements urging restraint while reaffirming Israel's right to self-defence. The United States, in particular, usually offers its "thoughts and prayers" but substantive action remains elusive.

The consequences of this unending cycle are not limited to one side of the conflict but it's obvious that's one side which bears the brunt of the pain and suffering. While the Palestinian people endure unimaginable suffering and despair, Israel, in its quest for self-preservation, finds itself mired in actions that have been widely criticised as illegal and inhumane. The occupation of the West Bank, the construction of settlements, and the ongoing encroachments into Palestinian territories are all deemed violations of international law. Yet, despite global condemnations, these practices persist.

The narrative of "self-defence", repeatedly invoked by Israel, has been stretched to its limits. How can the killing of over 8,000 civilians, mostly women and children, be an act of "self-defence"? The conflict has long ceased to be a matter of self-preservation, transforming into a multifaceted crisis that encompasses indiscriminate bombing, the targeting of hospitals, collective punishment, and what amounts to ethnic cleansing. The world watches, often unwilling to do anything, as these grave violations unfold.

In this unfolding tragedy, the glaring question remains: who speaks up for the Palestinian people? While criticism must also be directed towards Palestinian groups such as Hamas involved in the conflict, it is essential to recognise that they operate in a complex and deeply entrenched environment. The situation defies easy solutions and presents multifaceted challenges. Palestinian leaders and representatives are always asked to condemn the actions of Hamas, which they rightfully do. But why are Israeli leaders never asked to condemn the actions of the Israeli military? Why are they never asked to condemn the ethnic cleansing carried out by their own military? Their actions are likely to be identified as war crimes. Why are their actions never condemned in the Western media?

Within Israel, there exists a significant segment of the population that vehemently opposes these actions and yearns for a just and lasting resolution. Why do we never hear from the Israelis who strongly oppose this military action against Gaza?

The arrival of international troops and military support in the region from the United States, Australia, and other countries raises concerns about the effectiveness of external intervention in such a deeply rooted conflict. Will the deployment of troops yield tangible results or merely perpetuate the cycle of violence?

Ultimately, this crisis indicates that retaliations and counteractions will never arrive at a military or political solution. Civilians in Gaza are caught in a precarious and volatile situation, cut off from basic necessities like electricity, water, and food. It is a situation that demands an urgent and equitable resolution. The criticisms voiced here are not a judgment of entire citizenries but are aimed at the political organisations perpetuating this cycle of violence: the Israel military and Hamas.

As the crisis in Gaza continues to escalate, the world watches on, hoping that amidst the chaos and destruction, there might still be some hope for dialogue and a pathway forward, however unlikely that outcome might be.

ISRAELI GOVERNMENT'S CONFRONTATIONAL STANCE IN SPARKS OUTRAGE AND INTERNATIONAL CONCERN

As the crisis in Gaza continues to worsen, and as the conflict escalates, the Israeli government's actions are coming under further scrutiny and the rhetoric emanating from the Israeli government has deepened concerns about the trajectory of the crisis. The government's behaviour, resembles that of a rogue state, and its recent statement about "teaching the UN a lesson" has sparked outrage and unease.

It's worth noting that such confrontational language, akin to what one might expect from leaders like Vladimir Putin, is hardly characteristic of Western democracies. In a departure from diplomatic norms, this statement came in response to a speech by the Secretary General of the United Nations, António Guterres, who voiced deep concern about the dire situation in the Middle East, particularly in Gaza. Guterres expressed worry over clear violations of international humanitarian law in Gaza and unequivocally emphasised that no party to an armed conflict is above international humanitarian law.

Guterres's measured speech called for an immediate humanitarian ceasefire, emphasising the cessation of the collective punishment of the Palestinian people and the ongoing violence. His words were a plea for the international community to recognise the suffering of the Palestinian people, who have endured decades of occupation, territorial losses, economic stifling, displacement, and the destruction of their homes.

However, the Israeli military continues its relentless bombing campaign, resulting in over 8,000 innocent Palestinian casualties. The government's subsequent declaration to "teach the UN a lesson" in the face of international criticism has only added fuel to an already incendiary situation. This confrontational stance is a matter of grave concern, especially when the world is witnessing the immense human cost of the conflict.

It is essential to clarify that criticism is directed at the Israeli government, its military, and hardline elements within the country, particularly those who draw inspiration from extremist religious doctrines. Just as Hamas does not represent all Palestinian people—there are other political entities in the Palestinian territories—the actions of the Israeli government and military do not reflect the perspectives of all

Israeli citizens. There exists a significant portion of the Israeli population, as well as Jewish communities around the world, who are horrified by the Israeli government's actions and seek a different path toward peace and stability.

The repercussions of this crisis extend far beyond the borders of the Israeli–Palestinian conflict. The continued violence and turmoil jeopardise the security and stability of the entire Middle East region. It's a situation of immense complexity and depth, and despite the immense challenges, hope remains that the international community can help defuse the situation.

While world leaders, including President Joe Biden, have expressed criticism and concerns about the Israeli government's actions, it is apparent that the situation may deteriorate before any semblance of improvement emerges. What is paramount is the hope that a resolution can be found that minimises harm to innocent victims and paves the way for a more peaceful and secure Middle East. The current crisis demands an immediate re-evaluation of strategies and a concerted effort to prevent further suffering on all sides.

AUSTRALIAN POLITICAL FIGURES TREATING A COMPLEX ISRAEL–PALESTINE CONFLICT AS JUST ANOTHER OPPORTUNITY

As the conflict in Gaza rages on, it's crucial to recognise the far-reaching implications and how they resonate even in countries far removed from the immediate theatre of conflict. The war may be centred around Gaza, but its political reverberations are being felt across the globe, including in Australia and recent statements and actions by Australian political figures highlights the complexity of the issue and the potential impact on domestic politics.

One such instance that drew significant attention was when the leader of the opposition, Peter Dutton, suggested that Prime Minister Anthony Albanese should visit Israel while *en route* to meet President Biden in the United States. It was unclear what the Prime Minister's visit to Israel would achieve, but Dutton decided to push this agenda, cause trouble for the Labor government and create the perception that Albanese had failed to act—what he failed to act on wasn't articulated by Dutton but given the state of Australia's mainstream media, it never needs to be articulated: it creates news copy and a point of attack on the Albanese government.

Dutton's opportunistic suggestion and the ensuing debate highlighted the delicate and nuanced nature of the Israel–Palestine conflict. It is a matter that defies easy solutions, and while passionate voices on both sides advocate for their perspectives, the complexity of the situation remains.

The government minister Ed Husic, spoke out on behalf of Palestine, emphasising the collective punishment faced by Palestinians and the obligation of governments, particularly the Israeli government, to adhere to international law. His words reflected a growing concern about the disproportionate use of force and the impact on innocent lives.

Senator Fatima Payman also made a passionate speech in the Senate, condemning the killing of innocent civilians on both sides and calling for an immediate ceasefire. Her remarks highlighted the need for the international community to take a clear stand and push for a peaceful resolution to the crisis.

All these comments add to the plurality of debate in a diverse Australian community—and who doesn't want a hostile war to end for the sake of all sides—but for the modern Liberal Party, every issue presents as a political opportunity to attack the Labor government, irrespective of how delicate an international issue might be.

The Deputy Liberal Party leader Sussan Ley, sought to focus on the points of difference and announced as loudly as possible that the Labor government was "divided" over Palestine and the entire party was fracturing over the issue. And, of course, the media duly responded where an interview with a hyperbolic Ley on the friendly outlet of Sky News, became magnified and amplified: who's got time for nuance when we can listen to the words of Sussan Ley, which were uttered purely for political reasons? Labor is divided, obviously: Sussan Ley said so and, therefore, it must be true.

The question of sending the Australian Prime Minister to the Middle East raises an important consideration. While diplomatic efforts are essential, it's uncertain how such a visit would contribute to resolving the deeply entrenched conflict. Following Dutton's foolish suggestion, should the leaders of every country now visit Israel?

As the crisis evolves, the priority should remain on diplomatic solutions, as sending troops might escalate the situation further. However, the realities of international relations and the complexities of the conflict often mean that wishes and moral considerations take a backseat to political and strategic priorities.

While the Israel–Palestine conflict remains a highly intricate and emotionally charged issue with significant global implications, how long can the international community stand by, watch on and witness one of the most one-sided conflicts in history?

What is the tipping point for the international community when it decides that enough is enough? Is it 10,000 civilian deaths in Gaza? Is it 20,000? Twelve of Gaza's 35 hospitals cannot be used because of damage from bombing or lack of fuel and electricity. Will the international community act when the last remaining hospital switches off its lights? At least 221 schools and 180,000 dwellings have been damaged and destroyed over the past three weeks. Is 500 schools the tipping point? Or 500,000 dwellings destroyed?

While Australia, like many other countries, grapples with how to respond and engage with this crisis, the primary goal should be a resolution that minimises the suffering of innocent civilians on both sides. But the current destruction of Gaza cannot continue. The political discourse surrounding the conflict requires careful consideration and a commitment to engaging in constructive dialogue that paves the way for a just and lasting solution. At the moment, that seems a long way off.

***

THE WORLD SITS IDLY BY AS GAZA BURNS

4 November 2023

The United Nations held a critical vote during the week, with a focus on the ongoing Gaza conflict, calling for a ceasefire and a humanitarian truce. The numbers were comprehensively in favour of the ceasefire, as 120 countries voiced their support for the resolution, emphasising the global demand for an end to the violence. However, there was a surprising and controversial twist in this international response, as fourteen countries voted against the resolution, including the United States and Israel.

It's bewildering to imagine a nation opposing a ceasefire, especially when the conflict's grim human toll has captured the world's attention. Gaza has faced daily and indiscriminate bombing of dwellings, hospitals, schools, universities and shopping precincts for almost a month, resulting in thousands of deaths. What else would be needed to support a call for ceasefire?

This big division in the vote revealed a complex web of international relations, with certain countries choosing to align themselves with the United States. The reasons for such alignment ranged from historical favours to the pursuit of future diplomatic advantages.

For example, Croatia, which cast its vote in favour of the United States: this is viewed as a "thank-you" gesture for the U.S. support during their quest for independence in 1991. This historical camaraderie influenced Croatia's decision to stand with the United States and similar motivations can be attributed to other nations keen on securing favourable arrangements with the United States in the future.

While 120 countries supported the call for a ceasefire, 45 countries abstained from voting altogether, raising questions about their stance on the issue. One of those countries was Australia, which claimed that it refrained from supporting the resolution because it did not explicitly condemn the actions of Hamas. Do they need to go onto the streets of Gaza and ask the Palestinian families of those who have died to also condemn the actions of Hamas before they could support the resolution? What is Australia's limit of tolerance to the wanton destruction, ethnic cleansing and genocide that's happening in right front of our eyes?

This decision, however, highlights a broader and more difficult aspect of international diplomacy at the United Nations. For Australia, a country with its own interests and global diplomatic considerations, such a choice was made in an effort to avoid offending powerful allies and retain a delicate balance, rather than any human rights issues.

The non-binding nature of the United Nations resolution also raises questions about its practical impact and in the realm of international law, even if it were a binding resolution, enforcing it can be a daunting task. However, resolutions like these serve as opportunities for nations to express their positions on crucial global issues, making it a platform for countries to state their stance for the world to see, and built on further action.

In this case, the resolution was an unequivocal call to halt the destruction in the Gaza Strip. Countries such as France,

New Zealand, Norway, and Slovenia voted in favour of the resolution, demonstrating a significant alignment with the resolution's objectives. It's essential to emphasise that this was not a scenario where "third world" countries were ganging up on Israel; rather, it was a global consensus urging an end to the hostilities.

Australia's abstention in the vote, however, has raised concerns and controversy domestically and the decision to refrain from taking a clear stance on the issue was perceived by many as a failure to express solidarity with those affected by the conflict. It is crucial to note that the Gaza conflict has been characterized by humanitarian crises, and the world has watched with growing concern as the violence continues to escalate.

In addition, the conflict's nature, with its heavy civilian toll—over 10,000 Palestinians, mainly women and children, have been killed in Israel's retaliation to the events of 7 October, where 1,195 Israelis were killed mainly by Hamas—has led to strong condemnations against the Netanyahu government.

As a diverse and multicultural nation, Australia must tread carefully to avoid stirring anti-Jewish or anti-Muslim sentiments. A call for a ceasefire may not have radically altered Australia's domestic landscape, but it would have conveyed a message of compassion and concern for the people residing within its borders, regardless of their cultural or religious backgrounds.

Australia's abstention was a passive stance, leading to criticism that it lacked decisiveness and assertiveness in the global arena. Australia's decision to abstain from the United Nations resolution on the Gaza conflict raises questions about the nation's foreign policy priorities, its commitment to humanitarian values, and its role on the international stage. The move has sparked debate and disappointment from those within the electorate, who expected a more principled and proactive approach from their government, including the Prime Minister and the Minister for Foreign Affairs.

AUSTRALIA'S ABSTENTION AND ITS GLOBAL MIDDLE-POWER POSITION

A non-binding United Nations resolution may not appear as a decisive step in resolving a pressing and deadly conflict like the one in Gaza. However, it lays the foundation for future international diplomacy and action, offering a glimmer of hope in what is a grim scenario. With 193 member states in the United Nations, a diverse range of geopolitical interests must be considered when addressing global issues, including conflicts like the one in Gaza.

The purpose of such resolutions is to set the stage for further diplomatic efforts, which might encompass a broad spectrum of actions. These actions could involve lobbying for peace, implementing a UN peacekeeping force, or establishing a UN protectorate. However, these measures remain distant prospects, contingent on international support and cooperation, primarily from influential players like the United States.

The immediate and primary goal of this United Nations resolution was to halt the relentless targeting of civilians in the Gaza Strip by the Israel military, an issue that required immediate attention and international consensus. The abstention by Australia in the vote, though, reflects the intricate web of global relations that Australia finds itself entangled in due to security alliances like AUKUS and its historical alignment with the United States.

Australia's decision to abstain in the vote highlights the complexities and constraints it faces on the global stage. While Australia's abstention might seem like an independent decision—the U.S. voted against the resolution, whereas

Australia abstained—but a closer look at the background commentary and statements made by Australian envoys at the United Nations reveals a different story.

In reality, Australia's choice to abstain appears to be a less assertive, less committed position in the eyes of the international community and is in contrast to the crucial role Australia played in the creation of the United Nations in 1945, where figures such as Herb Evatt—who became the president of the UN—John Curtin, and Francis Forde played important roles in establishing the organisation, with the vision of providing smaller countries around the world a meaningful voice in international affairs.

However, nearly eight decades later, the global landscape has shifted significantly, and Australia's ability to independently influence major world issues has dwindled. Despite its role in creating the United Nations and the ideals of providing a voice for smaller nations, Australia now finds itself struggling to assert its independent stance on the international stage.

In retrospect, a "yes" vote in favour of the United Nations resolution would have increased Australia's international standing and potentially improved its relations with countries other than the United States. While Australia's commitment to its alliances and its global partners is crucial, the abstention has exposed the nation to criticism and has raised questions about its place as an independent participant on the world stage. The consequences of this decision are likely to ripple through Australia's foreign policy and diplomatic relations, making it interesting to observe how the nation will navigate its global role moving forward.

AUSTRALIA'S ALIGNMENT WITH THE UNITED STATES

The question of what special favours Australia secures by consistently aligning itself with the United States is a pertinent one, and it harks back to the days when Australia was often referred to as the "deputy sheriff" during the era of former Prime Minister John Howard. However, it is essential to scrutinise whether this alignment truly serves Australia's interests, especially when considering specific cases.

An illustrative case in point is the ongoing matter of Julian Assange, the Australian citizen who remains incarcerated in Belmarsh Prison in London, facing extradition to the United States on charges widely perceived as politically motivated. Prime Minister Anthony Albanese has met with President Joe Biden on multiple occasions to discuss the release of Assange, emphasising that "enough is enough" and that the case has dragged on for "far too long", yet this plea has seemingly fallen on deaf ears.

Despite the diplomatic rhetoric and repeated assurances, the situation remains unresolved, with Assange's legal plight continuing to drag on. Biden's position, emphasising the separation between politics and the judiciary, suggests a reluctance to intervene in Assange's case, causing frustration among those advocating for his release. Given Australia's consistent alignment with the United States, one would expect some reciprocal goodwill or diplomatic support, especially in securing the release of one its own citizens facing a potential extradition. But, it is yet to happen.

Australia's cooperation with the United States extends beyond political rhetoric. The recently formed AUKUS alliance, which the Albanese government inherited from the Liberal–National Coalition, highlights the nation's alignment with its powerful ally. However, the reasons for such unwavering loyalty and co-operation are not always clear, considering the apparent lack of *quid pro quo* when it comes to crucial matters such as Julian Assange's fate.

In the broader context of the Israeli–Palestinian conflict, Australia's foreign policy choices are being scrutinised closely. The recent letter of condemnation of Hamas and unequivocal support for the Israel government, signed by six former Australian prime ministers, has raised further concerns and ignited debate. The letter, signed by John Howard, Kevin Rudd, Julia Gillard, Tony Abbott, Malcolm Turnbull, and Scott Morrison, expressed support for Israel and its lauded its "promise" of avoiding civilian casualties, surely a naïve level of support, considering that over 10,000 Palestinian civilians have been killed, which raises the question of what measures the Israeli military have been taken to avoid civilian casualties, with such a high level of death and severe injuries.

Paul Keating, the only former prime minister who refrained from signing the letter, articulated concerns about its sharp and biased tone, advocating for a more balanced approach. This division within Australia's political leadership—even if it former Prime Ministers—highlights the complexities of its approach to the Israeli–Palestinian conflict.

Moreover, the media discourse in Australia concerning the conflict is another point of contention and the narrative in the Australian media leans strongly towards the interests of the Israeli government. Palestinian representatives, when given a platform, are often pressed to condemn the actions of Hamas, while Israeli counterparts are seldom asked to address the actions of the Israeli military or the issue of ethnic cleansing in Gaza.

In light of these observations, Australia's diplomatic and political stance in international conflicts, particularly in the context of its alignment with the United States and the Israeli–Palestinian conflict, remains a subject of intense debate and scrutiny.

COMPLEX DIPLOMATIC AND DOMESTIC DYNAMICS IN AUSTRALIA'S STANCE ON THE ISRAELI–PALESTINIAN CONFLICT

As the Israeli–Palestinian conflict continues to unfold, it is increasingly evident that diplomatic challenges and domestic debates are mounting globally. Egypt, for instance, has condemned the recent bombings and attacks, expressing its concern over the escalating violence. Several South American countries have also taken the unprecedented step of severing their diplomatic ties with Israel. These reactions highlight the gravity of the situation and the need for the international community to address the crisis urgently.

However, when examining Australia's position, the response appears one-sided, with limited room for nuanced or reasoned discussion. Senator Penny Wong's call for Israel to heed the international community's pleas for a ceasefire was met with harsh criticism from the Liberal Party and from Israel lobbyists in Australia, illustrating the polarised nature of the discourse.

Senator Wong's warning that the international community will not tolerate ongoing civilian casualties in Gaza, while echoing global sentiments, was also met with similar resistance and the line between supporting a different countries diplomatically and expressing humanitarian concerns becomes blurred in such a polarised context, leaving Australian politicians navigating a difficult political terrain.

Another contentious issue arose when the Canterbury–Bankstown Council decided to fly the Palestinian flag, in solidarity with the people of Palestine. This move was met with significant local support, particularly in the federal minister Tony Burke's constituency in the seat of Watson. In response to this decision, Burke defended the council's choice, highlighting the importance of recognising Palestinian lives lost in the ongoing conflict.

Burke's impassioned defence resonated with many in his electorate, where the tragic consequences of the conflict are felt acutely. The decision to fly the Palestinian flag was seen as an act of solidarity and acknowledgment of the Palestinian people's grief and suffering. While the question of whether local councils should engage in international politics is a separate debate, Burke's support for his constituents received wide approval.

However, the reaction from some quarters, including Sky News, News Corporation, the Liberal Party, and pro-Israeli lobbying groups, was predictably negative. This polarisation highlights the lack of space for constructive and balanced discussions on the Israeli–Palestinian conflict within Australia. The struggle to find a middle ground hinders the identification of the core problem and the application of a suitable solution. In essence, the Israeli–Palestinian conflict remains a contentious and polarised subject in Australia, mirroring global debates. While there are no easy solutions to such a deeply rooted and historically charged conflict, the lack of room for nuance and reasoned discourse in Australian politics poses a challenge to finding a path toward a more balanced and constructive approach to the issue.

Representatives like Burke, who advocate for their constituents' interests and concerns, play a crucial role in shaping Australia's response to the Israeli–Palestinian conflict. The complexities and sensitivities of the issue demand careful consideration and balanced perspectives to navigate the domestic and international landscapes effectively.

The Israeli–Palestinian conflict presents a multifaceted challenge for Australia, with repercussions on both diplomatic relations and domestic politics. The ongoing debate highlights the need for constructive dialogue, diplomatic measures, and nuanced discussions to help address the crisis and bring about a meaningful resolution to the conflict. The destruction of Gaza and the continuing acts of ethnic cleansing are not the solution, and the actions by the Israel military and the Netanyahu government must be stopped now.

***

THE ESCALATING CONFLICT AND THE INTERNATIONAL OUTCRY

18 November 2023

The conflict in Gaza continues with devastating consequences, with the Israeli military intensifying its bombing campaign, resulting in a rising death toll among civilians—over 13,000, which includes over 5,000 children and over 3,500 women—and the forced displacement of 1.7 million Palestinians from their homes. International pressure on the Israeli government to halt its military actions and seek a resolution has grown, to what is now being referred to as the "second Nakba".

"Nakba" refers to the catastrophic events of 1948 when 700,000 Palestinians were violently expelled from Palestine, marking a major historical turning point in the Middle East region, while it could be argued that the continuous displacement and ethnic cleansing endured by Palestinians over the past 75 years constitutes an ongoing Nakba, an unsettling reality that has never truly ceased. The public's increasing awareness of the situation in Gaza and a better understanding of the historical context has fueled global public outrage—if not by governments—against the Netanyahu government and the actions of the Israeli military.

Despite growing international calls for a ceasefire, closer to home, the Australian government remains steadfast in its support for Israel's "right to defend itself", refusing to advocate for a cessation of hostilities. The parliamentary debate on the matter reached a boiling point, featuring a confrontational exchange between the Leader of the Opposition, Peter Dutton, and Prime Minister Anthony Albanese.

Dutton, who seems more intent on scoring political points than expressing genuine concern, invoked historical parallels between the current situation in Gaza and the horrors witnessed during the Second World War and urged the Prime Minister to stand united with the Jewish community—even though this is exactly what Albanese had done—accusing him of a lack of solidarity and a divisive approach. Albanese, on the other hand, accused Dutton of overreach, condemning his attempts to weaponise anti-Semitism for political gain. This clash in Parliament reflects a broader polarisation, with political leaders grappling with the challenge of fostering unity in the face of deep social divisions, especially when the conservative side of politics insists on politicising the events in Gaza for its own political benefit.

This division in Australian politics is exemplified by Dutton's attempts to exploit fears and inflame tensions for advantage. The issue at hand, which essentially is to stop the loss of innocent lives in the first instance and push back the Israel military, is further complicated by the spread of misinformation. Reports, such as the debunked claim of a list of Palestinian operatives found in a Gazan hospital basement— which turned out to be a wall calendar—contribute to the complexity of discerning truth in the midst of conflict.

Both sides of the conflict—the Israel government and Hamas—find themselves lacking in widespread popular support: the Likud Party in Israel is deeply unpopular, as is Prime Minister Benjamin Netanyahu, and average polls during 2022 and 2023 show political support for Hamas at just 34 per cent. The nature of war, with its array of unverified claims and the unfortunate toll on non-combatants, highlights the urgency for a ceasefire. However, the international response, including the abstention of countries such as Australia and Canada in crucial votes at the United Nations, remains a point of contention.

The Australian Jewish Association's criticism of Penny Wong, accusing her of 'heading in a worrying direction' after she offered a small slither of support for Palestine, shows how difficult any meaningful discussion on a resolution in this crisis is, whether it's in an international forum, or for a domestic audience.

Dutton's approach has lacked subtlety and nuance, reflecting a concerning lack of depth in addressing the complex issues of the conflict. But this is Dutton at his worst: failing to avoid division, fear and loathing, because he knows no other way.

DUTTON'S DIVISIVENESS ON ISRAEL–PALESTINE

The domestic situation is becoming increasingly precarious, as tensions spill over into acts of violence and clashes between supporters of Israel and those standing in solidarity with Palestine. The recent firebombing of Burgertory, a burger shop owned by a pro-Palestinian advocate in the Melbourne suburb of Caulfield by purported supporters of Israel adds a dangerous dimension to the conflict. Although authorities denied political motivations—possibly to alleviate an already tense situation—there is a palpable risk of further escalation within the community.

In response to the attack, supporters of the Palestinian business organised a rally in Caulfield, unknowingly near a synagogue. Accusations of attempting to cause trouble arose, reflecting the heightened sensitivity surrounding the issue. Meanwhile, there have been calls from conservative members of the Jewish community to "prevent" Palestinians

THE SHADOW OVER PALESTINE

from entering Caulfield—as if to import the Israel brand of apartheid into Australia against people they do not like—indicating a disturbing level of polarisation within the community.

The incidents in Caulfield highlight the importance of political leaders treading carefully on international issues to prevent the exacerbation of tensions at a local level. Dutton's approach, geared towards inflaming divisions, aligns with his track record of utilising populist rhetoric on a wide range of issues: walking out during the Apology to the Stolen Generations in 2008; the "African gangs" rhetoric during 2018 and claiming the community was too scared to go out to restaurant in Melbourne; his concerns about non-white immigration and exploitation of terrorism issues.

This tendency to exploit divisive topics contrasts sharply with the need for subtlety and nuanced thought and, as the French politician Georges Clemenceau suggested, it's far easier to make war than peace, and the responsibility of a wise politician lies in fostering peace rather than perpetuating discord. Dutton's inclination towards trouble and division in domestic matters is evident across various contexts, and it raises questions about his suitability to navigate complex issues diplomatically.

The ongoing protests further highlight the contrast between the peaceful expressions of both pro-Israeli and pro-Palestinian sentiments. Demonstrations in Hyde Park, with thousands in attendance, demonstrated passionate but non-violent protests. While there have been instances of arrests, they have been minimal and related to minor infractions rather than serious offenses.

The importance of allowing peaceful protests, even on highly contentious issues, cannot be overstated. However, it necessitates responsibility from both organisers and participants to avoid exacerbating tensions. Dutton's failure to comprehend the distinction between disruptive yet peaceful protests and violent demonstrations further highlights the challenges in his approach.

In the midst of heightened emotions and deep-seated divisions, the call for political leaders to act responsibly and promote unity becomes more urgent than ever. The potential consequences of mishandling domestic tensions are immense, and the role of leaders in diffusing rather than escalating conflicts cannot be overstated.

DR. FRANCESCA ALBANESE'S BOLD WARNING ON ISRAEL–GAZA

During the week, Dr. Francesca Albanese, the United Nations Special Rapporteur on the occupied territories of Gaza and West Bank, visited Australia and addressed the National Press Club in Canberra.

In a series of exchanges with journalists from the mainstream media, Dr. Albanese unflinchingly addressed the severity of the crisis, going so far as to warn of the risk of genocide by Israel. Her responses challenged attempts to downplay the impact on civilians, emphasising the need for a nuanced understanding of the conflict. The exchanges also revealed the challenges faced by experts attempting to communicate the gravity of the situation amid differing interpretations.

The questions posed by journalists were poor and uninformed, chose the side of the Israel government, and deliberately misrepresented what she had actually said. The following exchanges are a sample, but a clear representation of the paucity of intellect that inflicts many journalists within the mainstream media, who mislead, misinform and search for the prize of "clickbait journalism", rather than informing the public:

Dr. Francesca Albanese: "There is a risk of genocide being committed by Israel, and also the capacity to do that..."

Tom Connell (Sky News): "if it wanted to, probably would have done, to be blunt about it—yes, it's a dire situation with civilians, but Israel did say civilians, 'please leave, this is where we're targeting'. So that wasn't them actually targeting civilians at that point."

Dr. Albanese: "...I don't mean to be rude. But can you really keep a straight face as you asked me this question?"...

Matthew Knott (Nine Media): "You've said previously, that it should ultimately be up to Palestinians to decide who governs in Gaza, and that Israel should be open to making a peace deal with Hamas. Given that Hamas leaders since October 7, have said repeatedly that they would like to repeat these attacks, is that really possible? Is Hamas really a potential partner for peace? Or would the defeat or surrender of Hamas be part of any realistic peace agreement in Gaza?"

Dr. Albanese: "Sorry, I cannot answer the question, because you are basically basing yourself on something that has been reported, that it has been completely distorted... you have some media who's really as manipulative as those in Italy! I said something else, that the military response cannot be war—must be peace, and the peace must be done with the Palestinians. I'm also speaking of a non-legal peace, at peace, reconciliation with the idea that Palestinians have same humanity and same entitlement to rights, freedom and dignity as the Israelis. I'm sorry, but this [what you've suggested] is not what I said—that has been completely distorted."

And the procession of gormless and uninformed journalists continued, only too happy to show their disregard for facts and information and, seemingly, to display their ignorance to a national audience. Dr. Albanese staunchly defended her choice of language, framing it within the context of international law and the existence of an apartheid regime, challenging journalists to refer to the apartheid convention for clarity.

Notably, Dr. Albanese's expertise and assertiveness provided a powerful counterpoint to the political dynamics at play. Her statements, delivered with conviction, resonated beyond the National Press Club, prompting reflection on the international stage.

However, as the discourse shifts from international perspectives to domestic considerations, the connection between Australia and Israel's military industries also needs to be considered. The potential use of Australian-made military hardware in the conflict raises ethical questions about Australia's role in supplying weaponry to a conflict zone. Have any Palestinian civilians been killed with Australian-supplied military hardware? It's likely. The lack of transparency around military exports to Israel, coupled with the substantial value of such exports, adds a layer of complexity to Australia's stance on the conflict.

The financial interests at play, evident in the significant military export licenses granted to Israel—52 so far during 2023, and over 350 since 2017—offer a potential explanation for the Australian government's unwavering support for Israel's "right to defend itself". The connection between political decisions and economic interests highlights the need for transparency in international relations, particularly when it comes to matters of conflict and human rights.

As the Israel–Gaza conflict continues to unfold, the dichotomy between international perspectives represented by figures like Dr. Francesca Albanese and domestic political considerations, influenced by economic interests, raises critical questions about Australia's role in the broader geopolitical landscape. The call for transparency in military exports and a reassessment of political stances in light of evolving circumstances becomes imperative in navigating the delicate balance between global ethics and national interests.

A DIPLOMATIC PARADIGM SHIFT AND MORE INTERNATIONAL ACCOUNTABILITY

In the context of the Israel–Gaza conflict, there is a critical need for a shift in approach in the management of international affairs. The reflexive use of claims of "anti-Semitism" to deflect criticism of the Israeli government, Benjamin Netanyahu, or the Israel military is not only counterproductive but may be working against the long-term interests of Israel itself. The international community must move beyond merely urging restraint and exert more substantial pressure on the state of Israel to bring about a resolution in Gaza: simply reiterating that Israel has a right to defend itself is simply avoiding the issue and won't result in any meaningful resolution.

Repeated calls for a resolution in the past month highlight the urgency of the situation. The international community's inability to resolve the Israel–Palestine conflict was compared with U.S. President Jimmy Carter's tenure in the late 1970s, standing out as a rare instance of significant progress. Carter's tough approach, contrary to his public persona, demonstrated that Israeli leaders respond to firmness. The subsequent decades, marked by a lack of assertive international intervention, have contributed to the current impasse.

It is a sobering reminder that when political leaders are allowed unchecked power, they will act in their self-interest: history has confirm this basic fact. For Israel, this highlights the need for a change in approach within its political leadership. The international community must not shy away from demanding accountability and promoting a resolution that respects the rights and dignity of all involved.

President Carter's success in negotiating peace in the Middle East, resulting in the Camp David Accords, stands as a testament to the potential impact of resolute leadership. In a complex geopolitical landscape, it is essential to recognise that firmness, not complacency, is required to address deeply entrenched conflicts.

Noam Chomsky's characterisation of Israeli governments as "spoiled children" demanding their own way—a comment repeated by the President of Turkiye, Recep Tayyip Erdogan in 2011—aligns with the need for a recalibration of diplomatic strategies. The current desperation and internal challenges faced by Netanyahu further complicate the situation. As he confronts serious corruption charges and waning public support, his actions in the international arena become increasingly unpredictable and it's always best to treat a desperate political leader firmly.

In essence, the Israel–Gaza conflict reflects broader geopolitical challenges that demand thoughtful, assertive diplomacy. It requires a departure from conventional approaches and a commitment to addressing the root causes of the conflict. International pressure must be wielded judiciously, focusing on fostering a just resolution that considers the rights, security, and dignity of all parties involved.

As the situation continues to evolve, the world watches with a high level of concern, acknowledging the delicate balance required to navigate the complexities of the Israel–Gaza conflict. The need for international leaders to learn from history, leverage diplomatic tools effectively, and prioritise a just and lasting resolution remains paramount.

***

THE DOUBLE STANDARDS OF
REPORTING THE GAZA CONFLICT

2 December 2023

A concerning revelation has come to light in the war reporting in Gaza, raising questions about the objectivity of the mainstream media coverage on the conflict. Over 70 journalists and editors from mainstream media outlets have had "re-education" trips and junkets to Israel over the past decade funded by the Israeli government, with a significant majority of these individuals are affiliated with News Corporation, Nine Media, with some from the ABC and *The Guardian* as well.

Unsurprisingly, these effects and influence of these trips and junkets has resulted in media outlets taking actions against journalists who have expressed support for the Palestinian cause. Nine Media, in response to an open letter demonstrating solidarity with journalists covering the Gaza conflict, has banned journalists who endorsed the letter. While the ABC didn't ban journalists, it did issue a warning to its staff regarding the open letter, adding to the growing concerns about media impartiality. These developments follow a prior directive from the ABC, which explicitly banned the use of terms such as "genocide" and "apartheid" to describe the actions by Israel in Gaza and West Bank.

These directives were in response to the open letter initiated by the Media, Entertainment and Arts Alliance, which aimed to offer support and camaraderie for journalists covering the war in Gaza and also emphasised the importance of adhering to journalistic principles, including holding power accountable and accurate reporting on war crimes, genocide, ethnic cleansing, and apartheid, and suggesting that there was a risk of losing "the trust of our audiences if we fail to apply the most stringent journalistic principles and cover this conflict in full". It's hard to disagree with the contents of the open letter.

The backdrop to this media controversy is the ongoing conflict in Gaza, which has resulted in the deaths of over 55 journalists, with a notable number allegedly targeted by the Israeli Defense Forces. In the open letter, journalists were also expressing outrage over the loss of over 15,000 Palestinian lives, demanding that mainstream media uphold the fundamental tenets of journalism, such as reporting truthfully and freely on the realities of war.

News reporting in Australia has a discernible pro-Israel stance, which compromises the principles of an open and fair media. The conflict in Gaza, essentially ongoing since 1946 but reignited on 7 October when Hamas led an assault which killed 1,195 Israelis, has highlighted the need for objective journalism, particularly in democracies reliant on a free and open media environment.

Amidst these challenges, it is crucial to emphasise—yet again—that criticising a government, in this case, the Israeli government, should not be equated with hostility towards any particular religious or ethnic group. The complexity of the Israeli–Palestinian conflict extends beyond religious or ethnic lines, and journalists play a vital role in navigating these nuances while adhering to the principles of responsible reporting.

The issue has been further compromised to attempts by the Israeli government to use accusations of anti-Semitism as a means of stifling criticism and debate. The condemnation of anti-Semitism, anti-Arab sentiment, anti-Muslim attitudes and Islamophobia should be a given, and there needs to be a diversity of opinions within both the Palestinian and Israeli communities. However, concerns persist about the influence of the vocal Zionist lobby in Australia—small but loud—raising questions about the authenticity of accusations and the potential impact on unbiased reporting.

A FURTHER EROSION OF TRUST IN THE MAINSTREAM MEDIA: WHO DO WE TRUST?

The recent revelations about these close ties between the Israeli government and Australian journalists and media outlets continues a pattern of influence over media reporting, not only in Australia, but also in the United States and Britain. The Israeli lobby's substantial sway over the Australian media has become a focal point of scrutiny, with echoes of previous incidents highlighting these biases.

In 2014, when the Israel government instigated yet another conflict in Gaza, journalist Mike Carlton was pressured to resign from the *Sydney Morning Herald* for using offensive language in responses to Jewish readers—private correspondences—who criticised one of his articles on the conflict, and a cartoon by Glenn Le Lievre was removed due to claims of offensiveness by the Australian Jewish Association. These incidents shows the existence of double standards in reporting on Israel and Palestine, where similarly offensive anti-Palestinian content, such as cartoons produced by News Corporations' Bill Leak, received little scrutiny. The perception that journalists may be compromised by their acceptance of sponsored trips from the Israeli government adds fuel to concerns about the integrity of media reporting on the conflict.

Figures such as Bevan Shields, editor at the *Sydney Morning Herald*, and Lenore Taylor, editor at *The Guardian*, have also received sponsored trips to Israel in the past. While the journalistic community defends their right to engage in such visits, the lack of disclosure raises questions about potential conflicts of interest.

Last week, at least two of the four panelists on the ABC's *Insiders* program were revealed to have traveled to Israel on sponsored trips: should the audience have been informed of this information? The editor of the *Herald Sun*, James Campbell, pushed his own one-sided views and racist attitudes when he commented:

"Do you really think that refugees from the Ukraine would potentially [pose] security risks the way people from Gaza are? There's also an unfortunate truth that they are unlikely to hold sanguine views about Jews... people don't leave those sorts of attitudes when they hit the check-in".

Why should a journalist be allowed to push forward these divisive attitudes to a national audience? How much of Campbell's commentary is taken from the talking points provided to him by the Israel lobby in Australia? The broader concern is that journalists on sponsored trips or pressure from specific interest groups are likely to be swayed in their reporting due to their experiences, creating a distorted narrative that compromises journalistic integrity. There are comparisons to the "cash for comment" scandals in 1999, where the radio broadcasters Alan Jones and John Laws were paid—$18 million in total—to make favourable comments about corporations without disclosure, which ultimately forced changes to the *Broadcasting Services Act* to ensure tighter disclosure regulations. Should tighter rules be instigated for political reporting?

In 2019, the media industry launched a "Right to Know" campaign, claiming that governments has been "passing laws that make it harder and harder for people to tell the truth about what the government is doing in your name". Where is the public's right to know about where information that's being provided to the media is coming from? Shouldn't the public be aware of the distortions of this information and be informed about when the news is real or based on propaganda provided by the Israel government? The need for transparency in this area is essential: how would Australians react if other governments, such as Russia, were funding journalists and providing "re-education" tours to the Kremlin, to reshape perspectives on conflicts in countries such as Ukraine?

While there are instances where governments may sponsor journalists for positive reporting—trade shows or tourism purposes—the call for transparency is paramount and even in these instances, disclosure is usually provided. Journalists, when sponsored by governments, should disclose such ties to maintain trust in their reporting: even better; refuse the junkets in the first instance. This would allow audiences to better assess the potential influences on a journalist's perspective and encourage critical examination of the narratives presented. Ultimately, the hope is that a more transparent approach will lead to a media landscape that is less susceptible to external influences and better serves the public's right to unbiased information.

CONTROVERSIAL EDITORIAL CHOICES MAR THE ISRAELI–PALESTINIAN COVERAGE

Australian journalists have previously expressed support for colleagues in war zones, particularly in Ukraine, condemning Russian actions and President Vladimir Putin for instigating the invasion almost two years ago. However, there are no half-measures or equivocation about Ukraine: the ABC and Nine Media have published many articles accusing Russia of war crimes, genocide and ethnic cleansing—and rightly so—and there was no censorship imposed by news editors or management at the time. This perceived inconsistency in treatment has fueled the argument that similar scrutiny and denouncement should be applied to Israel for its actions in Gaza.

If Russia can be accused of war crimes and attempted genocide in Ukraine, the same standards should apply to Israel in the context of Gaza. The ABC's editorial decision to ban certain terms such as "genocide" and "war crimes" in reporting on Gaza and Israel was inappropriate, but if it's correct to accuse Russia of war crimes, then it must be correct to accuse Israel, because the actions committed by both the Russian and Israeli military forces appear to be identical, if not far more severe in Gaza.

The decisions of Nine Media and the ABC to interfere with the reporting of war on such a level is a failure of journalism, although it's evident that the public is becoming increasingly aware of such editorial decisions and seeking news and information from other more reliable avenues.

Social media is providing many platforms for a wider range of unfiltered opinions, allowing for more diverse perspectives on the Israeli–Palestinian conflict. Despite the challenges of navigating misinformation and confirmation bias, this is encouraging critical thinking and evaluation on the Middle East politics and shifting public opinions, however slightly, particularly among younger generations, and providing an opportunity re-evaluate essentially what has been a barrage of Israel government propaganda appearing in much of the mainstream media in Australia.

The geopolitical implications of the Israeli government's actions today are quite different to events from the past, which have usually been tacitly condoned by Western governments and after initial concerns, a level of indifference from the public: a faraway and confusing conflict can hold the attention span of the public for only so long.

However, there is a different global response in 2023. The Israeli government, under Benjamin Netanyahu, has overplayed its hand, losing its precarious and perfunctory political support in the Middle East region but potentially losing the substantial support it holds in Europe, the U.S. and within Australia, whose populations are becoming more outraged with the continuing tragic loss of innocent lives, and the continued domination of Israel in Gaza and the West Bank.

CEASEFIRE'S GLIMMER OF HOPE WIPED OUT

The recent ceasefire in Gaza, which Australia abstained from voting on just a few weeks ago, brought a glimmer of some hope amid the darkness of war. Initially planned for four days, the ceasefire was extended by an additional two days, and there were hopes that it could become a permanent agreement. United Nations Secretary–General António Guterres expressed optimism about the ceasefire, seeing it as an opportunity to increase humanitarian aid to the suffering population in Gaza.

However, this current ceasefire has since been broken by Israel and it's a reminder that there's still a long road ahead in this conflict, which has been substantially one-sided. The civilian casualties have been disproportionately high, with over 15,000 Palestinians killed since October, compared to 1,195 Israelis and, beyond the grim statistics, there's a pressing humanitarian crisis in Gaza that requires urgent attention.

The outcry against this conflict on the international stage has been larger than in previous Israeli conflicts, raising awareness and prompting outrage globally and the narrative surrounding the conflict, often controlled by mainstream media filters, is undergoing a transformation. The traditional controls on how stories are disseminated and framed are dissipating, indicative of the broader changes in media reportage and communication through social media and access of material, in general, through the internet.

While geopolitical changes move at a glacial pace, mainstream political parties in the Western world are facing challenges, both electorally and philosophically, and the disillusionment with established parties and their dwindling memberships becoming contributing factors. The changing narrative around the Palestinian people—once only portrayed in a negative light—is breaking down. Even among those who may not entirely support the notion of Palestine, there is a growing recognition that the situation is more complex than previously thought, that the situation cannot continue for ever and needs a long-lasting and peaceful resolution.

THE GEN Z AND MILLENNIAL IMPACT

The evolving landscape of public opinion on the Israeli–Palestinian conflict is significantly being influenced by social media, particularly among younger demographics. Platforms such as TikTok and emerging independent media outlets in 2023 provide alternative perspectives beyond mainstream narratives. Younger audiences are less receptive to historical propaganda, and are increasingly critical of Israel's actions, perceiving them as practicing apartheid, attempting genocide, and likely committing war crimes.

This shift in perception is not confined to Australia but extends globally, prompting a re-evaluation of Israel and Palestine's dynamics. The Gen Z and Millennial demographic, in particular, are more likely to be advocating for international action against injustices, and this demographic's influence is spreading to other age groups, creating a sizable shift in popular opinion that may impact Middle East politics in the future. Beyond changing public sentiment, geopolitical factors are also at play. The slowly diminishing reliance on oil will reduce the strategic importance of Israel for Europe and the United States.

Recent developments at the United Nations, including Australia's vote against a resolution for Israel to withdraw from the occupied territories in the Golan Heights—as well as abstaining from a vote for a ceasefire—reveal a disparity between Australia's stated positions and its actions. While Australia supports the idea of a two-state solution, its voting record suggests a gap between rhetoric and practical steps.

Despite the international lobbying efforts of the Israel government and Zionist support groups in many countries, public support for the actions Israel is waning, and the consequences of overplaying their hand may be irreversible. The Israeli government's challenge now is to navigate this changing landscape, where reshuffling the deck may not guarantee a favourable outcome, leaving them with limited options to regain public favour. Obvious acts of war crimes, attempts at genocide, ethnic cleansing and apartheid will always outrage the international community, even if it has taken over 75 years to get to this stage.

***

THE FRAGILE STATE OF THE CEASEFIRE AND A HUMANITARIAN CRISIS

9 December 2023

In the wake of a shattered ceasefire in Gaza, tensions continue to escalate, drawing international attention and concern. Initially, there was a glimmer of hope for a lasting peace, but this optimism has been dashed by recent developments, when the Israeli Defense Forces broke the ceasefire—blaming this on Hamas, without providing proof—and resumed their operations, leading to an increased number of Palestinian casualties, including women and children, and a situation that is rapidly evolving into a humanitarian crisis.

James Elder, a spokesperson from UNICEF, provided a grim outlook on the conditions in Gaza, specifically the so-called "safe zones", which, in reality, are anything but safe. These areas lack basic necessities such as water, sanitation, and shelter, turning them into potential hotbeds for disease and suffering. Elder highlighted the dire situation in these zones, where basic facilities are woefully inadequate or entirely absent, exacerbating the plight of the displaced population.

The international community's response to this crisis has been a focal point of debate and the calls for more decisive action against Israel's actions in Gaza and the West Bank are growing louder. While they don't have great influence in current politics, Young Labor in Australia has passed a resolution urging the federal government to support an immediate ceasefire and to hold Israel accountable for its adherence to international law, as have 40 other Labor Party branches across Australia.

In the Australian Parliament last week, Labor MP Stephen Jones echoed these concerns, advocating for a peaceful resolution through a two-state solution, emphasising the importance of secure and internationally recognised borders for both Israelis and Palestinians and, importantly, stressed that peace is the only viable long-term solution to the ongoing hostility in the Middle East.

While these are fine sentiments—who doesn't want a ceasefire, except for the Israel government, their assorted lobbyists and the Liberal Party here in Australia—the ground realities paint a different picture. Despite the international outcry and political rhetoric, the situation in Gaza remains dire and this disconnect between political discourse and on-the-ground actions highlights the complexity and difficulty of resolving this long-standing conflict. Adding to the complexity is the intertwining of political ideologies and ethnic identities. The U.S. Congress's recent legislation equating anti-Zionism with anti-Semitism has sparked controversy, with a conflation of the two issues of political criticism of Israel and ethnic prejudice—even though the two are mutually exclusive issues—an oversimplification of a multifaceted issue, and a sign of further evidence of the influence the Israel lobby has within U.S. politics.

Both Israeli and Palestinian leadership face accusations of corruption and self-preservation at the expense of their people. The conflict, which disproportionately affects the innocent, is increasingly seen as a struggle between corrupt political factions rather than a representation of the will of the people. The pro-Netanyahu faction in Israel, in particular, faces diminishing moral and intellectual defences as the conflict continues and support within the international community is waning, and is testing the patience of the U.S., which seems to support any actions performed by the Israel government against Palestine, irrespective of how violent and destructive this action might be.

As the situation remains volatile, the hope for a return to ceasefire is more urgent than ever. The consequences of prolonged conflict are unpredictable, and the need for a peaceful resolution is paramount to prevent further loss and suffering.

AN INTERNATIONAL CONFLICT WITH LOCAL RAMIFICATIONS

In Australia, the conflict in Gaza is resonating deeply, particularly among the Jewish community, where these is a significant segment standing in opposition to Israel's actions. This divergence of opinion, often overshadowed by Australian media, is gradually gaining recognition. Louise Adler, the noted publisher and cultural figure, offered her perspective on her encounters with the Zionist lobby in Australia, which always seeks to suppress criticism of Israel and counters any negative perceptions.

Adler's experiences date back to the 2000s, beginning with a confrontation with the Israeli ambassador over a book she published as the CEO of Melbourne University Press—*My Israel Question* by Antony Lowenstein—the release of the book marked the start of her ongoing interactions with these lobby groups, and in this case, resulting in conservative politicians demanding her dismissal from the University of Melbourne.

Adler also highlighted the controversy surrounding the Adelaide Writer's Week, where the inclusion of Palestinian literary culture was also met with vehement opposition from the Israel lobby. Despite pressures, including calls for withdrawal of sponsorship and political interventions, the festival stood firm in its decision, underscoring the importance of representing diverse narratives, including those of Palestinians.

This situation is not a monolithic representation of Jewish opinion. Many Jewish individuals, both in Australia and globally, do not align with the Israeli government or its policies under Benjamin Netanyahu and Adler's willingness to expose the behaviour of the Zionist lobby highlights the diversity of thought within the Jewish community, as there would be in any other community.

While there should be an acceptance of a diversity of views and opinions, tolerance seems to be selective and based on the message that is being promoted. A poignant example of this selective acceptance was seen in the inner west of Sydney, where a woman, during the inauguration of the Lewis Herman Reserve by Prime Minister Albanese, held a sign featuring a hand-drawn watermelon—symbolising Palestinian resistance and identity—with the words "Shame Albo", was swiftly removed by police, while she was holding the sign, along with her one-year old-toddler. Forty years ago, Albanese would have been the one holding up the sign, agitating for the rights of Palestinian people and forcing a change in the politics of the Middle East.

While there have been criticisms of Albanese since this conflict erupted in early October, over a stance where Australia initially abstained from a United Nations resolution for a ceasefire in Gaza, as well as voting against another resolution calling for Israel to withdraw from its occupation of the Golan Heights—seen as a requisite and precursor to the two-state solution that has been envisioned for Israel and Palestine—Australia has now engaged in a *volte-face*, and has now supported a ceasefire, along with 152 other countries. It's unfortunate that it's taken the deaths of at least 18,000 civilians in Gaza for Australia to reach this step, an action that seemed so obvious to so many other people around the world.

Of course, this recent decision to support a ceasefire in Gaza will see different responses in different communities within Australia, but the domination that the Israel lobby has previous held over politics—when it comes to issues relating to Israel and Palestine—has seen a shift in recent months, as more people from within the Jewish community speak out in support of Palestine. These reflections and responses to the Gaza conflict illustrate the complexity and multiplicity of perspectives within both the Jewish community and broader Australian society. They also highlight the ongoing struggle to balance political affiliations, personal convictions, and the demands of leadership in the face of global crises.

As the conflict in Gaza continues to unfold, the need for a comprehensive and humane approach to resolving it becomes ever more pressing. The voices of dissent and protest, both within and outside the affected regions, are crucial in shaping a future where peace and justice can prevail. This complex range of opinions and actions highlights the ongoing struggle to balance political power, personal convictions, and the urgent need for humanitarian intervention in a world increasingly fraught with conflict and division.

***

2024

INTERNATIONAL CONDEMNATION OF ISRAEL'S BRUTAL ACTIONS

12 February 2024

In the midst of escalating tensions and the ongoing humanitarian crisis in Gaza, recent actions by Israeli forces and the subsequent international response have drawn strong condemnation and raised questions about the principles guiding international relations and humanitarian aid. The suspension of funding for the United Nations Relief and Works Agency for Palestinian Refugees—based on unsubstantiated claims made by the Israel government—by countries such as the United States and Australia, has broader implications on international protocols and the plight of the Palestinian people.

Israeli forces have fired at crowds of Palestinians in Gaza for nine consecutive days, targeting individuals gathered to collect humanitarian aid and the severity of the situation is highlighted by the attack on trucks carrying humanitarian aid for northern Gaza. These actions have taken place against a backdrop of Israel blocking aid to the north of the Gaza Strip, exacerbating the dire humanitarian situation faced by the Palestinian population.

The suspension of funding for UNRWA by the United States and Australia marks a significant escalation in the international response to the conflict. This suspension, justified by unverified accusations from the Israeli government regarding UNRWA members' involvement in Hamas attacks against Israeli civilians, represents a worrying shift away from the established norms of evidence and investigation in international relations. The acknowledgment by U.S. Secretary of State Antony Blinken of the U.S. government's inability to independently verify the claims, while still considering them "highly credible," highlights the duplicity of Western governments. These governments have been all too willing to overlook the acts of genocide and ethnic cleansing carried out by the Israeli government.

This situation raises critical questions about the role of international aid organisations, the responsibilities of donor nations, and the impact of geopolitical considerations on the provision of humanitarian aid. The suspension of funding for UNRWA without a thorough investigation not only undermines the credibility of the international system but also deprives Palestinian refugees of essential services and support. The decision by Australia and other countries to follow suit, without concrete evidence, suggests a broader alignment with political pressures rather than an adherence to principles of justice and humanitarian need.

The implications of these developments are profound. Firstly, they highlight the vulnerability of international aid organisations to political manipulation and the potential for such actions to disrupt essential humanitarian services. Secondly, the lack of consistency and apparent double standards in the international community's response to the crisis in Gaza point to a broader erosion of trust in international norms and institutions. The immediate consequence of these actions is the further entrenchment of suffering among the Palestinian population, which finds itself caught between the violence of military actions and the political machinations that hinder the flow of aid.

The unfolding crisis in Gaza and the international response to it reveal deep-seated challenges in the realms of humanitarian aid, international law, and geopolitical strategy. The suspension of UNRWA funding on questionable grounds and the apparent impunity with which military actions are conducted against civilians highlight a troubling departure from the principles of evidence-based decision-making and respect for human rights. There is a critical need for a return to principled action that prioritises the wellbeing of vulnerable populations and the pursuit of peace over political expediency. This is not happening in Gaza.

NOT ALL POLITICIANS ARE LOOKING AWAY

The escalating humanitarian crisis in Gaza has not only drawn international condemnation but has also sparked significant debate within national governments, including Australia's. The Australian Greens have been vociferous in their criticism of the Australian Government's one-sided support for Israel, highlighting a broader discourse on the complexities of international alliances and the principles that should guide them. The Federal Labor member for Fremantle, Josh Wilson, provides a contrast within the Australian Labor government itself, offering a poignant insight into the devastating human toll of the conflict in Gaza:

"The truth is that Gaza is being bombed into rubble, with 70 per cent of buildings damaged and the entire population being squeezed further and further south in starvation conditions, without basic medical services. In four months, 28,000 civilians have been killed, two thirds of whom are women and children. It is wrong, and it has to stop—history tells us that violence almost never solves anything, and state sponsored violence almost always causes enormous disproportionate harm to innocent people."

Wilson's statement highlights the severe situation in Gaza, characterised by extensive bombing that has led to widespread destruction and a significant humanitarian crisis. However, there appears to be a lack of collective voice within the Labor government. While there have been some instances of isolated commentary, notably from Senator Fatima Payman and Minister Ed Husic, the response from Prime Minister Anthony Albanese and Foreign Minister Penny Wong has been underwhelming.

There is an urgent need for a commitment to peace and the protection of human rights, as opposed to militaristic strategies that invariably harm innocent individuals. The question arises as to when the Labor government will confront the actions and influence of the Israel lobby in Australia. How many innocent civilians must be killed in Gaza before governments finally denounce Israel's actions as genocide and ethnic cleansing? Is the threshold 30,000? Or 50,000? Does it need to reach 100,000, or even one million?

The behaviour of the Israeli government and the Israel Defense Force in Gaza is reminiscent of those willing to inflict extensive torture, as evidenced by the Stanford University Prison Experiment in the early 1970s and the abuses at Abu Ghraib within the Guantánamo Bay Naval Base in the 2000s. Israel acts like the unhinged psychopath who does not know when to stop, primarily because no one is telling them to stop.

The situation in Gaza and the international response to it raise critical questions about the responsibility of governments to act in accordance with international human rights standards and the principles of justice and peace. The disparity in the global reaction to crises, as illustrated by the contrasting figures in Gaza and Ukraine, highlights a perceived inconsistency in the international community's commitment to these values. This inconsistency not only undermines the credibility of international law but also exacerbates suffering by allowing political considerations to override humanitarian needs.

For meaningful progress to be made, there must be a concerted effort to bridge the gap between rhetoric and action. The growing calls for a reassessment of the situation in Gaza, both within Australia and internationally, reflect a broader demand for policies that prioritise human dignity and the protection of civilians in conflict zones. As more voices within government and the international community advocate for change, the pressure mounts for a re-evaluation of support mechanisms and for holding accountable those who violate international norms.

THERE ARE NO SAFE ZONES IN GAZA

The escalation of hostilities in Gaza, particularly in the city of Rafah, marks a critical juncture in the ongoing conflict between Israel and Palestinian factions. The Israeli Defence Force's actions in Rafah, including bombings and a planned ground offensive, have intensified the humanitarian crisis and raised significant international concerns. The reported killing of at least 112 people in Israeli air and sea attacks on Rafah, as stated by the Ministry of Health in Gaza, highlights the dire consequences of military operations on civilian populations.

The strategic significance of Rafah, coupled with the Israeli Defence Force's justification of its actions as being for the "safety" of Palestinians, reveals a disturbing aspect of the conflict. The bombardment of areas into which Palestinians have been forced into raises profound questions about the efficacy and ethics of such military strategies. In addition, the potential derailment of captive exchange negotiations by a ground offensive in Rafah, as indicated by senior Hamas leaders, highlights the intricate interplay between military actions and diplomatic efforts in the region.

The international reaction to the situation in Rafah has been muted. The communication between U.S. President Joe Biden and Israeli Prime Minister Benjamin Netanyahu, which emphasised the need for a "safety" plan for the over one million people sheltering in Rafah, reflects global concern over the humanitarian implications of a ground assault. However, similar to Senator Wong's meaningless rhetoric of "deep concerns", it is clear that no one in the West is prepared to take action to defend Gaza and halt the daily massacre of innocent civilians, including women and children.

Similarly, the obstruction of vital supplies, as evidenced by the blocking of a shipment containing a month's supply of food for Gaza at Israel's Ashdod Port, further exacerbates the humanitarian crisis and highlights the urgent need for international intervention to ensure the provision of aid.

Senator Wong's expression of concern about the "potentially devastating consequences" for the civilians of Rafah is in contrast to the growing international sentiment that calls for an immediate cessation of hostilities and a re-evaluation of military strategies that risk civilian lives. The "potential" that Senator Wong refers to has already been reached: Rafah is already being devastated and the war against innocent civilians is continuing.

In light of these developments, the international community stands at a crossroads. Just as we discovered the effectiveness and value of their actions during the massacres in Rwanda and Bosnia in the 1990s, and in Darfur in the 2000s, it has become evident that the United Nations functions as a "paper tiger"—incapable of responding to any international disaster or atrocity unless the permanent members of the Security Council are prepared to agree to act. Given their divergent fields of geopolitical interests, such consensus on Gaza is highly unlikely.

The events in Rafah demand a concerted and unified response that prioritises the protection of civilian lives, the facilitation of humanitarian aid, and the pursuit of peaceful resolutions to the conflict. The juxtaposition of military objectives with the humanitarian needs of the Palestinian population in Gaza necessitates a re-evaluation of the strategies employed in the conflict and a renewed commitment to peace, human rights, and international law.

The imperative to prevent further loss of life and address the humanitarian crisis in Gaza demands a recommitment to peace, non-violence, and the principles of international law. Only through such reorientation can the international community hope to resolve the conflict in Gaza and restore dignity and hope to its people. However, this goal is unlikely to be achieved as long as governments in the West lack courage and continue to acquiesce to and appease the genocidal behaviour of the Israeli government and the Israel Defense Forces.

***

THE IMBALANCE IN AUSTRALIA'S MEDIA COVERAGE OF GAZA

26 February 2024

In examining the complex and emotive issue of media coverage concerning the conflict in Gaza, particularly from the perspective of Australian reporting, one cannot help but confront a deeply unsettling narrative of imbalance and, arguably, misrepresentation. The contrast in casualties, with around 1,195 Israeli civilians and almost 30,000 Palestinians killed since 7 October, highlights not just a disproportionate scale of loss but also a fundamental question of how such events are framed and understood through the lens of media. This disparity in numbers, which by any measure suggests a grave imbalance in the human cost of conflict, raises significant ethical questions about the role of media in shaping public perception and, by extension, political discourse.

The media landscape in Australia, characterised by major outlets such as News Corporation and Nine Media, has been critiqued for a perceived one-sidedness in its coverage of the conflict. This critique extends beyond the borders of Australia, touching upon a broader concern about Western media's portrayal of the Israeli–Palestinian conflict. The ramifications of such reporting are profound, affecting not just public opinion but also the political will and policy-making that directly impact the region's future. The cycle of violence, perpetuated in part by this skewed narrative, continues unabated, fueled by a lack of balanced reporting that might otherwise foster a more nuanced understanding and, potentially, a more concerted effort towards peace.

Social media, meanwhile, has emerged as a counterbalance to traditional media narratives, providing a platform for the dissemination of images and stories that often go unreported or underreported in mainstream channels. The poignant images of children and civilians caught in the crossfire serve as a powerful testament to the human cost of the conflict, challenging narratives that seek to minimize or ignore Palestinian suffering. However, the role of social media is double-edged, serving both as a space for critical discourse and as a battleground for ideological clashes, where accusations of anti-Semitism and racism can sometimes overshadow the urgent need for dialogue and understanding.

The call for balanced and ethical journalism is not merely a matter of professional integrity but a crucial step towards addressing the underlying issues that fuel the conflict. Quality journalism should strive to present diverse perspectives, seeking to understand the complexities of the conflict beyond simple binaries of victim and aggressor. The recent legislative developments in Australia, such as the anti-doxxing legislation, highlight the influence of media narratives on political decisions, raising questions about the timing and motivations behind such measures. The implications of media bias extend beyond the Israeli–Palestinian conflict, influencing a wide range of political and social issues, from international diplomacy to domestic policy.

As we look deeper into the intricacies of media representation and its impact on the Israeli–Palestinian conflict, it becomes increasingly clear that the challenge lies not only in reporting the facts but in navigating the delicate terrain of historical grievances, cultural sensitivities, and political aspirations. The path to a more balanced and informed public discourse is fraught with obstacles, from the fear of defamation to the risks of oversimplification. Yet, the pursuit of a more nuanced and empathetic understanding of the conflict is not only a journalistic imperative but a moral one, demanding courage, integrity, and a steadfast commitment to the principles of fairness and justice.

The role of media in shaping the narrative of the Israeli–Palestinian conflict, particularly within the Australian context, highlights a pressing need for a reevaluation of how stories are told and whose voices are amplified. As we move forward, the imperative for media outlets, journalists, and society at large is to engage in a more critical and reflective discourse, one that acknowledges the complexity of the conflict and the shared humanity of all those affected. Only through such a balanced and ethical approach can we hope to contribute to a more informed and, ultimately, more peaceful resolution to one of the most enduring and divisive conflicts of our time.

ECHOES OF SILENCE: THE STORY OF HIND RAJAB AND THE MEDIA'S ROLE IN SHAPING WAR NARRATIVES

The tragic story of Hind Rajab, a six-year-old Palestinian girl caught in the brutal crossfire of the conflict in Gaza, encapsulates the profound human cost of war and the critical role of media in bringing such narratives to light. Her desperate plea for help, broadcast by Al Jazeera, contrasts the often sanitised and dehumanised portrayal of Palestinian suffering in parts of the Australian media landscape. This incident, where Hind and her family were allegedly lured to their deaths by the Israeli military, has been labeled by many as a war crime, yet its coverage—or the lack thereof—by major Australian news outlets highlights a disturbing disparity in the portrayal of victims based on their national or ethnic identities.

The relationship between media coverage and political influence is further exemplified by the response to Hind Rajab's story. Where international outlets and social media platforms provided a platform for her story to be shared and mourned, the silence or minimal coverage from certain Australian media entities raises questions about the impact of journalistic practices and affiliations on public perception and policy making. The fact that such a heart-wrenching narrative received limited attention in Australia, especially from outlets that have historically participated in state-sponsored educational tours provided by the Israeli government, highlights the intricate connections between media representation, political narratives, and the shaping of public opinion.

This imbalance in media coverage extends beyond individual tragedies, reflecting a broader trend of humanising Israeli victims while marginalising or ignoring Palestinian suffering. Such practices not only distort the reality of the conflict but also contribute to a skewed understanding of the dynamics at play, reinforcing stereotypes and entrenching biases. The criticism directed at public figures and entities that dare to challenge this narrative, including international dignitaries and members of the royal family, highlights the challenges faced by those seeking to promote a more balanced and equitable discourse.

The consequences of this media imbalance are far-reaching, influencing not only domestic policy in countries like Australia but also international responses to the conflict. The narrative that emerges from mainstream media coverage can shape the decisions made at the highest levels of government and international diplomacy, affecting the lives of millions and the prospects for peace. As the story of Hind Rajab and countless others fade from public consciousness, the imperative for a more ethical, balanced, and human-centred approach to journalism becomes ever more critical.

In addressing these challenges, the role of alternative media sources and social media platforms in providing a counter-narrative becomes increasingly important. As traditional media outlets face accusations of irrelevance and bias, the democratisation of information through digital platforms offers a glimmer of hope for a more nuanced and comprehensive understanding of the conflict. However, this shift also highlights the need for media literacy and critical engagement from the public, ensuring that the stories that shape our perceptions and policies are scrutinised and understood in all their complexity.

The narrative of the Israeli–Palestinian conflict, as presented in parts of the Australian media, serves as a poignant reminder of the power of media to shape our understanding of the world. It challenges us to seek out diverse perspectives, to question the narratives presented to us, and to strive for a more just and empathetic portrayal of those caught in the crosshairs of history. Only through such a collective effort can we hope to move towards a future where the stories of all victims are heard, where the cycles of violence are broken, and where peace is not just a distant dream but a tangible reality.

***

THE GREAT AUSTRALIAN SILENCE

16 March 2024

In his address at the National Press Club last week, Yanis Varoufakis, the former Greek finance minister and renowned economist, took a firm stance on the ongoing crisis in Gaza, shining a spotlight on the Australian government's weak and often contradictory one-sided position. Varoufakis, whose expertise stretches beyond economics to encompass a broad understanding of global geopolitical dynamics, criticised Australia's implicit support for Israel's actions in Gaza, East Jerusalem, and the West Bank, actions he described as deliberate war crimes.

Varoufakis's poignant words, "children are not starving in Gaza today; they are being deliberately starved," highlight a grave accusation against Israel's policies, which is an intentional strategy to subjugate and eventually displace the Palestinian population. By drawing parallels with historical instances of apartheid and the ideological justifications used to erase native populations, such as the doctrine of *terra nullius* in Australia, Varoufakis not only condemned Israel's policies but also called out Australia's complicity in these actions, arguing that Australia's diplomatic defence of Israel's actions, uncritically supporting the right to self-defence—for Israel, but not for Palestinians—and its decision to defund the United Nations Relief and Works Agency, the only agency capable of alleviating the humanitarian crisis in Gaza, has tarnished its international reputation.

Varoufakis urged Australia to lead a campaign against apartheid in Israel–Palestine, reminiscent of its historical campaign against apartheid in South Africa in the 1980s, to restore equal civil liberties to both Israelis and Palestinians.

The Australian government's lacklustre response to the crisis in Gaza, suggests that it's primarily parroting U.S. policies without forging an independent foreign policy stance. The ongoing violence in Gaza, resulting in the deaths of over 32,000 Palestinian people in just five months, has been met with a cowardly silence from Australia, marked by a failure to unequivocally condemn the actions of the Israeli Defense Forces. This stance is a significant stain on the legacy of the Albanese government, raising questions about the moral and ethical lines that must be drawn in international relations and human rights advocacy.

The dialogue surrounding this issue highlights a broader critique of global inaction and the need for a concerted effort to address the root causes of the conflict in Gaza. The lack of a strong, principled stance from countries like Australia not only undermines their moral authority but also implicates them in the ongoing humanitarian disaster. As the international community watches, the call for Australia to revisit its foreign policy priorities and stand on the right side of history grows louder, urging an end to the violence and a move towards lasting peace and equality in the region.

THE UNACCEPTABLE REASONS FOR AUSTRALIAN COWARDICE

If people such as Varoufakis—and many others in the world community—can be so critical of the actions of Israel, why is it so difficult for political leaders to make the same strident calls? What are the barriers that make Australian leaders such as Prime Minister Anthony Albanese and Foreign Affairs

Minister Senator Penny Wong so reluctant to call out the actions of Israel? What are the factors that have made them determine that supporting Palestinians—as well as being on the right side of history—will cause them far greater political and electoral damage, than calling out Israel for obvious war crimes, attempted genocide and ethnic cleansing?

At the heart of Australia's foreign policy are its strategic and diplomatic alliances, particularly with Western nations. The longstanding military and diplomatic co-operation between Australia and Israel, reinforced by mutual interests in the Middle East, highlights a significant aspect of this relationship. The alliance with Israel aligns Australia with its primary ally, the United States, which exerts considerable influence over Australian foreign policy. This alignment reflects a broader geopolitical strategy, positioning Australia within a network of Western democracies facing shared security concerns.

Domestic politics also play a crucial role in shaping Australia's stance. The influence of the Jewish community, while numerically small, is notable in political and business circles. This community's support is seen as vital for political leaders of the Labor and Liberal parties, and there is a palpable fear among politicians of alienating these and other pro-Israel voters. This fear is compounded by the broader Australian public's perception of Israel some kind of like-minded democracy in a turbulent region, which many politicians are loath to challenge. Whether this notion of democracy is the case or not—Israel currently has an extremist far-right government that doesn't seem to be representative of the will of the electorate—this is the perception that exists within the Australian community.

The media's portrayal of the Israeli–Palestinian conflict significantly influences public opinion and, by extension, political stances. Media coverage often sympathetic to Israel's security dilemmas tends to shape a narrative that discourages overt support for Palestine and Australian leaders, wary of backlash or accusations of not supporting Israel, often find themselves navigating a media landscape that can be hostile to nuanced positions on the conflict.

The conflation of criticism of Israel with anti-Semitism is a significant factor in the Australian political discourse. Politicians are acutely aware of the fine line between legitimate criticism and being perceived as anti-Semitic—maniacally monitored and pushed by groups such as the Zionist Federation of Australia and the Australian Jewish Association—and it's this fear leads to more cautious public statements that often favour Israel or express neutrality, even when faced with significant evidence of humanitarian crises or disproportionate responses in conflicts like that in Gaza.

And, of course, there is the grand old sentiment of racism in Australia, which has historically had a fear of outsiders and people who are 'different to us', and this is an issue that cannot be underplayed.

Australia's cautious approach to the conflict in Gaza and the broader Israeli–Palestinian conflict reflects a complex interplay of strategic, domestic, ethical, religious, and racial considerations. The challenge for Australia lies in navigating these multifaceted issues while maintaining its strategic interests and upholding its values, necessitating a more assertive and principled stance in foreign policy. Whether or not Australia will rise to this challenge remains to be seen, however, it is evident that many politicians in federal politics—particularly within the Labor government—prioritise their political careers over the lives of the 32,000 individuals who have been lost in Gaza over the past five months.

A MORE INDEPENDENT COURSE

For most governments, attempted genocide, ethnic cleansing and apartheid would be reasons for political leaders to speak out, irrespective of where it's occurring in the world, but especially in a case where we can see exactly what is happening and have been constantly outraged by these events. Should Australia cultivate a more autonomous foreign policy direction, distinct from the overarching influence of the United States, so it can discuss more openly—and more accurately—the events that are taking place in Gaza?

The relationship between Australia and the U.S. is undoubtedly deep-rooted, characterised by extensive military, security, and intelligence collaborations. However, this intertwined relationship has sparked debates over the extent of Australia's foreign policy autonomy, particularly in its current position on Israel and the ongoing situation in Gaza.

The unwavering support of the United States for Israel, epitomised by President Joe Biden's unequivocal backing—a self-proclaimed Zionist—raises questions about the implications of such alliances for Australian domestic and foreign policy. While the solidarity with Israel may resonate with American political narratives, it simultaneously tests the waters of Australia's political leadership, challenging the Prime Minister and Foreign Affairs Minister to navigate a complex geopolitical landscape.

Historically, figures such former prime ministers Bob Hawke and Paul Keating have demonstrated that Australian foreign policy can indeed be formulated with a degree of independence, mindful of the country's unique geographical and strategic interests. Their efforts to differentiate Australian foreign policy from that of its allies, while maintaining amicable relations, offer valuable lessons for the current administration. The proximity of nations like Indonesia, Papua New Guinea, India and China highlights the strategic imperative for Australia to pursue a foreign policy that not only respects its alliances but also recognises the importance of its immediate neighbourhood.

By positioning itself as a significant middle power within the South-East Asia region—where it geographically belongs—rather than merely acting as a subordinate player to the United States, Australia could assume a more impactful role in international affairs. This shift would not only enhance Australia's standing but also provide itself with greater moral authority on issues in the Middle East, allowing it to address the death, destruction, and suffering of the Palestinian people more effectively, rather than continually overlooking these grave concerns.

The challenges facing the Foreign Minister are considerable as she endeavours to navigate the intricate landscape of international diplomacy and her goal is to strike a balance between maintaining Australia's long-standing alliances and advocating for a distinctive and principled stance in foreign policy. At present, it is a balance that is not being achieved. The ongoing debate over Australia's autonomy in foreign policy, especially highlighted by the Gaza conflict, prompts a wider discussion about the nation's role on the global stage.

ANTI-SEMITISM HAS LOST ITS MEANING

In the evolving narrative surrounding Australia's position on the Gaza conflict, criticism towards the Foreign Minister and the Labor government has intensified, underscoring a perceived failure to navigate the diplomatic tightrope with the finesse expected of a nation with Australia's international standing. The delayed decision to restore funding to the UNRWA for humanitarian aid in Gaza, as highlighted by former Foreign Affairs Minister Gareth Evans where he urged the government to "stop sitting on the fence", epitomises this critique. The eventual reinstatement of aid, while a positive step, has been overshadowed by the protracted hesitation that preceded it, casting a shadow over Australia's commitment to humanitarian principles.

There have also been incidents where Palestinians in Gaza, having been granted visitor visas to Australia, managed to escape from Gaza into Egypt and board flights to Australia, only to be told mid-flight that their visas had been cancelled, forcing them to return. Although over 2,000 visitor visas have been granted to Palestinians—and more than 2,400 to Israeli citizens—only 400 have actually arrived in Australia. Many have been left stranded due to these mid-flight visa cancellations, a situation influenced by pressure from Israeli lobby groups in Australia and political figures such as the Shadow Home Affairs Minister, Senator James Paterson.

Once again, a lacklustre justification was offered by Minister Clare O'Neil, stating that the government was investigating the manner in which some of these visa holders had exited Gaza "without explanation"—just a guess, but perhaps the daily bombings, genocide, and ethnic cleansing in Gaza could provide some context? This situation highlights the influence of the Israeli lobby and demonstrates the Australian government's readiness to perpetuate the persecution of Palestinians, extending the suffering initiated by the state of Israel. It's reminiscent of the ships of Jewish refugees turned back from the ports of the United States during Word War II, under the belief by the U.S. State Department that they could "threaten national security". Short memories.

The conversation around Australia's diplomatic language and actions—or the lack of action—regarding the situation in Gaza is marked by a palpable frustration. The government's rhetoric often resorts to what could be best described as "weasel words," a diplomatic contortion that fails to adequately address the gravity of the conflict or the disproportionate number of Palestinian casualties.

Amidst these critiques, voices within the Labor government, such as Tony Burke, Ed Husic and Senator Fatima Payman, have been acknowledged for their condemnation of the violence in Gaza—their outspokenness serves as a reminder that strong, principled stances on international human rights issues do not necessarily precipitate political fallout and these example highlights the possibility for the Australian government to adopt a more unequivocal stance in condemning the actions of the Israeli government and advocating for a ceasefire, without fear of reprisal from domestic political opponents or lobby groups. It shouldn't be necessary to point this out, but surely it's acceptable for political leaders to condemn genocide, ethnic cleansing, apartheid and the slaughter of over 32,000 Palestinians in Gaza and not be accused of anti-Semitism. *Surely*.

The discussion around response to the conflict also extends beyond diplomatic and humanitarian concerns, touching on broader issues of identity, morality, and the politics of criticism. The controversy surrounding writer-director Jonathan Glazer's Oscar speech, wherein he called out the genocide in Gaza—only for him to be accused of anti-Semitism by the Combat Antisemitism Movement and Holocaust Survivors groups—encapsulates the fraught terrain of public discourse on this issue, where even a small and legitimate criticism of the state of Israel and the actions of the Israel Defense Forces—whether it's a real or perceived criticism—brings on the torrents and waves of abuse and claims of anti-Semitism. What is the meaning of anti-Semitism if every course of debate has the label throw at it?

As Australia navigates its response to the crisis in Gaza, the calls for a more assertive and morally consistent foreign policy grow louder and the aspiration for an Australian foreign policy that aligns with the nation's values and international human rights standards, while managing diplomatic relationships, presents a challenge. Yet, it is a challenge that Australia must meet if it is to fulfill its potential as a force for good on the world stage, advocating for peace, justice, and the protection of human rights for all, irrespective of political pressures or alliances. The path forward requires courage, clarity, and a recommitment to the principles that should guide international relations in the twenty-first century. We're not seeing that at the moment.

**

THE DEATH OF AID WORKERS SPARKS GLOBAL OUTRAGE

6 April 2024

In the wake of the killing of Australian aid worker Zomi Frankcom and her colleagues by the Israel Defense Forces in Gaza, a storm of controversy and outrage has developed, not only for those directly involved but also the response—or lack of response—by the Australian government. The reports of this killing—which seems to be an execution based on the use of artificial intelligence and predictive technology—were marred by initial disinformation from Mossad attributing the deaths to Hamas, and the event has rapidly evolved into a focal point for broader discussions about Israel breaching international humanitarian law, war crimes, the ethics of warfare, and the complex web of geopolitical relationships that dictate international responses to such events.

The Australian government's response, although more strident than most their commentary on Gaza over the past six months, has still been tepid and indecisive. Despite the gravitas of the situation, statements from Prime Minister Anthony Albanese and Foreign Minister Senator Penny Wong lacked the forcefulness for such a disaster, and played down the role of the Israel government. The killings in Gaza, which resulted in the deaths of seven aid workers from World Central Kitchen, should have been the clarion call for a stronger stance against the actions of Israel and the IDF, as well as lobbying for a ceasefire in Palestine and to end the war which has so far killed over 33,000 people in Gaza. Yet, the Australian leadership's reaction reflects a cautious approach, influenced by the intricate dynamics of international politics and Australia's strategic ties, especially with the United States, which maintains a complex and one-sided relationship with Israel.

While the world should have acted way before this specific event—the deaths of 33,000 Palestinians should have been the core reason for action—the deaths of the World Central Kitchen aid workers have ignited debates about the proportionality and justification of military actions performed by the IDF, the obligations under international humanitarian law, and the moral imperatives facing nations witnessing such conflicts. This incident constitutes a war crime—among many others committed by the IDF—and underlines the severity of the breach of laws designed to protect the most vulnerable, including those providing humanitarian aid in conflict zones.

The Australian government's lack of meaningful actions have not occurred in a vacuum. International reactions have varied, with some leaders, like U.S. President Joe Biden and U.K. Prime Minister Rishi Sunak, expressing more direct frustrations with Israel's actions—still with great limitations—and this divergence highlights the complexities of international diplomacy, where responses to conflicts are often tempered by strategic interests, historical relationships, and domestic political considerations.

The calls for tangible actions, such as recalling ambassadors and boycotting of Israeli products, are growing louder and reflects a growing impatience with this tepid diplomatic caution. Drawing parallels with the international isolation faced by the South African apartheid regime in the 1970s and 1980s, similar pressures could prompt a re-evaluation of policies and practices by Israel which are deemed in violation of international law and norms.

In this complex and evolving situation, it is clear that the Australian government faces a delicate balancing act. On one hand, there is a clear moral and legal imperative to condemn and seek accountability for actions that violate international humanitarian law. On the other, Australia must navigate its strategic relationships and the broader geopolitical landscape. But at what cost should this be, especially in the context of clear and obvious cases of apartheid, genocide and ethnic cleansing?

We should not only mourn the significant loss of lives in Gaza, but push the international community's commitment to uphold the principles of justice, accountability, and human dignity in the face of conflict and geopolitical complexities. Australia is part of this international community and domestic pressure must continue to be placed upon the Albanese government to also uphold these principles.

DOUBLE AND TRIPLE STANDARDS REMAIN IN VOGUE FOR POLITICAL LEADERS

Despite Prime Minister Albanese's historical advocacy for Palestinian rights and critical stance on Israeli policies—in 2002, his parliamentary comments openly and directly criticised the government of Israel for "creating a human rights and humanitarian crisis in Palestine", for provoking the Al-Aqsa Intifada, funding Hamas, and berated Israel for allowing "fundamentalists to build illegal settlements on Palestinian land"—his commentary in 2024, once he achieved the power where he could actually make a difference, has lacked vigour and the condemnatory force many people would have expected, based on his past positions. The cowardice from Albanese, now in a position to effect change, reveals that his strong statements and actions in 2002 were superficial and shallow words, and have shown him up as a politician who is weak and callow.

Of course, this shift in Albanese's tone highlights the complex pressures and responsibilities that come with leadership, especially on the international stage, where the balance between diplomatic relations and principled stances on human rights and international law must be carefully navigated. But how far can one's principles be bent and distorted, and credibility shredded in such a way? Albanese's past statements in Parliament, which emphasised the importance of adhering to international law and acknowledged the humanitarian crises faced by Palestinians, stand in contrast to his current commentary.

These criticisms should be extended beyond the Prime Minister and to other members of the Labor government, but this also highlights the divisions and the broader debate within Australian politics about the country's stance on the Israeli–Palestinian conflict. The frustration among rank-and-file Labor members highlights the tension between party unity and individual members' sympathies towards the Palestinian cause. This internal dynamic within the party mirrors the larger global debate on the conflict, where sympathies and political stances are often deeply personal and reflect a wide spectrum of views on justice, human rights, and national security.

The targeted IDF attack on World Central Kitchen has also been seen as a deliberate message to deter external aid to the Palestinian community in Gaza. This incident, referred to the British news presenter and commentator Richard Madeley as a "targeted execution", represents a significant escalation in the tactics employed in the conflict, raising serious questions about the rules of engagement and the protection of humanitarian workers in conflict zones. The Australian government's response to such incidents is not just about diplomatic relations with Israel but also about its commitment to upholding international humanitarian law and protecting civilians and aid workers in conflict zones. It's condemnation of Israel and the IDF should have been far stronger.

THERE IS SO MUCH MORE THE AUSTRALIAN GOVERNMENT CAN DO

There are many potential avenues through which Australia could exert pressure and signal its condemnation of the Israel government's actions, not only on the killing of one of its citizens performing humanitarian aid work, but of the 33,000 Palestinians in Gaza. Australia possesses a range of diplomatic and economic tools that could be deployed to express discontent and push for change, including recalling ambassadors, pausing military trade to Israel—52 Australian export licences were granted to Israel during 2023—and considering trade and cultural sanctions. These suggestions not only reflect potential policy actions but also highlight the expectations placed on Australian leaders to embody their historical stances on human rights and international law.

The local political ramifications of the government's stance, particularly for Prime Minister Anthony Albanese, suggest a broader discontent among constituents. The silent vigil outside Albanese's electoral office in Marrickville by the Palestine Action Group and his refusal to meet with them, illustrates a tension between political pragmatism and democratic responsiveness and a reflection of how the broader debate on Australia's foreign policy and can have implications for domestic politics. The electoral implications for Albanese in his historically safe seat of Grayndler, highlight the political cost of perceived inaction or inadequate response to international human rights concerns.

The potential for electoral backlash in Albanese's constituency, based on shifting public sentiment on the

Israeli–Palestinian conflict, indicates a broader trend of increasing political accountability. While Albanese won the seat of Grayndler at the 2022 federal election by a margin of 67–33 per cent in two party preferred voting, previous election results—54–46 per cent at the 2010 federal election—have shown that with the right candidate and with the right campaign, the Australian Greens do have the potential to unseat Albanese at the next election. The unique dynamics of the Grayndler electorate—which shares state boundaries with the NSW state seat of Newtown, held by the NSW Greens—reveal a heightened sensitivity to issues of human rights and justice, and this presents a potential vulnerability for Albanese.

While there might be a political cost for the Prime Minister at a local level, Australia's response to the destruction of Gaza and the broader Israeli–Palestinian conflict reveals the complex interplay between international diplomacy, domestic politics, and the moral imperatives of human rights and justice. As Australia manages its role on the global stage, the actions it chooses to take—or not take—will not only impact its international relations but also reflect its values and priorities to its own citizens and the electorate. The call for a more assertive stance on the Israeli–Palestinian conflict is not only about foreign policy and geopolitics, but about the very identity and moral compass of the Australian nation.

***

NAVIGATING THE COMPLEXITIES OF CONFLICT AND DIPLOMACY

21 April 2024

The escalation of the war in Gaza and its ripple effects extend far beyond the immediate conflict zone, touching on global politics and influencing national policies, including those of Australia. The recent increase in hostilities, marked by Iran's unprecedented direct missile and drone attacks on Israel, stems from a complex web of regional tensions and historical grievances. This act by Iran, a response to a provocative Israel Defense Forces attack on its embassy in Syria, signifies a dangerous broadening of the conflict's scope, which could lead to further instability in the Middle East.

This international conflict also has profound implications for Australian politics, especially concerning its foreign policy and domestic political discourse. Australia, with its significant Jewish and Muslim populations, finds itself in a delicate position, needing to balance its historical, if misguided, support for Israel with the growing calls for recognition of Palestinian statehood. The recent statements from Foreign Minister Senator Penny Wong highlight this shift, where she advocated a two-state solution as the only viable method to end the cycle of violence. It's inherently correct—the long-held view of a two-state solution can't be achieved if Palestine is not a state—and her comments have stirred controversy within Australia from the usual conservative players, reflecting a fractious debate on how the nation should navigate its diplomatic ties and moral positions on international justice and human rights.

The situation has also been a catalyst for wider discussions in Australia about the role of international law and the responsibilities of nations in upholding peace and security. The Australian government faces increasing pressure to align more closely with global consensus, which leans towards recognising Palestinian statehood. This is highlighted by the significant number of UN member states that support such a move—140 of the 193 members—though challenges remain, notably the potential for veto by permanent UN Security Council members, including the United States, which recently used its veto power to block Palestinian statehood.

Australian domestic politics also feels the strain as community groups and political factions express divergent views on the issue, mirroring the global division. The response from the conservative and self-interested Australian Jewish Association, which vehemently opposes recognising Palestinian statehood, contrasts sharply with the broader international and national movements towards a two-state solution. This dichotomy represents the deep ideological divides within Australia that mirror the global disagreements over the Israeli–Palestinian conflict.

The war in Gaza and the international responses to it, including from actors like Iran and Israel, significantly affect Australian political discourse and policy. As the conflict continues to evolve, Australia must navigate its diplomatic strategies carefully, balancing its domestic interests with its international obligations and moral stances on peace, justice, and human rights.

HOW THE ISRAELI–PALESTINIAN CONFLICT SHAPES AUSTRALIAN POLITICS

The domestic political landscape in Australia is intricately tied to its international relations, especially concerning the Israeli–Palestinian conflict. As the conflict escalates, comparisons are being drawn between Israeli Prime Minister Benjamin Netanyahu and former British Prime Minister Margaret Thatcher. Both leaders, facing political unpopularity, leveraged military actions to boost their domestic approval ratings. Netanyahu, like Thatcher with the Falklands conflict in 1982, is using the ongoing violence to solidify his position amid political instability.

This perception has sparked significant debate within Australia, impacting both public opinion and the stances of political leaders. Prime Minister Anthony Albanese and Senator Wong have faced considerable pressure, navigating the complex and often divisive reactions among the Australian populace—the Australian government, while officially supporting a two-state solution, appears to vacillate under the influence of powerful lobbies, such as the Australian Jewish Association. The situation is further complicated by Israel's actions, particularly under Netanyahu's leadership, are motivated by strategic interests in natural resources, such as gas reserves near Gaza, rather than purely security concerns.

Public response in Australia has varied widely, with community leaders and activists vocalising either staunch support for Israel or condemnation of its actions and calling for more robust support for Palestinian statehood. The Labor Party, historically more sympathetic to Palestine, has found itself at a crossroads, attempting to balance these complex international dynamics with domestic political consequences. The Australian government's approach has been characterised by caution, as it weighs the implications of fully endorsing

Palestinian statehood against the backdrop of international relations and domestic electoral fallouts.

The controversy over Senator Penny Wong's shifting stance on Israel and Palestine highlights the broader political and ethical dilemmas facing Australia. Her nuanced position—to put it very generously—reflects an attempt to mediate between the humanitarian crises in Gaza and the powerful domestic and international interests that influence Australia's foreign policy. This balancing act is indicative of the broader challenges that Australia faces on the world stage, where it must navigate its values, strategic interests, and international obligations.

THE IMPACT ON AUSTRALIAN POLITICAL LEADERSHIP

The Israeli–Palestinian conflict continues to cast a shadow over Australian politics, influencing not just foreign policy decisions but also the dynamics within domestic political arenas. The leader of the opposition, Peter Dutton, recently took a controversial stance that contrasts with the more measured approach of the government. Dutton's remarked that "whilst no one was killed during the protests... the events of the Sydney Opera House were akin to a Port Arthur moment in terms of their social and national significance ... Prime Minister Albanese has not driven risen to that moment, as John Howard did," a comment that was guaranteed to incite and cause yet another divisive debate within the community.

This discourse is not just about the events themselves but also about the role of leadership in times of national and international turmoil. Dutton's comments were intended to as a criticism of Prime Minister Albanese's handling of the issue of Gaza, suggesting a failure to rise to the occasion as past leaders have. However, this comparison has been met with backlash and ridicule from various quarters, including from within his own party, especially from the Liberal Party backbencher, Bridget Archer.

The government's Jason Clare commented that "if you want to run the country, you can't run your mouth. Last week, Peter Dutton took the sight of another country that killed an Australian citizen. This week, he is using the murder in cold blood of 35 Australians to try to make a political point. This bloke is all aggro and no judgment."

Dutton's behaviour resulted in a response that shows a broader discontent with what is seen as an opportunistic and divisive approach to politics and a style of irresponsible leadership that prioritises sensational rhetoric over substantive policy.

The fallout from Dutton's comments has also highlighted a schism within the Liberal Party, with figures such as Archer calling for a return to more principled politics, echoing a sentiment that many Australians find lacking in Dutton's approach. This internal party conflict mirrors the larger national debate over how Australia should engage with complex international issues like the Israeli–Palestinian conflict. The sharp critiques from within Dutton's own ranks—Archer wasn't the only Liberal Party to voice her dismay—suggest a party at odds with itself on the direction and tone of its leadership.

The broader Australian political landscape is witnessing a shift towards more grassroots movements, as indicated by the Climate 200 initiative's plans to support candidates in upcoming elections. This movement signifies a growing public demand for new political narratives that diverge from traditional party lines and address global issues like climate change and international conflict with a fresh perspective. Such movements pose a challenge to established figures like Dutton, who are perceived as out of touch with the evolving political consciousness of the Australian public.

The discourse surrounding the Israeli–Palestinian conflict not only shapes foreign policy but also deeply influences Australian domestic politics, challenging leaders to adapt to a rapidly changing political environment. As Australia deals with these complex global interactions, the political responses at home reflect a nation striving to reconcile its international engagements with domestic political accountability and integrity of leadership.

***

A UN VOTE AND AUSTRALIA'S INCONSISTENT FOREIGN POLICY

11 May 2024

There was another vote at the United Nations on the weekend, aiming to provide Palestine with additional observer status rights. Unlike the vote in April, which the United States blocked through the UN Security Council, this time the draft resolution had undergone changes to address the previous objections. The revised vote was passed by the United Nations by a substantial majority of 143 votes to 9, despite the vehement protests from the Israeli Ambassador. Although this change was small, it signified progress in the pathway for Palestine being fully recognised as a state. This vote did not concern full UN membership for Palestine, which typically involves a cyclical pattern of vetoes from permanent members of the United Nations—the United States vetoed the vote in April and is expected to do so again if a resolution for full Palestinian membership arises, and in the unlikely event that it did either support the vote or abstain, the permanent members usually conspire so that one of the other members—either Britain or France—can find some fault with the resolution, perpetuating the diplomatic stalemate.

Australia's stance on this matter continues to highlight the inconsistency in its foreign policy regarding the Israeli–Palestinian conflict. The rhetoric of a two-state solution, frequently reiterated by Australian officials, rings hollow without recognising both Israel and Palestine as sovereign states. Australia's abstention from the vote in April—to provide Palestine with full UN membership—reflects a lack of courage and commitment to meaningful progress in the region and while it did support this vote, it did it's best to downplay the significance of this support, leaving people wondering why they supported it in the first place. Foreign Minister Penny Wong had been engaged in discussions with ministers from Germany, the United Arab Emirates, and New Zealand, yet substantial political will is still lacking. In an election year for the United States and Britain—and possibly Australia—these countries are unlikely to shift their positions, further complicating efforts for change.

Comparisons have been also been made between the situation in Palestine and the historical context of East Timor in 1999. Indonesia's long-standing control over East Timor, driven by strategic interests in the region's resources, seemed intractable until international pressure and political will culminated in an end to the Indonesian occupation and East Timor's independence in 2002. While each international situation is unique, there are lessons to be learned from East Timor that could be applied to Palestine and the broader Middle East. However, this requires a significant shift in political will from the international community, which is currently absent concerning Gaza and Palestine.

Australia's involvement in East Timor was also marred by controversial actions, including the disproportionate appropriation of gas resources and allegations of spying on the East Timorese government. These actions highlights the importance of supporting smaller nations rather than exploiting them, a lesson that seems not fully absorbed when it comes to Gaza. The ongoing reluctance to join the global consensus in protecting Palestinian rights and sovereignty reflects a persistent failure in Australian foreign policy. This failure is particularly stark given the context of Palestinian resistance against what they view as foreign interlopers taking their land, especially when consideration of Australia engaged in exactly the same action in 1788 which its own Indigenous population. It is crucial for Australia, and the international community, to engage in self-reflection and adopt a more just and proactive stance on Palestine.

DEBATE OVER PALESTINIAN STATEHOOD HIGHLIGHTS HYPOCRISY AND INACTION IN AUSTRALIAN FOREIGN POLICY

The ongoing debate over what constitutes a Palestinian state has also dominated international discussions recently. Central to this debate is whether the borders should be based on the pre-1967 lines or include Gaza and the current West Bank, which has been increasingly encroached upon by illegal Jewish settlements over the past 57 years. The pre-1967 borders are unequivocally unacceptable to the current Israeli leadership. Yet, it's crucial to acknowledge that, as a state founded on Zionism, Israel is unlikely to ever accept the establishment of any kind Palestinian state, irrespective of how small it is. Consequently, any vote on the state of Palestine is improbable to succeed in the near term, especially during an election year in the United States. Australia, with an election looming possibly by the end of this year or by May 2025, is likely to maintain its pro-Israel stance under Prime Minister Anthony Albanese's government.

Albanese's recent actions contradict his positions when he was in opposition. This perspective was evident in his conversation with former Liberal Party treasurer Josh Frydenberg—who appears to be revelling in role of director of pro-Israel propaganda documentaries for Sky News—when Frydenberg asked Albanese if the phrase "from the river to the sea" extremely violent and said it had no place on Australian streets, Albanese readily agreed. And to further show which side he now supports, in a recent 3AW interview when asked to comment on the pro-Palestine university protests and encampments, Albanese said "I reckon if you asked those people chanting it [from the river to the sea], heaps of them wouldn't have a clue, wouldn't be able to find the [river] Jordan on a map". Not much solidarity with the people who Albanese would have been protesting with on campus, in his previous life in student politics. But, as Lord Acton once said "power tends to corrupt and absolute power corrupts absolutely".

This stance raises questions about the perceived violence of words versus actions. While the phrase is deemed offensive and violent towards Israelis, the massacre and bombing of over 35,000 Palestinians, predominantly women and children, is not similarly condemned by these leaders. This selective outrage reflects a profound hypocrisy. Frydenberg, Albanese and many other leaders seem to overlook the equally inflammatory and violent rhetoric from Israeli leaders. Not long ago, Israeli Prime Minister Benjamin Netanyahu asserted that Israel must control the entire area "from the river to the sea"—so, it seems, words are deemed violent and unacceptable if uttered by Palestinians, but appear to be ignored when the same words come from an Israeli leader.

The double standard extends further. Albanese recently reprimanded Education Minister Jason Clare for his balanced stance on protests and slogans, where Clare emphasised that while protests are a fundamental part of democracy, there is no place for hate, prejudice, discrimination, intimidation, anti-Semitism, or Islamophobia, and pointed out the ambiguous interpretation of slogans like "from the river to the sea," which have been used by both Palestinian advocates and Israeli political parties. Clare's call for a two-state solution, where two peoples could live side by side in peace without fear, terrorism, checkpoints, or occupation, was a plea for reason and balance. Yet, Clare's very moderate comments and statements on Israel were shut down by Albanese, and criticised as being highly inflammatory and anti-Semitic by the Israel and Zionist lobby groups, and News Corporation.

The hypocrisy is obvious. The selective condemnation of rhetoric depending on its source highlights a broader issue in international politics regarding Palestine. The same words are branded as violent when spoken by Palestinians but are brushed off when articulated by Israeli officials. This double standard not only undermines the legitimacy of calls for peace and justice but also perpetuates the cycle of violence and occupation in the region. Albanese's shift in stance from opposition to leadership further exemplifies the political expediency that often trumps genuine efforts towards a fair resolution of the Israeli–Palestinian conflict.

Australia's lack of action and the inconsistency in its foreign policy reflect a broader unwillingness to confront the complex realities of the Israeli–Palestinian conflict. This reluctance to take a firm and principled stand, whether driven by electoral considerations or international alliances, ultimately contributes to the ongoing suffering and instability in the region. It is imperative for leaders to transcend partisan politics and adopt a genuinely balanced approach that advocates for the rights and sovereignty of all peoples involved.

ALBANESE'S SHIFTING STANCE ON PALESTINE UNDERMINES HIS CREDIBILITY

Albanese's stance on Palestine presents a troubling inconsistency that has become increasingly evident over his tenure. While Albanese has shown strong leadership on various issues, his approach to the Israeli–Palestinian conflict contrasts with his earlier, more principled positions.

True leadership entails adhering to values consistently, and deviating from these values can erode a leader's credibility over time. This divergence is particularly glaring given Albanese's history of pro-Palestinian advocacy and other issues, such as his previous support for increasing social welfare payments. His current positions not only diminishes his moral authority but also raises questions about his commitment to justice and human rights.

Albanese's shift on Palestine, alongside his reluctance to support raising Jobseeker payments, marks a significant departure from his past advocacy and this change reflects a broader trend in politics where electoral calculations often outweigh moral imperatives, and it's a pragmatic but ethically dubious approach, especially given the ongoing humanitarian crisis in Gaza. As reports of massacres and uncovered mass graves continue to emerge, Albanese's support for Israel becomes increasingly indefensible. Certainly, the electorate may not prioritise Middle Eastern policy in their voting decisions on election day, and this is a calculation that both Albanese and U.S. President Joe Biden are relying on. However, dismissing the ethical and moral dimensions of the Gaza conflict undermines the very principles that should guide leadership.

When leaders abandon long-held beliefs, they need compelling reasons for doing so. In the case of Albanese, such reasons have not been convincingly presented. He was pro-Palestine when he was in opposition but now that he's a leader of government, he's pro-Israel and dismissive of any calls for action on alleviating the situation for the people of Gaza. This lack of transparency and deviation from core values is troubling. The government must rediscover its soul, purpose, and reason for being. Albanese's leadership on this issue—or lack thereof—demands a re-evaluation of priorities, guided by the principles of justice, equality, and human rights.

The ongoing developments at the United Nations regarding Palestine highlight the need for strong, principled international leadership. Australia's failure to take a decisive stand on this issue reflects broader systemic problems in how foreign policy is conducted. The hypocrisy in supporting Israel despite the clear humanitarian crisis in Gaza cannot be justified by electoral pragmatism alone. Leaders must be held accountable for their actions and the values they espouse.

True leadership requires unwavering commitment to one's values, especially in the face of complex international issues. Albanese's shifting stance on Palestine not only undermines his credibility but also reflects a deeper problem within political leadership today. The international community, including Australia, must take a more active and principled role in resolving the Israeli–Palestinian conflict, guided by a genuine commitment to human rights and justice for all.

***

ISRAEL INCREASINGLY ISOLATED OVER GENOCIDE IN GAZA

25 May 2024

The International Criminal Court has issued arrest warrants for Israeli Prime Minister Benjamin Netanyahu, his defense minister, and the leadership of Hamas, on the grounds of war crimes and crimes against humanity. This move, while contentious, is a significant step in the ongoing conflict between Israel and Palestine. For decades, the Israeli–Palestinian conflict has been marked by violence predominantly perpetrated by the state of Israel, extreme political machinations, and international diplomatic interventions, with both sides committing actions that have drawn widespread condemnation. In this case, however, the ICC's decision is based on extensive documentation of alleged war crimes, particularly since the escalation of violence since October last year.

Israel has faced accusations of committing war crimes and genocide against Palestinians over many years, a claim that has gained traction especially since the intensification of hostilities. On the other hand, Hamas's actions, particularly those on 7 October 2023, have also been classified as crimes against humanity. The international response to these developments has been polarised—support for Israel, while still significant, appears to be waning, with many advocating

ISRAEL INCREASINGLY ISOLATED OVER GENOCIDE IN GAZA

for adherence to international law and due process as stipulated by the ICC.

Domestically, reactions have also been divided along political lines. Prime Minister Anthony Albanese has refrained from commenting on the legal proceedings, maintaining a stance of non-interference with the judicial process. Conversely, the Leader of the Opposition, Peter Dutton, has vehemently criticised the ICC's actions, describing them as "an abomination" and threatening to withdraw Australia from the ICC's jurisdiction if the Liberal Party were to come into power after the next election, a reaction which is consistent with his historical stance of ignoring legal processes that conflict with his political agenda.

Internationally, the situation is equally complex. Albanese has the dubious distinction of being the first Australian political leader referred to the ICC for his support of Israel in their actions in Gaza, a position that contrasts sharply with the ideals he once held about ending the Israeli occupation of Palestine. Meanwhile, the Netanyahu government is increasingly seen as morally compromised, especially as the death toll among innocent Palestinians rises—over 36,000—and protests within Israel grow louder. The shift in global sentiment is further evidenced by countries such as Norway, Spain, Malta and Ireland recognising Palestine as a state, indicating a significant change in the international community's stance.

The potential repercussions of the ICC's actions are profound. There is a possibility that the court itself could face challenges to its authority, particularly from powerful nations such as the United States, which usually seeks to undermine its legitimacy when its decisions are not favourable to the political and military agenda of the U.S. As more Western countries without direct ties to the conflict begin to voice their support for Palestine, it becomes evident that a significant shift is underway. Whether this will lead to a peaceful and just resolution remains to be seen, but the changing dynamics suggest that the status quo is no longer tenable.

AUSTRALIA'S RESPONSE REFLECTS A PREDICTABLE STANCE

Closer to home, the responses in Australia have been predictable and politically unsophisticated. The Australian government has largely disengaged diplomatically from the Israeli war on Gaza and seems content not to position itself as a leader with any gravitas or independence in this conflict. Dutton has criticised Albanese for what he perceives as equivocation regarding the ICC's announcement, while most politicians have lined up to condemn the ICC. Prominent Liberal figures such as Senators Simon Birmingham, James Paterson and Jane Hume have all taken pot shots at both the Labor government and the ICC decision, while government MPs have all been in unison that there is no "moral equivalence" between Hamas and Israel, voicing their strong support for the state of Israel, reflecting a broader trend of political appeasement towards the Israel lobby in Australia.

It is undeniable that Hamas and the Israeli government are not equivalent entities; they have distinct motivations and methods. However, both have committed war crimes and crimes against humanity. Hamas's actions on 7 October 2023 and Israel's sustained violence—36,000 deaths in Gaza, the continual operation of an apartheid state since 1948 and oppression of Palestinians in both Gaza and the West Bank—are egregious and have been widely documented. Statements from Israeli Defense Force leaders, the Israeli government, and Prime Minister Benjamin Netanyahu himself have confirmed these actions.

Palestinian human rights lawyer Diana Butu, commenting on the ICC announcement, has emphasised that while it is a significant step, it has taken "far too long to reach this point". The occupation of Palestine has persisted for almost 80 years, and starting the timeline on 7 October 2023 rather than when Palestine signed on to the ICC in 2015 reflects a lack of context and depth to this case. Nonetheless, she sees this as an essential first step towards holding Israeli leaders accountable for their actions. Butu hopes that this will lead to more substantial actions, including indictments, to bring an end to what she describes as Israel's genocide.

The prolonged suffering in Gaza must end, regardless of who has committed the crimes. In the case of the alleged war crimes, punishment and sanctions are necessary for those responsible but the priority at this stage must be to halt the extensive human suffering. The global community is growing increasingly intolerant of the ongoing violence, and Netanyahu must face accountability for his actions. His continued aggressive policies are efforts to avoid internal prosecution in Israel for historical corruption, but this cannot justify the immense loss of life in Gaza. The world demands an end to the violence and a move towards justice and peace.

IRELAND LEADS EUROPEAN RECOGNITION OF PALESTINE

"On January 21, 1919, Ireland sought international recognition of its right to be an independent state, emphasising its distinct national identity, historical struggle, and quest for self-determination and justice. Today, Ireland uses the same language to support the recognition of Palestine as a state, grounded in the belief that freedom and justice are fundamental principles of international law and that permanent peace can only be secured through the free will of a free people."
Prime Minister of Ireland, Simon Harris, announcing that Ireland will recognise the state of Palestine.

In his statement, Simon Harris highlighted the powerful political and symbolic value of recognition, asserting that Palestine holds the full rights of a state, including self-determination, self-governance, territorial integrity, and security. This recognition also places obligations on Palestine under international law and supports those in Palestine advocating for a future of peace and democracy.

The Irish government announced its intention to recognise Palestine as a state, a move to be followed by Spain, Slovenia, Norway, and Malta, with speculation that France and Belgium might soon join. This shift in recognition from influential European nations signals a major impetus for change—historically, Palestine's recognition was often limited to smaller, less influential countries, but now, significant European states are taking a stand, reflecting a growing global consensus against Israel's immoral and illegal actions in Gaza and the West Bank.

This movement is not confined to diplomatic recognition alone—the International Criminal Court has issued arrest warrants for Israeli leaders on war crime charges; the International Court of Justice has brought a case of genocide against Israel; a recent United Nations vote increased the rights of the state of Palestine, albeit slightly; FIFA is considering banning Israel from the Football World Cup. Protests and awareness of the plight of Palestine around the world is increasing, with a global outcry demanding an end to the occupation of Palestine.

Israel is becoming increasingly isolated due to its actions in Gaza and the West Bank—the United States remains a steadfast ally, as does Britain, and the upcoming general election in the U.K. is likely to delay any significant change in their stance. However, the international community's patience with Israel's ideological, political, and military overreach is wearing thin, and it can no longer look away.

Despite this international momentum, Australia's response to these developments has been weak and embarrassing. By closely aligning itself with the United States' unwavering support for Israel, Australia has chosen a path of least political resistance domestically, despite knowing about the human rights abuses, war crimes, and genocide. The Liberal Party's overwhelming support for Israel and Zionism contrasts sharply with the more cautious stance of the Labor government. However, the government's response to the events in Gaza and Israel has been disappointing, reflecting a lack of courage and clarity compared to the governments of Ireland, Spain, Norway, Slovenia, and Malta, which have taken decisive and principled stands.

The Australian government should look to these European nations for direction. Despite some commentary from parliamentarians such as Senator Fatima Payman, Tony Burke, Ed Husic and several others, the overall support for Palestine has been insufficient. Many federal cabinet members, including the Prime Minister, had previously supported the rights of Palestinians, and while foreign affairs are complex and subject to change, being on the right side of history is a goal worth striving for.

As support for Palestine gains momentum in Western Europe, it signifies a significant shift in global politics. Australia should aim to facilitate this change rather than cling to the status quo, and the recognition of Palestine and the end of the genocide in Gaza are crucial steps toward a more just and peaceful world. The international community's increasing intolerance of Israel's actions should serve as a wake-up call for Australian political leaders to show greater courage and align themselves with the global movement for justice and peace.

***

NAVIGATING ISLAMOPHOBIA IN THE MEDIA AND POLITICS

13 July 2024

The narrative surrounding multiculturalism and media representation in Australia presents a complex and often contradictory narrative. The recent remarks by the Leader of the Opposition, Peter Dutton, exemplify a troubling pattern where political rhetoric not only reflects but exacerbates societal biases. Dutton's comments, which linked the prospect of a minority government with the inclusion of Muslim candidates from Western Sydney, implicitly cast these potential representatives as threats to political stability, in his words, "a disaster". Such statements are not isolated incidents but are part of a broader narrative that often surfaces in Australian political discourse.

The recent resignation of Senator Fatima Payman from the Labor Party to sit as an independent further fueled the media's engagement with themes of race and religion. Payman, a refugee from Afghanistan—*and visibly Muslim*—has been at the centre of what can be described as a media spectacle, with her actions and statements scrutinised and interpreted through a lens of racial and religious stereotypes. The coverage by various media outlets, from Seven West Media, the ABC and through to News Corporation, has varied in tone, but a common undercurrent of skepticism and fearmongering about Islam and its adherents persists.

Commentary provided by figures such as Andrew Bolt— who breached the *Racial Discrimination Act* for publishing racist material in 2009—claiming that with Payman's shift, "Australian politics just got more dangerous", illustrates how media figures can influence public perception by perpetuating narratives of fear and *otherness*. Bolt's derogatory remarks about Muslim victimhood and his targeting of Payman's background as a refugee highlights a broader media trend that often borders on—and surpasses—Islamophobia. Such narratives not only distort public discourse but also reinforce societal divisions by emphasising differences rather than commonalities.

This media portrayal does not exist in a vacuum. It interacts with and shapes the political landscape, where the fear of the 'other' can be a powerful tool in mobilising electoral support. The political utility of Islamophobia, as seen through the actions and words of some Australian politicians, raises questions about the role of media in either challenging or perpetuating these divisive strategies. While there are exceptions, such as the efforts of broadcasters like SBS to present a more nuanced and diverse perspective, the dominant media narrative tends to favour a portrayal of Australian society that prioritises Anglo-centric views and marginalises minority voices.

The presence in the media of figures such as Waleed Aly, Stan Grant, and Fauziah Ibrahim does offer alternative viewpoints, yet they often face a paradox. While their perspectives are crucial in fostering a more inclusive dialogue, their acceptance and success are contingent upon aligning with a predominantly conservative mainstream narrative. In Grant's case, when he strayed away from this narrative and offered his perspectives as an Indigenous Australian, he was severely criticised and ushered out of the media industry.

This dynamic illustrates the challenges faced by minority voices in gaining traction within a media landscape that is predominantly Anglo, male, and oriented towards centre-right political narratives.

Media representations and political rhetoric in Australia reveals a landscape fraught with challenges for minority communities, particularly for Muslims and especially since the events of 9/11 in the United States in 2001. The narrative not only reflects existing societal biases but also has the potential to shape political and social outcomes. Understanding and addressing these dynamics is crucial for moving towards a truly inclusive and representative Australian society.

THE STRUGGLE FOR SECULARISM AND DIVERSITY IN AUSTRALIAN PARLIAMENT

As Australia manages the ideals of multiculturalism and secularism, the practices within its political institutions reveal a continuing struggle to reconcile tradition with a diverse and changing demographic landscape. The recitation of the Lord's Prayer to commence Parliament—reintroduced by the Howard government in 1996—symbolises this tension. This ritual, ostensibly benign and reflective of moral aspirations, inadvertently highlights the incongruence between Australia's secular commitments and its ceremonial practices, marginalising non-Christian parliamentarians and, by extension, the diverse populace they represent.

The use of the Lord's Prayer as a parliamentary opener is more than just a formality; it is a symbolic act that highlights the perceived primacy of Christian values at the core of governmental proceedings, alienating members of other faiths and those with no religious affiliation. It also highlights how deeply embedded and normalised Christian norms are within the structures of Australian governance, despite the nation's secular policy and diverse religious landscape.

The representation in Parliament, although becoming more diverse, still lags behind the actual demographic makeup of Australia. The 2022 federal election brought in more representatives from various backgrounds, yet the political and cultural infrastructure has been slow to adapt. This sluggishness in embracing true diversity is further compounded by the media and political narratives that often view non-Christian participation, particularly Islamic, with suspicion and as a potential threat rather than a reflection of societal diversity.

The historical context of Australia's foundation as a secular nation, highlighted by the *Australia Act* of 1986, provides a constitutional backing for broader religious freedom and representation. The legacy of figures such as Alfred Deakin at the time of Federation in 1901 and his engagement with spiritualism and theosophy highlight the varied spiritual undercurrents that have shaped Australian public life, which are often overshadowed by the dominant Christian narrative.

The discussion around whether to remove the practice of reciting the Lord's Prayer in Parliament is not only about a procedural detail; it is emblematic of a larger debate about what values Australia wants to project and whose interests and beliefs it aims to reflect. The persistence of such a debate reveals the challenges that lie in fully actualising a secular and inclusive governance structure that respects and represents its citizens' diverse religious and cultural backgrounds.

This situation calls for a thoughtful re-evaluation of traditions that no longer serve the intended purpose of inclusivity and unity in a modern, multicultural society. Such re-evaluation is not an indictment of Christianity or any religion but a recognition of the need for Australia's political practices to mirror its democratic, pluralistic, and secular ideals. This ongoing tension between tradition and modernity in Australian politics highlights the need for a more conscious and deliberate approach to inclusivity, one that not only recognises diversity in parliamentary representation but also respects it in practice.

THE WANING INFLUENCE OF THE MAINSTREAM MEDIA ON AUSTRALIAN POLITICS

The downward spiral of media influence in Australia, particularly in the context of political outcomes, reflects a complex interaction between traditional media power and the shifting dynamics of public engagement and technological change. This transformation is evident in the declining ratings and influence of legacy media outlets, which have traditionally played a central role in shaping political debate and public opinion in Australia.

The decreasing relevance of mainstream media is highlighted by significant shifts within the industry itself, such as staff redundancies at major corporations like News Corporation, which is the largest employer of journalists and media staff in Australia. These changes are symptomatic of a broader transformation where the diversification of media platforms and the advent of digital media have fragmented the audience, offering alternatives that cater to a wider array of interests and viewpoints.

This fragmentation is mirrored in the political sphere, where the rhetoric of politicians such Dutton, who frequently frames Islam as a threat, or commentators like Bolt, who perpetuates negative stereotypes about Muslims, no longer uniformly sway the electorate. Instead, there appears to be a growing scepticism towards the media's portrayal of these issues, suggesting a deeper, more critical consumption of media content by the public. This shift implies that while mainstream media still has the power to reinforce existing prejudices, its ability to convert or significantly alter political views is waning.

The recent political events such as the election of the Albanese government in 2022 and the results of the Voice to Parliament referendum illustrate this nuanced role of the media. In both instances, despite strong media campaigns for opposing outcomes, the public voted differently, indicating that while media narratives can influence public opinion, they do not dictate it. This scenario suggests a more discerning electorate that engages with media content that aligns with their pre-existing beliefs rather than being passively shaped by it.

In addition, the general distaste for Dutton's public offerings, despite media efforts to bolster his image as a decisive leader, further demonstrates the limits of media influence in modern Australian politics. The public's disappointment with the Albanese government, on the other hand, reflects not just media criticism but also broader societal expectations and the complex realities of governance.

This evolving media landscape highlights a significant shift from a passive reception of media content to an active, critical engagement by the public. The growing schism between the politicians and media on one side and the electorate on the other indicates a changing dynamic where traditional media must adapt to remain relevant—if, indeed, it is not too late. This suggests that while the media still plays a critical role in political debate, its influence is modulated by a more informed and critical electorate capable of independent analysis and decision-making.

CAN POLITICAL BEHAVIOUR ADAPT TO THE CHANGING MEDIA LANDSCAPE

In the evolving dynamics between Australian politics and media, the relationship, although altered by digital transformations and shifting public perceptions, remains fundamentally interconnected. Politicians, irrespective of their ideological leanings, continue to rely on mainstream media to disseminate their messages, despite the decline in the media's sway over public opinion. This persistent dependency highlights a deep-seated inclination towards traditional platforms of communication, which, though waning in effectiveness, still hold symbolic and practical value for political figures.

The media's influence, while diluted, is far from extinguished and maintains a psychological hold over politicians, who often measure their own relevance and the impact of their policies through the lens of media coverage. This is reflected in the attention they pay to headlines and news stories, where visibility in mainstream outlets is still equated with political potency. Consequently, even as the power of these outlets wanes in the digital era, their endorsement or criticism remains a coveted prize in political circles.

This enduring relationship reveals a conservative approach to political communication, where innovation is often sacrificed for familiarity. The reluctance to fully embrace newer, more direct methods of engagement such as social media or alternative news platforms highlights a hesitancy to break away from established norms. This is not only a matter of habit but a calculated decision rooted in the perceived risks of alienating traditional media power bases, most notably players such as Kerry Stokes and Rupert Murdoch. Politicians, aware of the media's capacity to shape narratives, are cautious of incurring their ire, which can amplify opposition and stir public sentiment.

However, this dynamic is not without its critics and potential for reform. The suggestion of a governmental inquiry into media ownership and the regulation of media licenses points to a growing recognition of the need for greater media diversity and accountability. Such measures, though fraught with political risk due to potential backlash from powerful media conglomerates, could significantly alter the landscape of political communication. By diminishing the concentrated power of a few media entities, the government could encourage a more pluralistic media environment that better represents Australia's diverse population and offers a wider array of viewpoints.

Taking these issues into account, the challenge is one of courage and political will. The transformation of the media–political nexus would require not only regulatory changes but also a cultural shift within politics itself, where short-term gains through conventional media channels are weighed against the long-term benefits of a more engaged and representative public discourse. The inertia of the status quo is a formidable barrier, with governments often opting for the path of least resistance, which sustains existing power structures and communication strategies.

While the influence of mainstream media on political outcomes may be diminishing, its role within the political process remains significant and the future of this relationship hinges on the ability of politicians to adapt to new realities of media consumption and public engagement. Forging a new path will involve rethinking not just the tools of communication but also the underlying assumptions about power and influence in the digital age. As Australia continues to go through the challenges of racism and Islamophobia, the evolution of this media–political landscape will be crucial in shaping more inclusive and effective governance.

***

ICJ RULING CONDEMNS ISRAEL'S OCCUPATION

27 July 2024

The International Court of Justice has unequivocally ruled that Israel's occupation of Palestinian territories is illegal under international law and the court's findings highlight numerous breaches of international statutes by Israel, mandating an immediate cessation of the occupation and full reparations for the extensive damage inflicted since 1967. This landmark ruling represents the most definitive legal condemnation of Israel's actions by an international judicial body to date.

Despite the historical tendency of major powers to dismiss unfavourable rulings from international institutions, the ICJ's decision has intensified calls for tangible actions, particularly from the Australian government. In response, Foreign Minister Senator Penny Wong issued a statement urging Israel to halt the expansion of settlements and to curb settler violence in the West Bank and the Albanese government, which keeps saying it is "committed to a two-state solution" without doing anything to move towards that position, is now evaluating potential measures, including financial sanctions and travel bans on specific Israeli settlers and groups implicated in violence.

Senator Wong emphasised that sanctions are "a significant measure", usually reserved as a last resort in foreign policy, with individuals targeted by these sanctions have been involved in severe acts of violence against Palestinians in the West Bank, including beatings, sexual assaults, and torture, resulting in serious injuries and fatalities. While Senator Wong insists that these sanctions reflect careful consideration, the measures have been criticised as insufficient, reflecting a continued reluctance to alienate influential pro-Israel lobbies within Australia.

The actions of the Israel Defense Forces are undeniably acts of genocide, particularly given the deliberate targeting of non-combatants, children, and the destruction of essential infrastructure such as schools and hospitals, and this factor adds a grave dimension to this issue—despite what the government of Israel continues to claim, this is not a conventional military conflict but a systematic campaign against a civilian population, demanding a swift and robust international response which, so far, has been lacking.

Senator Wong's call to stop settlement expansion in the West Bank without an equal demand to withdraw, also suggests a tacit acceptance of the current status quo, which many argue is insufficient and advocates insist on a reversion to the pre-1967 borders, a stance supported by a substantial segment of the international community. Some commentators argue that a return to the 1948 borders is critical, though this is viewed as politically impractical by most experts—at this stage. The two-state solution, while contentious among Palestinians, remains the most widely endorsed framework for resolving the conflict.

The Australian government's position, while rhetorically firm, continues to navigate the delicate balance of international diplomacy and domestic political pressures. The ICJ's ruling, however, injects renewed urgency into the debate, compelling nations such as Australia to reconcile their foreign policy with the imperatives of international justice and human rights, and ignore the demands and influence of domestic conservative Israel lobby groups. This path forward is fraught with challenges, but the strong calls for justice and accountability cannot be ignored forever.

AUSTRALIA CAN ASSERT INFLUENCE AND SUPPORT PALESTINE THROUGH STRONGER DIPLOMATIC ACTION

While the Australian government would not be expected to take extreme measures such as physically or militarily intervening in the conflict, there remains a broad spectrum of actions it could undertake to support Palestine, including imposing sanctions on the Israeli government, severing trade relationships with Israel, recalling the Israeli ambassador, and recognising the state of Palestine—which the Labor Party promised when they returned to government—and extending travel bans to more Israeli citizens involved in the occupation and violence. Such actions would signal a significant shift in Australia's foreign policy, demonstrating a commitment to holding Israel accountable for its violations of international law.

Critics may argue that these measures will not immediately halt the ongoing violence in Gaza, and they would be correct. However, the weight of the ICJ's ruling provides a legal and moral foundation for these actions. By aligning its policies with international law, Australia can exert increased pressure on Israel to change its behaviour in the occupied territories, including a withdrawal from the West Bank and Golan Heights, as well as ceasing and removing the military slaughter in Gaza. The initial sanctions targeting seven Israeli settlers and a youth group are a minimalist first step, but they must be expanded to create meaningful impact.

Drawing parallels with the anti-apartheid movement in South Africa, history has shown that sustained economic and diplomatic pressure can lead to significant political change. It took years of concerted international efforts to dismantle apartheid, and a similar approach is necessary to address the Israeli occupation. While immediate political solution for those suffering in Gaza is unlikely, a robust and persistent stance by the international community, including Australia, can contribute to longer-term solutions. However, Palestine cannot wait as long as South Africa did to end apartheid, which essentially took over 30 years: immediate action is required by the international community to end the genocide in Gaza and bring lasting peace to the Middle East.

The role of Australia's foreign minister is undeniably complex, particularly in the delicate arena of Middle Eastern politics. Directly confronting allies, such as the United States, is not a straightforward option, given Australia's limited influence in the region and its broader strategic interests and this geopolitical reality necessitates a nuanced approach, balancing diplomatic relations while advocating for justice and human rights.

Despite these constraints, Australia can still assert its independence and express strong, principled views. Diplomatic channels can be used effectively to convey Australia's stance without jeopardising essential alliances. Senator Wong—or any foreign minister—must navigate this fine line, articulating Australia's positions firmly but tactfully. The challenge lies in reconciling Australia's strategic interests with its commitment to upholding international law and supporting human rights.

Recognition of the state of Palestine would be a powerful statement, aligning Australia with the growing number of countries acknowledging Palestinian statehood. Such recognition would not only bolster Palestine's international standing but also highlight Australia's commitment to a just and lasting peace in the region. Similarly, recalling the Israeli ambassador and severing trade ties would send a clear message of disapproval of Israel's actions, reinforcing the international community's calls for accountability.

Extending travel bans to more Israeli citizens involved in the occupation and violence would further isolate those responsible and increase pressure on Israel to change its policies. While these measures alone will not resolve the conflict, they represent critical steps towards a comprehensive international response. However, these actions also involve political courage and the Australian government has shown little empathy for the plight of the Palestinian people so far. Certainly, the diplomatic path is fraught with challenges, but the pursuit of justice and peace demands bold and decisive action.

CHINESE-BROKERED UNITY DEAL MARKS A MAJOR DEVELOPMENT IN MIDDLE EASTERN DIPLOMACY

A significant event has also taken place that has largely gone unreported in the Australian media: a unity deal brokered by the Chinese government involving Hamas, Fatah, and twelve other Palestinian political groups. This development is particularly noteworthy as Fatah and Hamas have been political adversaries for decades and the accord, which fosters political accommodation among these fourteen groups, marks a potential turning point for Palestinian governance and unity.

The efficacy of this accord remains uncertain as it has not yet been tested. However, it represents a crucial step towards the full recognition of the state of Palestine. One common criticism has been that Palestine lacks a unified government capable of effectively governing, yet, it is crucial to consider the severe constraints faced by any Palestinian administration: governing an area likened to an open-air concentration camp, under blockade by land and sea, subjected to apartheid-like conditions by Israel, deprived of free movement, and continuously bombarded and attacked by Israeli Defense Forces and settlers in the West Bank. The conditions are such that running an effective government is an extraordinary challenge.

This unity deal is significant for several reasons, not least because it signals China's entrance into Middle Eastern diplomacy in a substantial way. By brokering this deal, China is stepping into a role traditionally occupied by Western powers, which have historically exacerbated problems in the region and this move can be seen as China asserting that it can resolve conflicts in the Middle East more effectively than the West. While the deal will not end the conflict immediately, it is a critical development that could pave the way for more significant changes.

Historically, the disunity among Palestinian resistance groups has been a major obstacle and this lack of cohesion among these groups has meant that the Palestinian people had little choice but to follow fragmented leaderships. The unity brokered by China could be a game changer, and bringing together factions that have historically despised each other means there is now a potential for concerted and effective action.

China's intervention also signifies its growing role on the world stage. By facilitating this unity deal, China is demonstrating its capability and willingness to engage in high-stakes international diplomacy, a domain where it has previously been reticent. This development is likely to provoke a strong reaction from Western media outlets, especially those aligned with the interests of the News Corporation empire, as it highlights a diplomatic achievement that the West has failed to secure.

The United States, in particular, has been largely dormant in Middle Eastern diplomacy over the past couple of decades and its current approach is a relic of Cold War politics, inadequate for addressing the contemporary complexities of the region. China's proactive stance in brokering the Palestinian unity deal exposes the limitations of the American and broader Western diplomatic strategies, potentially heralding a new era of Chinese influence in the Middle East. The impact of this deal remains to be seen, but it undoubtedly represents a critical shift in the dynamics of the Israeli–Palestinian conflict and the broader geopolitical landscape.

LABOR PARTY FACES INTERNAL TENSIONS AND ELECTORAL RISK OVER PALESTINE

Amidst these international developments, the recent NSW Labor Conference held at Sydney Town Hall highlights the growing internal tensions within the Australian Labor Party regarding the recognition of Palestinian statehood. The conference—again—voted to urge the Australian government to promptly recognise Palestine as a sovereign and independent state, echoing a similar motion approved at the previous year's national conference. This repeated call, which also reflects the contents of the Labor Platform agreed to in 2021, raises a critical question: what is the Labor government waiting for?

A clear schism is developing between the parliamentary members and the Labor rank-and-file membership, where the latter are striving to adhere to core Labor values of justice, human dignity, and solidarity, while the former appears indifferent and cautious, potentially gambling on the belief that this issue will not critically affect their safe seats in Western Sydney at the next election. However, this assumption may prove to be a significant miscalculation.

The frustration and impatience within key Labor-held electorates are palpable. Western Sydney, with its substantial and vocal pro-Palestinian community, is particularly aggrieved by the federal government's inaction. This discontent was visibly manifested when a large crowd of pro-Palestinian protesters gathered outside the Town Hall during the conference, some of whom heckled delegates as they exited. The activists voiced their frustrations over the government's failure to recognise Palestine and demanded more robust diplomatic actions against Israel, which has been responsible for the deaths of over 40,000 Palestinians in Gaza over the past 10 months and, according to *Lancet* magazine, possibly up to 186,000 deaths.

This growing dissatisfaction poses a potential electoral risk for the Labor government and the party's traditional support base in Western Sydney, which has historically delivered safe seats, may not be as secure as assumed. If the government continues to delay decisive action on Palestinian statehood, it risks alienating a significant portion of its voter base, who are deeply committed to justice for Palestine. This issue could become a focal point in the next federal election, with voters seeking to hold their representatives accountable for their stance on this critical international issue.

The broader implications of inaction extend beyond electoral politics. By failing to respond decisively to the calls for recognising Palestinian statehood, the Labor government undermines its own professed values and principles, and it also risks diminishing Australia's credibility on the international stage as a nation committed to upholding human rights and international law.

Of course, the current hesitation to take stronger action will be influenced by various factors, including geopolitical considerations and domestic political calculations. However, the growing discontent within the party and among the electorate suggests that the Labor government cannot afford to remain passive. Recognising Palestine as a sovereign state would not only align with international legal standards, as emphasised by the decision by the ICJ, but it would also resonate deeply with the values and expectations of many Labor supporters, as well as many members of the general community.

The Labor government's lack of action in addressing the concerns of Palestinians and recognising Palestinian statehood may have significant repercussions in the next election and the discontent within the party and among key electorates in Western Sydney cannot be ignored. The government must reconcile its policies with the core values of justice and human dignity that it professes to uphold, or it risks facing a strong electoral backlash. Recognising Palestinian statehood and taking decisive diplomatic actions will not only fulfill a moral and legal imperative but also secure the trust and support of its voter base, ensuring a stronger and more unified party moving forward.

***

ISRAEL'S ESCALATING WAR CRIMES IN LEBANON

28 September 2024

The expansion of Israel's war beyond the Gaza Strip into Lebanon marks another terrible chapter in the region's escalating violence, further entrenching the cycle of destruction that has already been inflicted upon Palestine for decades. Israel's bombardment of southern Lebanon, now stretching up to Beirut, echoes a familiar and devastating pattern of military aggression and war crimes, displacing up to a million people who have fled their homes in fear of further strikes, and killing thousands of civilians.

These attacks follow in the wake of previous tragedies, such as the pager-bomb explosions—suspected to be orchestrated by Mossad—that killed around 300 people and injured over 3,000 others in Lebanon. The scale and intensity of Israel's military operations in Lebanon are an extension of its ongoing campaign in Gaza, where evacuation orders for civilians often presage devastating strikes, disproportionately affecting women and children.

Israel's military operations, whether in Gaza or now in Lebanon, have repeatedly violated international law, defying United Nations resolutions and conventions designed to protect civilians. The bombardment in Lebanon, just like the massacres in Gaza, appears to have been premeditated and unrelated to the events in Israel from October the previous year, which were used as a justification for the mass killing of well over 40,000 Palestinians in Gaza. By extending its war beyond its borders, Israel is deepening the humanitarian crisis in Lebanon, and even more troubling are Prime Minister Benjamin Netanyahu's threats to expand the war into Jordan, a nation with which Israel has a long-standing peace treaty. The international community is witnessing an escalation that threatens to destabilise the entire region, yet there is an alarming passivity in global responses.

In Australia, the government's weak stance on Israel's actions reflects a broader issue of political inertia in the face of blatant human rights abuses. Many Australians, along with political commentators, continue to question what their country *can actually* do in response to this conflict and have suggested that the Foreign Minister, Senator Penny Wong and the Australian government are being unfairly targeted for their inaction. Yet the reality is that there is a considerable range of diplomatic tools and practical actions that Australia could employ to signal its opposition to Israel's aggression and contribute meaningfully to international efforts to halt the violence.

For example, recalling its ambassador to Israel; expelling the Israeli ambassador in Canberra; imposing high-level trade sanctions; halting military exports to Israel, and reducing cultural and sporting ties are just a few of the options available to Australia. These are not unprecedented measures; Australia has a history of using such tactics to oppose apartheid in South Africa during the 1970s and 1980s. At that time, few people questioned whether such actions would make a difference: aside from people such as Margaret Thatcher in the U.K. and a young Tony Abbott in Australia, it was accepted that standing up to systemic human rights abuses and racial injustice was a moral imperative, and Australia played a significant role in that global effort. The same rationale should apply today in the case of Israel's ongoing war crimes in Palestine and Lebanon.

The Israeli government is on a dangerous path, and if it continues, it risks self-destruction, and hard diplomacy, sanctions, and international pressure are essential to stop Israel from perpetuating further violence and violating the rights of Palestinians and Lebanese civilians. The silence and inaction from the western countries, particularly from countries such as Australia that hold considerable diplomatic and economic influence, allow these atrocities to continue unchecked.

When nations fail to act, they become complicit in the violence they passively observe. If countries like Australia had taken decisive action when it became clear that Israel was committing war crimes and engaging in genocidal practices in Gaza, we might not now be witnessing the tragic extension of these actions into Lebanon and further afield. The unchecked military campaign Israel has launched across its borders further exposes the need for international intervention, not just to protect the lives of those caught in the conflict but to uphold the principles of international law and human rights that are supposed to govern relations between states.

AUSTRALIA'S COMPLICITY IN MIDDLE EAST INJUSTICE: FAILING MULTICULTURALISM, HUMAN RIGHTS, AND GLOBAL PEACE

Australia's consistent alignment with Israel in the Middle East, often at the expense of acknowledging the grievances of the Arab world, reflects a broader failure in its foreign policy. This approach not only undermines Australia's claim to being a global advocate for human rights and peace but also neglects its own multicultural values, which should inherently drive more balanced diplomatic stances.

Former prime minister Scott Morrison's decision to move Australia's embassy from Tel Aviv to Jerusalem in 2018 stands as an example of this, a move that pandered to a narrow ideological worldview, one rooted in apocalyptic and religious interpretations rather than rational, diplomatic considerations. This decision, deeply offensive to Palestinians and the wider Arab world, was largely ignored by the mainstream media in Australia, and this lack of critical discourse around such a significant diplomatic blunder revealed how deeply embedded the bias toward Israel is within Australian political and media establishments.

The question arises: why can't Australia implement a range of actions against the state of Israel, or even express solidarity with the Lebanese people, who are being devastated by Israeli bombs? Australia's Lebanese community has played a significant role in shaping the nation's modern identity, yet their voices are conspicuously absent in policy discussions concerning the Middle East. For a country that prides itself on multiculturalism, it is baffling that the federal government is unwilling to take a stand that reflects the values of its diverse population, particularly when it comes to condemning the illegal actions of a foreign government. The Labor Party, which touts itself as a champion of multiculturalism, has been disappointingly silent on this front.

Despite the United Nations condemning Israel for its continued illegal actions, Australia, along with the United States, the United Kingdom, and a few other nations, persists in shielding Israel from any meaningful consequences. Australia's foreign policy toward the Middle East also reflects a broader indifference to the suffering of innocent civilians, particularly in the Arab world. The government's refusal to condemn Israel's actions, while simultaneously turning a blind eye to the suffering of Lebanese and Palestinian civilians, is a profound moral and political failure. Surely, it is possible to condemn the actions of extremist groups and criminal factions on all sides without ignoring the reality that it is overwhelmingly innocent civilians who are caught in the crossfire. It is these civilians—whether they are Palestinians in Gaza, Lebanese in Beirut, or refugees fleeing the region—who deserve Australia's solidarity and protection.

A MORAL CRISIS AND THE LOOMING POLITICAL CONSEQUENCES

The weak and ambiguous response from the Australian government, exemplified by Senator Penny Wong's carefully worded statements, reflects a longstanding issue in Australia's foreign policy regarding Israel and the broader Middle East. The statements are familiar: *deeply concerned*, *gravely concerned*, and calls for *de-escalation* echo across the media but lack real conviction or specificity. The situation was even extended to Wong's meeting with Iran's Foreign Minister Seyed Abbas Araghchi, with firm discussions about pressing *Iran* for "regional de-escalation and restraint". Yet, there was no mention of "pressing" Israel, despite its efforts to destabilise the region and escalate tensions with Lebanon, Iran, Jordan and Egypt. The omission of Israel's name, particularly in instances where it is directly responsible for military actions and civilian casualties, speaks volumes about the government's reluctance to challenge the narrative propagated by Israel and its allies. Even when the death of Australian aid worker Zomi Frankcom, killed in a missile attack by the Israel Defense Forces, cannot prompt a direct acknowledgment of Israel's role, it is clear that Australia's political establishment is deeply entrenched in a policy of *both-side-ism*—careful not to offend Israel, and cautious to the point of cowardice.

The foreign minister's failure to explicitly condemn Israel in instances where its military actions have clearly crossed ethical and legal boundaries highlights an alarming reluctance to hold the state accountable. This failure is not born of ignorance; the Australian government knows full well the role Israel has played in escalating conflicts in Gaza, Lebanon, and beyond. The use of vague language and diplomatic equivocation allows the government to avoid any substantial policy shifts or criticisms, effectively continuing a status quo that props up a regime currently led by Netanyahu, a man whose political survival hinges on perpetuating conflict.

The ongoing support for Israel, particularly under the Netanyahu regime, raises questions about why Australia continues to follow this path. Of course, the answer lies in a combination of political influence, strategic alliances, and a deeply ingrained reluctance to deviate from U.S. foreign policy, which remains steadfastly pro-Israel. The influence of a powerful ultra-conservative Israel lobby within Australia, particularly in Sydney and Melbourne, also ensures that any significant political pushback against Israeli policies is stifled before it gains momentum.

The consequences of this approach are more than just moral; they have real political implications, especially within Australia's diverse and multicultural electorate. The Lebanese community in Australia, particularly in Western Sydney, is large and politically active. The community's roots in Lebanon, a country now under bombardment from Israeli forces, create a strong connection to the conflict that the government can no longer afford to ignore. While the Lebanese–Australian community is diverse, with various religious, political, and regional differences, the escalating violence in Lebanon could galvanise parts of the electorate that feel abandoned by the government's refusal to condemn Israel's actions.

While there is undoubtedly frustration within the Lebanese and broader Arab communities, it is difficult to predict whether this will be sufficient to influence voting patterns at the next federal election in a significant way. However, it would be a mistake for the Australian government to assume that foreign policy issues like Israel's aggression in Lebanon will have no bearing *at all* on domestic politics. The Lebanese community, along with other Arab and Muslim communities in Australia, is growing increasingly aware of the gap between Australia's professed values and its actions on the global stage. This disconnect could lead to a loss of support for the Labor government, particularly in key electorates in Western Sydney, where disillusionment with the party's failure to act is driving voters toward alternatives, such the independent candidates supported by Muslim Voice and the Australian Greens.

The political inertia that has characterised Australia's foreign policy toward Israel is unsustainable in the long term. As the conflict deepens and more innocent civilians are killed, the government's refusal to take a firm stand will become harder to justify to both the international community and the Australian electorate. The current approach, dictated by an unrepresentative Israel lobby and a fear of upsetting powerful allies, is fundamentally at odds with the values that Australia claims to represent.

Ultimately, the Australian government must decide whether it is willing to continue supporting a foreign policy that is driven by political expediency and alliances rather than principles. Certainly, the next federal election will not hinge on foreign policy, but it will be influenced by the broader sense of whether the government truly represents the values of the electorate. Whether or not the current government is willing to listen to community concerns remains to be seen— and so far, they haven't—but one thing is certain: the era of blind support for Israel without consequence is drawing to a close, and the political consequences for this delusion may arrive sooner than anticipated.

***

AUSTRALIA'S UNQUESTIONING SUPPORT FOR ISRAEL

5 October 2024

The conflict in Lebanon, spurred by Israel's expansion of military action beyond Palestine, brings into sharp focus a long history of territorial aggression, misrepresentation in Western media, and cynical political games in countries like Australia. The escalation into Lebanon is not a new chapter but rather an extension of Israel's aggressive posturing, a strategy it has employed for decades with impunity.

Since the invasion of Lebanon, the Israeli Defense Forces have pushed forward with strikes that have caused considerable devastation. Iran's response, in the form of missile attacks, follows a predictable script of retaliation that gets highlighted and exaggerated by the global media, which in turn paints Lebanon and Iran as the primary antagonists. This media narrative—especially in Australia—glosses over the fundamental reality that Israel is the *main aggressor* in this scenario, continuing its campaign of occupation and violence.

Since the most recent eruption of conflict, with its beginnings on 7 October 2023, the human cost has been staggering. By many estimates, at least 42,000 Palestinians have been killed—potentially rising to 200,000, according to the medical journal *Lancet*—and over 2,000 Lebanese lives, while, during this time, 1,700 Israelis have been killed.

These numbers are not presented to create a hierarchy of suffering but to highlight the asymmetry of the violence. Around 99 per cent of *all* deaths have been inflicted by Israeli forces and settler paramilitary groups in the West Bank, while 1 per cent can be attributed to Hamas, Hezbollah, and the state of Iran. This disparity makes it clear who the primary perpetrators of violence are yet, this critical perspective is conveniently absent from mainstream Australian discourse, where figures such as leader of the opposition Peter Dutton seek political capital in the conflict.

Dutton's exploitation of this conflict for domestic political gain is clearly evident. His remarks about the Australian government's response paint a picture of weakness, casting Prime Minister Anthony Albanese as 'failing in his leadership duties'. His criticism, however, conveniently ignores the broader historical and ethical context of Israel's actions, reducing a complex international crisis into an opportunity for political point-scoring and appealing to the Australian right-wing base, eager to see a more testosterone-fuelled response in alignment with the West's pro-Israel stance.

Senator Bridget McKenzie—not known for any expertise on Middle East affairs at all—also chimed in, selectively championing the United Nations' call for Hezbollah's removal from the northern border of Israel, conveniently ignoring Israel's continued violation of countless UN resolutions. Such one-sided rhetoric not only fuels Islamophobia and xenophobia but also contributes to the further alienation of Arab and Muslim communities in Australia.

This marginalisation was further exacerbated by statements from Home Affairs Minister Tony Burke and, as an MP representing a western Sydney seat, where 25 per cent of voters come from an Islamic background, he should know better. Burke linked claims of hate speech and symbols to the Islamic community, even threatening to revoke the visas of those displaying the Hezbollah flag or images of its recently assassinated leader, Hassan Nasrallah.

The political responses in Australia reveal the extent to which the conflict is being manipulated for ideological and political gain. The reflexive alignment Australian political parties with pro-Israel rhetoric, while casting any dissent or criticism as support for terrorism, reveals an intellectual and moral bankruptcy. These positions rely on a wilful ignorance of historical facts and a cynical exploitation of the fear and anxiety surrounding Middle Eastern conflicts. For politicians such as Dutton and McKenzie, it is easier to stoke division and fear than to engage in the complex realities of the conflict, where Israel's actions must be critically assessed against the backdrop of decades of occupation, violence, and expansionism.

The reduction of complex historical, cultural, and political issues into talking points meant to fuel ideological divisions only makes the conflict worse. It reduces the Australian public's understanding of a deeply nuanced issue to simplistic narratives of *good versus evil*, perpetuating the myth that Israel's actions are purely defensive. It also contributes to the larger global problem of how Western countries, including Australia, uncritically accept and support Israel's militaristic approach, further emboldening it to expand its aggression into countries like Lebanon and beyond.

HOW AUSTRALIA'S NATIONAL SECURITY RHETORIC FUELS ISLAMOPHOBIA

Ever since the late 1990s, when John Howard's Liberal–National Coalition government began to sharpen its focus on asylum seekers and border security, national security has been the Achilles' heel of the Labor Party. Key events such as the Tampa crisis in 2001 and the September 11 attacks in the U.S. dovetailed perfectly with these narratives, creating a political environment where security could easily be exploited to generate fear, division, and justify far-reaching, authoritarian policies. Over the years, these issues have grown to become a permanent fixture of Australian politics, linking internal policies with Middle Eastern geopolitics, particularly Palestine.

What is remarkable is how, more than two decades later, the Labor Party has still not devised an effective strategy to counter these conservative national security narratives. Rather than challenging the framing or interrogating the supposed links between domestic security and foreign conflicts, Labor often capitulates to the Liberal Party's agenda, whether they're in government or not. This reluctance to push back results in poor legislation that not only infringes on civil liberties but also disproportionately affects marginalised communities. The willingness of both major parties to prioritise "security" over human rights perpetuates harmful stereotypes, further marginalising communities that are already under immense social and political pressure.

In recent years, this tendency has intensified, particularly when it comes to Palestinian solidarity movements in Australia. Pro-Palestine events in cities like Sydney and Melbourne have drawn large crowds, reflecting the deep sense of hurt and suffering felt by many in the Arab and Muslim communities, especially in response to the violence in Gaza and the West Bank. Despite the peaceful nature of these gatherings, media narratives and political rhetoric often paint these protests as *dangerous* or *extremist*.

It is in these moments that national security rhetoric is deployed most cynically, conflating peaceful protest with terrorism, and using symbols like the Hezbollah flag to justify police crackdowns and oppressive legislation—the presence of a yellow flag is deemed by the establishment to be more threatening than the ongoing violence in the Middle East, where tens of thousands of people have been killed by Israeli forces. This rhetoric reveals how national security is used as a blunt tool to suppress expressions of solidarity with oppressed peoples, even when those expressions are peaceful and legal.

The escalating crackdown on Palestinian solidarity movements in Australia sets a dangerous precedent. It not only criminalises symbols of resistance but also reaffirms a broader pattern of equating national security with the suppression of dissent, particularly when that dissent is tied to Muslim or Arab communities. The focus on security becomes less about protecting the Australian public and more about reinforcing the dominance of a particular narrative—one that positions Israel as the victim only and any critique of its actions as inherently dangerous. This framing not only distorts the realities of the Middle East conflict but also stifles the political discourse necessary to hold both Israel and Australia's political establishment accountable.

By treating these solidarity movements as a national security threat, Australia is aligning itself with a broader global trend that seeks to criminalise criticism of Israel while bolstering support for its continued occupation of Palestinian land and beyond. This trend is not unique to Australia—but a very common trait of the settler-coloniser states of Britain, Canada and the United States, whose support for Israel has been most vociferous—where the government's commitment to security at all costs has consistently led to the erosion of civil liberties and the marginalisation of communities deemed *the other*.

HOW POLITICS AND MEDIA SILENCE PALESTINIAN AND ARAB VOICES

The Australian political class, along with the mainstream media, have long taken a one-sided approach when it comes to Israel and its ongoing occupation of Palestine, a position that is mirrored in the country's broader discourse on the Middle

East—it paints Israel as a nation under siege, constantly threatened by an aggressive Arab world, while ignoring or minimising the suffering inflicted upon Palestinians, Lebanese, and other Middle Eastern communities. Even the illustrations and cartoons in mainstream media must reflect a pro-Israel bias, ensuring that everyone is aligned in promoting the cause.

A narrative that is rarely heard in Australia is that the Arab world, particularly the 57-member Arab and Muslim coalition, is ready to guarantee Israel's security in exchange for an end to the occupation and the creation of an independent Palestinian state. This is a narrative of peace, a plan for co-existence, but it is also a plan that the Israeli government continues to ignore. Instead, Israel perpetuates cycles of violence with no long-term vision for peace.

Australian politicians and media, aligned with Israel's narrative, fail to critically interrogate this lack of an endgame. They instead propagate the notion that Israel's security can only be guaranteed through military dominance and suppression of Palestinian resistance, ignoring decades of diplomatic efforts from the Arab world that have sought a two-state solution.

What remains bewildering is how little the Australian public knows about these alternatives, largely because the media and political elite focus on a singular, distorted narrative that portrays Israel as a beleaguered nation fending off existential threats and is the true partner for peace that is ignored by the Arab world. The reality, however, is far more complex, with Israel being a military powerhouse that has consistently pursued expansionist policies at the expense of Palestinian lives and land. And yet, discussing Israel's role as an aggressor is virtually taboo in Australian political discourse. Any deviation from the mainstream narrative, especially in defence of Palestine and now, Lebanon, is often framed as radicalism or extremism, once again marginalising voices that seek to highlight the brutal realities of occupation.

In Australia, mainstream political figures are entirely comfortable supporting Israeli policies that many human rights organisations have labelled as apartheid, while paying lip service to human rights in their rhetoric. The term *apartheid* itself, when applied to Israel, is met with accusations of anti-Semitism, even though it is a well-documented reality for Palestinians living under occupation, subjected to different laws, movement restrictions, and systemic violence. This complicity in maintaining Israel's oppressive regime is troubling, particularly given the increasing global recognition of Israel's violations of international law.

The Australian media also plays a significant role in perpetuating these distortions—media outlets regurgitate the same pro-Israel talking points, framing the conflict in binary terms: *Israel as a democracy defending itself against barbaric, radical forces*. The violence and suffering inflicted on Palestinians and Lebanese civilians, often framed as unfortunate collateral damage, rarely make the headlines in a way that captures the depth of the human tragedy.

In Australian politics, the Australian Greens have consistently raised concerns about these issues, but their voices are also marginalised. The broader political class, including the Labor government, tends to fall in line with the dominant narrative, perhaps out of fear of being branded anti-Israel or anti-Semitic. Yet, this silence does not only reflect a lack of political courage; it speaks to a deeper failure to represent the diversity of opinion within Australia itself.

The Arab and Muslim communities have contributed significantly to Australian society yet, they remain an easy target for demonisation, especially when tensions flare in the Middle East, and this is compounded by a simplistic understanding of those communities and Islam itself.

Australian media and politicians often lump the diverse range of Islamic thought and practice into a monolithic category, focusing primarily on the most radical elements while ignoring the rich diversity of opinion within the faith.

The demonisation of Middle Eastern Muslims in particular mirrors broader Western tendencies to ignore the progressive and peaceful voices within Islam, an approach that is not only intellectually lazy but dangerous, as it fuels further Islamophobia and alienates Australian Muslims from the political process.

In contrast, Australia's political class demonstrates an unwavering commitment to conservative Zionism, conflating the interests of the Israeli state with those of the Jewish people. This conflation is not only inaccurate but harmful, as it silences critical voices within the Jewish community itself, many of whom oppose the Israeli government's policies. Figures such as Noam Chomsky and many other Jewish intellectuals have long critiqued Israel's expansionism, yet their voices are often ignored or sidelined in favour of maintaining a simplistic narrative that casts any criticism of Israel as inherently anti-Semitic. Newer local voices such as the Jewish Council of Australia are also frequently ignored, mainly because they also present an alternative progressive perspective to the prevailing conservative Zionist narrative.

Ultimately, what is needed is a more honest and open discussion about these issues, one that acknowledges the complexities of the Israel–Palestine conflict and allows for diverse perspectives within Australia. Politicians need to move beyond the tired and lazy security rhetoric that demonises the Arab world and Muslims, and instead, engage with the root causes of the conflict, including calling out Israel's ongoing occupation and systemic violence. Such a shift would not only help improve Australia's foreign policy but also foster a more inclusive and empathetic domestic discourse, where all communities are respected and their contributions to society are recognised.

***

THE POLITICS OF PROTEST: UNDERMINING FREE SPEECH

11 October 2024

The Premier of New South Wales, Chris Minns, has raised the controversial idea of shutting down the pro-Palestine protests that have become a regular occurrence in Sydney. Minns' primary justification revolves around the costs associated with policing these protests, suggesting that such financial burdens on the state are unsustainable. However, this rationale, presented as a pragmatic response to budgetary constraints, fails to address the broader implications for freedom of speech and protest in Australia. What we are witnessing is a deliberate attempt to suppress a significant political movement under the guise of fiscal responsibility.

The suggested costs associated with these protests, claimed to be upwards of $5.4 million over the past year, seem questionable. The pro-Palestine gatherings in Sydney, have been largely peaceful, where the attendees chant, wave signs, and give speeches—hardly the kind of activities that demand such a heavy police presence and each event, which typically lasts for about two hours, does not resemble the kind of disruptive or violent events that would justify an inflated price tag on law enforcement. The NSW police union has already dismissed the idea that patrolling these protests is preventing them from addressing crime elsewhere. This raises the question: what is the real motivation behind Minns' push to ban these protests?

At the core of his argument is a thinly veiled pandering to Sydney's influential pro-Israel lobby. It is a familiar tactic: drown out dissenting voices, particularly when they challenge entrenched interests. The pro-Palestine protests represent a growing public consciousness about the ongoing crisis in Gaza and the Middle East, and these protests serve as a legitimate expression of outrage at the actions of the Israeli government and the Israel Defense Forces. By attempting to silence these voices, Minns is not only undermining free speech but aligning himself with a particular political agenda that seeks to shield Israel from criticism in the public sphere.

This move also flies in the face of historical precedent in Australia, where the right to protest has long been regarded as a fundamental aspect of democratic engagement. Minns seems to have forgotten, or is wilfully ignoring, the labor movement's own historical roots in public protest and civil disobedience. The Labor Party, under whose banner Minns serves, was itself forged in the collective action and resistance against a government. To now attempt to limit or shut down peaceful protests against a foreign government's actions, as well as to protest against the inaction of the Australian government—especially when those actions and inactions are increasingly seen as unjust and oppressive—is a betrayal of the principles Minns should be defending.

The argument about cost ignores an obvious solution: scale back the unnecessary and excessive police presence at these events. The protests have consistently remained peaceful, and the several skirmishes that have occurred over the past year have been primarily caused by Zionist agitators. Many attendees bring their children; there are no signs of the violence or chaos that would justify lining the streets with police officers. Reducing the police force at these gatherings would not only cut costs significantly but also reflect the reality of the situation—the fact that these are *not* dangerous protests.

The leadership of Minns has been a disappointment for many who hoped for a progressive and dynamic direction since he became Premier in March 2023. Instead, he has come across as a continuation of the same policies and approaches seen under his Liberal Party predecessors, Dominic Perrottet and Gladys Berejiklian and his handling of the pro-Palestine protests is just one more example of this conservative, risk-averse approach. By framing the protests as a financial burden, Minns is diverting attention from the real issue at hand: the right of people to protest against what they can see is an ongoing genocide. In a world where political leaders are increasingly expected to take bold and principled stands, Minns seems content to sidestep controversy and cater to established power structures.

ALIENATING COMMUNITIES AND UNDERMINING LABOR VALUES

The commentary provided by Minns over the pro-Palestine protests—to the right-wing shockjock, Ben Fordham at Radio 2GB—not only signal a disconnect from Labor's historic values, but they also reveal a troubling pattern of double standards that risks alienating a significant portion of the NSW community, particularly the Islamic and pro-Palestine groups.

By focusing on the financial cost of these protests while simultaneously remaining silent on other, arguably more costly and disruptive protests, Minns is sending a clear message: the voices of some communities are more burdensome and less welcome than others. This is a dangerous road for any political leader, but especially for one leading a party that traditionally prides itself on inclusivity and justice, and seem to be designed to stoke division within the community.

Rather than engaging in meaningful dialogue with the pro-Palestine protesters, or addressing the legitimate concerns of the Islamic community, Minns has chosen to position these protests as a costly inconvenience. Yet, if the federal and NSW governments and political class had not been so steadfastly one-sided in their support of Israel, or if they had engaged in more balanced and open dialogue with these communities, such protests might not even be necessary. The protests themselves are a direct response to being systematically ignored, and Minns' attempts to shut them down without addressing the root cause will only exacerbate the issue.

There is also glaring inconsistency in the NSW Government's approach to protest. While the pro-Palestine gatherings are labelled as too costly and are viewed as disruptive, other protests, such as the anti-lockdown and anti-vaccine demonstrations that took place during the pandemic, went on for nearly two years without similar complaints from the government. Some of these protests were openly hostile, with participants openly calling for the execution of political leaders, yet there was no outcry over the police resources needed to manage them. Similarly, neo-Nazi rallies have been treated with far more leniency, with police presence often seen as more of an escort than a control measure. Where is the outrage over the costs of these events? Where is the call for them to be banned or scaled back?

Minns' failure to apply a consistent standard suggests that his actions are less about fiscal responsibility and more about political posturing. The fact that Minns would never dream of asking the Jewish community to refrain from public shows of support for Israel due to cost only highlights the double standard further. If he were to make such a suggestion, the backlash would be swift and severe, and rightly so. Yet, when it comes to the Islamic community, their right to peaceful protest is treated as expendable.

Even within his own party, Minns is facing backlash for this stance. Several Labor MPs have spoken out against his push to ban protests on the basis of cost, warning that such actions threaten civil liberties. This criticism highlights a growing concern that Minns is out of touch not only with the values of his own party but with the broader electorate as well. There is also a notable reluctance among many Labor MPs to openly support Palestine, fearing political retribution or alienation, and this reflects the broader atmosphere of suppression around the issue, where open support for Palestine is often stifled or discouraged, even within supposed progressive circles.

Ultimately, Minns' approach to these protests raises serious questions about his fitness to be a Labor Premier. His failure to engage with the concerns of the pro-Palestine community, coupled with his consistent appeasement of pro-Israel lobby groups, suggests he is a leader more interested in maintaining the status quo than in representing the diverse voices of his electorate. This behaviour might be more fitting for a leader on the conservative side of politics, but it has no place in a party that claims to champion the rights of the oppressed and marginalised.

The Labor Party, at its best, is a party of inclusion, social justice, and equality. Its leaders are expected to stand up for all communities, not just the ones with the most political capital or influence. Chris Minns has not only failed in his leadership responsibilities but has alienated a significant part of the population he is meant to represent. If he continues down this path, he risks not only losing the trust of these communities but also jeopardising the very fabric of the multicultural society that Sydney prides itself on being.

**

ALBANESE'S MISTAKE OF ENDLESSLY APPEASING THE ISRAEL LOBBY

14 October 2024

The commemoration of 7 October 2023 Hamas attacks in Israel has become a flashpoint in Australian politics, showing the deeply polarised differences between Labor and the Liberal Party. When Prime Minister Anthony Albanese introduced a motion in parliament to mark the first anniversary of these tragic events—1,195 deaths in Israel and the start of a genocide in Gaza—his words were measured, designed to strike a delicate balance, where he sought to acknowledge the pain felt by Israeli and Palestinian communities, to emphasise the sanctity of innocent life, and to reaffirm Australia's commitment to a two-state solution.

While critics have said that his actions have been meaningless gestures and called on the Australian government to do more to act against Israel, his remarks highlighted the Australian government's consistent call for a ceasefire, the protection of civilians, and a path toward peace that acknowledges both Israeli and Palestinian suffering.

Any statement on such a volatile issue would inevitably invite criticism from all sides. Yet, his approach reflected the need for bipartisanship, or at least the appearance of it, in handling such a sensitive international conflict. His speech demonstrated an effort to engage with multiple communities—Jewish, Palestinian, Lebanese—and to appeal to the broader Australian public, who, after witnessing a year of devastation in Gaza, are increasingly disillusioned with political and media narratives that minimise or obscure Palestinian suffering.

But whenever there is a need for political bipartisanship, the Leader of the Opposition Peter Dutton cannot be relied upon, whose response to the Prime Minister's motion was predictably combative and divisive. Dutton's objection—that Albanese's call for a ceasefire and peace efforts went beyond the scope of a commemoration—revealed his endless unwillingness to engage in constructive dialogue, where he portrayed Albanese's balanced stance as duplicitous, accusing the Prime Minister of political opportunism. Dutton's insistence that the motion should focus solely on the lives lost in Israel, while ignoring the broader humanitarian crisis in Gaza, speaks volumes about his political strategy: one of narrowing the conversation to suit his agenda while sidestepping the complex realities of the conflict.

Dutton's reaction is emblematic of a broader pattern in his leadership, where he thrives on division, seizing on moments of national or international significance to sow discord rather than fostering unity. In this instance, his refusal to engage with the humanitarian disaster in Gaza reveals a lack of empathy not just for Palestinians but for the broader Australian electorate, which increasingly recognises the importance of addressing the root causes of conflict.

This approach to leadership may have short-term political benefits for Dutton, especially in electorates that are predisposed to his hardline stance, however, it also carries significant risks. The Liberal Party, under Dutton's leadership, appears increasingly disconnected from the diverse, multicultural makeup of Australia and many immigrant communities, who might traditionally lean toward the Liberal Party for its economic policies, are finding themselves alienated by Dutton's divisive rhetoric on social and international issues.

His tactics—focused on driving wedges between communities rather than uniting them—are out of step with a growing desire among Australians for political leaders who can offer genuine solutions to global challenges. As the Australian political landscape continues to shift, the need for bipartisanship on international crises such as the Israeli–Palestinian conflict is becoming more urgent. But Dutton's divisive approach stands in the way of that possibility. Instead of offering a vision for peace and cohesion, he has chosen to exploit this tragedy for political gain, revealing once again how unfit he is to lead the country.

LABOR'S UNWAVERING SUPPORT FOR ISRAEL BACKFIRES

While Dutton has been busy sowing the seeds of division, the situation surrounding the Labor government's handling of the Israeli–Palestinian conflict over the past year illustrates a deeper problem: the pursuit of appeasement, especially toward pro-Israel lobby groups, with little regard for the Islamic community or traditional Labor supporters. This dynamic has unfolded as the government bends over backward to maintain a pro-Israel stance, hoping this will quell tensions domestically and secure political favour. However, despite their efforts, the government, Prime Minister and Foreign Minister Senator Penny Wong, are receiving no political reward, and instead, they find themselves criticised from all sides.

At the outset of the conflict following the 7 October attacks, it appears that the Albanese government calculated that expressing unequivocal support for Israel, while minimising criticism of Israeli military actions in Gaza, would be a pragmatic short-term choice, where historically, conflicts between Israel and Palestine since 1987 have often faded from the spotlight after a short period, allowing governments to weather the storm domestically without long-term consequences. This time, however, the situation has dragged on for over a year, with humanitarian crises and continued military actions forcing the issue to the forefront of political discourse in Australia and around the world.

What Albanese would not have anticipated is how entrenched and enduring this crisis would become. The political pressure on the Labor government has mounted, especially from progressive factions within the party and the broader Australian community, many of whom are appalled by the loss of life and destruction in Gaza. Labor's initial instinct was to support Israel and sideline the Palestinian cause, yet, despite this one-sided support for Israel, the government is still being lambasted by pro-Israel groups, as was shown by the hostile reception Albanese received during the commemorative event in Melbourne, where he was jeered while Peter Dutton was cheered.

This reflects a clear political reality: no matter how much the Labor government tries to appease the pro-Israel lobby, they will never satisfy their demands. Groups like Zionism Victoria have criticised the government for not being "steadfast" enough in their support of Israel, even though the Labor government has gone to great lengths to avoid harsh criticism of Israel's actions. As a result, the Labor government has alienated their traditional base without gaining any new support from the pro-Israel factions they sought to placate and, in any event, they were unlikely to receive any political support from these groups who are traditionally conservative, right-wing and hostile to the interests of the Labor Party.

This political conundrum has left the Labor government appearing weak and reactive. Instead of taking a principled stand from the beginning—one that recognised the complexity of the situation and the need to balance the rights and lives of both Israelis and Palestinians—they chose the path of least resistance and, in doing so, they underestimated the long-term consequences of their approach. Labor's reluctance to condemn Israel's military actions, coupled with its failure to offer meaningful support to Palestinian communities, has exposed a disconnect with the progressive values many of their supporters hold dear.

Their attempts to please the pro-Israel community have not only failed to garner support but have also given the opposition, particularly Peter Dutton, ample ammunition to criticise them. Dutton has seized upon this opportunity, using the government's wavering stance to paint Albanese as indecisive, while he positions himself as a staunch defender of Israel. This opportunistic strategy may resonate with parts of the Liberal Party's base, but it further polarises the political landscape and damages Australia's reputation as a neutral arbiter in global conflicts.

The Attorney–General Mark Dreyfus's attempt to label the term "Zionist" as an anti-Semitic slur reflects the broader challenges facing the Labor government. While it is crucial to combat anti-Semitism, conflating all criticism of Israel with anti-Jewish sentiment is a dangerous oversimplification, as it undermines legitimate political discourse and fails to recognise the diversity of views within the Jewish community itself, many of whom oppose Israel's actions in Gaza. By pushing this narrative, the government risks alienating those who seek a more nuanced understanding of the conflict and further distances itself from the Islamic community, which has long felt marginalised by Australia's foreign policy stance.

This capitulation to powerful lobby groups, rather than standing firm on principles of justice and human rights, only weakens the Labor government, as it always has. Australia's historical stance, particularly under leaders such as Gough Whitlam, was one of neutrality and fairness, recognising the need to avoid involvement in foreign conflicts and to condemn the loss of civilian lives wherever they occur. Today, however, the government appears beholden to a small but influential group, and this influence shapes policy decisions that fail to reflect the will of the broader Australian community.

COULD LABOR'S PRO-ISRAEL POSITION COST IT AT THE NEXT ELECTION?

The Labor government's one-sided support for Israel is setting the stage for a political fallout in the next federal election. The disconnect between Labor's foreign policy stance and the concerns of many of its supporters, particularly those aligned with progressive values and the Islamic community, is becoming increasingly difficult to ignore. As the crisis deepens and the death toll in Gaza, West Bank and Lebanon continues to rise, a growing number of Australians recognise the extent of the violence as genocide, and Labor's failure to address this head-on, risks alienating a crucial part of its voter base.

The Australian Greens, led by outspoken MPs such as Max Chandler-Mather, have been unwavering in their criticism of Israel's military actions and the Australian government's complicity. Chandler-Mather's pointed questions in parliament—demanding to know how many more atrocities must be committed before the government sanctions Israel— reflect the frustration of many Australians who feel that Labor has abandoned its moral compass. The Greens' position has exposed a fundamental weakness in Labor's strategy: their reluctance to condemn Israel's actions forcefully and to end military cooperation with a nation that is, by many accounts, inflicting widespread destruction on civilians in Gaza.

This unwillingness to act decisively is not without consequence. Labor may believe that it is striking a careful balance to avoid inflaming tensions with Israel's supporters in Australia, but this strategy has already proven to be a political miscalculation. Zionist organisations, such as the Zionist Federation of Australia, are now pressuring Labor government to preference the Australian Greens last on election ballots, a clear sign of how entrenched the influence of the Israel lobby has become in Australian politics.

This interference in electoral processes—where external organisations are seeking to dictate preference deals—demonstrates a troubling erosion of democratic integrity. Yet, the most significant political damage from Labor's position on Israel is likely to come from within its own ranks. By failing to stand up for Palestinian civilians and aggressively distancing itself from the Greens' more assertive stance, Labor risks bleeding votes to its left flank. The Greens, who have long positioned themselves as the true progressives on issues of social justice and foreign policy, can capitalise on this discontent, especially in urban and multicultural electorates where Labor's voters are increasingly frustrated by their party's complicity in what they see as a humanitarian catastrophe.

Albanese's categorical rejection of any coalition with the Greens seems like a defensive posture designed to maintain a fragile sense of party unity. However, the strategic calculus behind such a declaration may be shortsighted. If the Greens continue to gain ground, particularly in seats in inner-city parts of Brisbane, Melbourne and Sydney, Labor may find itself forced into some form of collaboration post-election. Albanese's reluctance to engage with the Greens on foreign policy issues such as Israel and Palestine could come back to haunt him if Labor loses critical seats to the Greens. For many voters, particularly younger Australians and those in immigrant communities, Labor's perceived indifference to Palestinian suffering may be a decisive factor in how they cast their ballots.

The next election will likely be fought on multiple issues, and while foreign policy may not always be the top priority for most voters, the situation in Gaza is unique. The scale of the devastation and the perception that a genocide is being carried out under the watch of complicit governments could galvanise voters in unexpected ways. Labor's failure to offer a more balanced approach—one that acknowledges the rights of both Israelis and Palestinians—could cost it dearly, particularly if the Greens continue to gain traction by positioning themselves as the party of principle.

In rejecting any formal alliance with the Greens—as has been suggested by their leader Adam Bandt—Albanese may be playing to the immediate political gallery, attempting to secure a majority government without reliance on minor parties. Yet, this strategy ignores the broader shifts happening within the electorate. Voters are increasingly savvy, and many are no longer willing to accept the kind of mealy-mouthed foreign policy that sidesteps the hard truths of international conflicts. For Labor, the risk is clear: if it continues to toe the pro-Israel line while ignoring the growing humanitarian outcry over Gaza and Lebanon, it could lose not just the next election, but the moral authority that has historically set it apart from the conservative parties.

***

THE UNMASKING OF THE WEST
REVEALS AN UGLY FACE

16 November 2024

In recent years, the narrative surrounding the behaviour of Israel has become a mixture of political rhetoric, selective outrage, and, at on many occasions, *blatant distortion*. The recent football match in Amsterdam, where Maccabi Tel Aviv supporters turned a sporting event into a festival of violence, highlights the power that mainstream media and political figures wield in shaping public perception in favour of the state of Israel—often to align with a particular political agenda. For those who witnessed or later learned of the events as they truly unfolded, the gap between media reports and reality was glaring and unsettling, raising pressing questions about the manipulation of truth in service of political allegiances.

At the heart of this incident were Israeli supporters who arrived in Amsterdam to watch their team play Ajax in the Europa League (yes, *Israel* plays in a *European* league), ostensibly to support their team but quickly transformed the city into an arena for provocations, aggression, and racism where bystanders and residents were not simply caught in crossfire but were specifically targeted. Eyewitness accounts and independent media revealed that Maccabi Tel Aviv fans shouted racist slurs directed towards Palestine, harassed and physically assaulted people they perceived as 'Middle Eastern', and tore down Palestinian flags in brazen acts of provocation.

In an even more disturbing event, they disrupted a moment of silence meant to honour victims of recent floods in Spain, turning a display of respect into yet another arena for their anti-Palestinian vitriol. The next day saw more aggression on the city streets, ultimately leading to inevitable confrontations between the Israeli hooligans and Dutch locals, who retaliated in defence against the repeated provocations.

Yet, in the media, the narrative that reached international audiences was drastically different. Rather than highlighting the Maccabi fans' violence and bigotry, reports widely focused on the backlash from the Dutch public, depicting it as an outburst of anti-Semitic violence against innocent Israeli fans. Mainstream outlets drew dramatic parallels, likening the incidents to the *Kristallnacht* from 1938, casting the Dutch response as an attack on Jewish identity itself, rather than a defensive reaction to aggression. This shift in focus, this reinterpretation of events, served to shield the instigators and reframe the incident within a context that evoked collective Western guilt and sympathy, minimising the violent role the Israeli supporters played.

Australian politicians were also quick to adopt this skewed narrative, with Foreign Minister Senator Penny Wong condemning what she described as "anti-Semitic attacks" on the Israeli fans. There was no acknowledgment in her statement of the cause of these tensions—and certainly no recognition of the actions of Maccabi supporters that led to the confrontation—and it demonstrated an unwillingness, either out of convenience or political strategy, to question the origins of the conflict. Instead, Wong's statement reinforced a long-standing pattern in Western politics: denouncing anti-Semitism while remaining silent on provocations and violence perpetrated by Israeli supporters and Zionist sympathisers.

While anti-Semitism must be confronted—*as we must always point out*—and violence unequivocally condemned, this one-sided response contributed to a narrative that holds one group immune from accountability. This is not a new pattern in matters related to Israel and Palestine, where narratives are often shaped to protect or justify Israeli actions while minimising or vilifying Palestinian responses. This selective outrage has, over time, solidified a concerning pattern in Western foreign policy and media coverage, where Israeli actions are never held to the same standards. For politicians such as Senator Wong, the optics of appearing 'neutral' or 'aligned with allies' often come at the cost of truth.

SHIELDING ISRAELI AGGRESSION FROM ACCOUNTABILITY

This was just a game, but the tolerance shown towards Israel's actions extends far beyond football violence. Israel has long enjoyed vast financial and military support from the United States, despite persistent human rights abuses in Palestine since 1946, and accelerated since October 2023. Billions of U.S. dollars are funneled to Israel each year, supporting military operations that result in significant Palestinian casualties, destruction of homes, and widespread displacement. Meanwhile, countless Americans struggle with economic hardship, job insecurity, and rising living costs. Although there isn't a direct correlation between U.S. domestic policies and its unwavering support of Israel, the vast sums allocated to Israel reveal a priority in U.S. foreign policy that many American citizens are beginning to question, especially when they themselves lack adequate social support.

This disconnect between the public's interests and the priorities of political leaders was one factor in the Democrats' recent defeat in the U.S. elections. Despite widespread calls for a foreign policy shift that emphasises human rights and equitable treatment of all nations, President Joe Biden continues to authorise funding for Israel's military, supporting its airstrikes and operations in Palestinian territories. This disparity in treatment—both in terms of resources and diplomatic immunity—sends a clear message: Israel, despite its actions of genocide and ethnic cleansing, remains a protected ally.

This immunity raises questions about the underlying factors that influence Western leaders' responses to Israel. The influence of intelligence and information-gathering agencies, such as Mossad, has long been speculated as a force shaping global attitudes toward Israel. While these claims are difficult to substantiate, the pattern of unwavering support, even in the face of clear misconduct, suggests that many political leaders feel compelled to maintain favourable relations with Israel, irrespective of how repulsive, repugnant and violent its behaviour is, fearing potential political backlash or fallout.

HOW AGGRESSION ABROAD REFLECTS PRACTICES IN PALESTINE

The behaviour of the Maccabi Tel Aviv hooligans in Amsterdam also mirrors the broader dynamics of Israeli conduct in the occupied Palestinian territories. Their aggression, racially charged provocations, and disregard for local norms were more than just instances of football hooliganism; they were symptomatic of a larger pattern of behaviour rooted in entitlement, impunity, and a pervasive disregard by Israel for accountability. Just as these fans acted as though they were beyond reproach in Amsterdam, Israel's actions in Gaza and the West Bank similarly proceed unchecked, unchallenged by the same Western leaders and media who regularly demand human rights and accountability from other nations.

Many observers, including governments worldwide, now openly call Israel's actions in Gaza a genocide. Ireland—a European country with similar political values to many

Western democracies, including Australia, recently passed a resolution condemning Israel's actions as genocidal, highlighting that it's not just a radical viewpoint but a global concern recognised by many governments.

Meanwhile, Western media and political leaders seem not only reluctant to confront these realities but actively complicit in perpetuating a narrative that excuses Israel's actions, often resorting to what can only be described as propaganda to shift blame onto Palestinians. The deliberate and systemic targeting of Palestinian homes, the near-daily bombings, the destruction of essential infrastructure, and the enforced famine are all documented in independent media and widely condemned by human rights organisations. However, Western politicians, such as Senator Wong, continue to offer only hollow expressions of "deep concern" while stopping short of real condemnation or action. How can they continue to deny and ignore the actions that everyone else can see with their own eyes?

The events in Amsterdam exemplify this pattern. The international media portrayed the Israeli supporters as *victims* rather than *aggressors*, just as it often frames Palestinians as the instigators of violence in their own territories, rather than resisters to an occupying force. Politicians who should be speaking out against such flagrant behaviour instead default to condemning anti-Semitism, a stance that overlooks the racist, violent actions directed toward Arabs and Palestinians. This selective condemnation reveals a troubling hypocrisy that extends beyond political alignment to reflect a deeply ingrained bias in how Western media and political institutions view and report on the Israeli–Palestinian conflict. It is a bias that allows Israel to act with impunity, assured that the media will obscure its actions and redirect blame to the Palestinians, who are framed as perpetually at fault, regardless of the evidence.

The United States plays a central role in this double standard. Despite Israel's escalations, from daily bombings to a planned annexation of the West Bank, the U.S. government continues to stand by Israel unequivocally, dismissing the grave human rights violations occurring under its watch. American leaders have issued ultimatums to Israel, cautioning against further violence or expansionist measures, but these warnings have never been enforced. It is a cycle of empty threats and inaction, enabling Israel to continue its policies without fear of repercussion. The result is a situation where U.S. politicians condemn violence in principle but fail to hold the region's most aggressive actors accountable.

For many—not all, but a substantial number—this is the "mask-is-off" moment, revealing the true nature of Western political and media complicity in Israel's actions. Politicians who proclaim to be defenders of human rights reveal their selective application of these values, as they ignore or justify the violence inflicted on Palestinians. This selective blindness exposes a deep-seated bias that elevates Israeli interests over Palestinian lives, allowing a campaign of dispossession and oppression to continue unchecked. Zionism, in its most extreme manifestations, presents itself as an ideology that sees no limit to Israel's expansion and control over Palestinian land. This belief system fuels the violence in Gaza and the West Bank, and it is precisely this worldview that played out on the streets of Amsterdam, where Maccabi supporters felt entitled to act as they pleased, assured that they would face no consequences.

In this double standard, we can see the *ugly face* of the West—a face that prioritises political alliances over justice, that condones and accepts racism when it comes from a preferred ally, and that perpetuates a system where Palestinian suffering is either ignored or justified. The events in Amsterdam may seem minor in the global scope of Israeli-

Palestinian relations, but they are a microcosm of the larger narrative that plays out daily in Gaza, the West Bank, and Western media.

It's a selective empathy, a refusal to confront reality, and perpetuates an environment where the violence against Palestinians is normalised, while any form of Palestinian resistance is condemned. But it's the actions and inactions of Western leaders and their supporters in the media, that has to be condemned—whether it's on the football field or in occupied territories.

***

NETANYAHU ARREST WARRANT COULD
SEE A RAPID CHANGE

3 December 2024

The arrest warrant issued by the International Criminal Court for Israeli Prime Minister Benjamin Netanyahu over alleged war crimes in Gaza has cast a spotlight on international justice and the geopolitical issues that arise when principles of law collide with political alliances. This decision by the ICC has prompted a debate in Australia which, of course, has fallen along predictable party lines.

Foreign Minister Senator Penny Wong has emphasised Australia's respect for the ICC's independence and its role in upholding international law and pointed to the principle that adherence to international law is not only a *moral* obligation but also serves Australia's strategic interests. This stance aligns with the broader framework of ensuring accountability for war crimes and maintaining Australia's credibility as a nation committed to international norms.

The Liberal Party Senator Michaelia Cash, has fiercely criticised the ICC's decision—her response is based on two key points: alignment with the United States' unequivocal rejection of the arrest warrant and an assertion that there is no moral equivalence between the actions of Israeli leaders and those of Hamas. Cash also raised the possibility of Australia re-evaluating its membership in the ICC, suggesting the court's actions as 'overreach' that jeopardises key international alliances. This reaction not only mirrors the stance of the United States but also reveals a deeper discomfort within certain conservative circles about the ICC's *perceived* bias and its focus on allies of the West.

However, such arguments sidestep Australia's historical commitment to the ICC, a commitment that began under the conservative Howard government in 2002. The court's role in prosecuting war criminals from regions such as the former Yugoslavia, Rwanda, and Sudan highlights its importance in delivering justice for atrocities and crimes against humanity. Calls to abandon the ICC now, when its focus shifts to leaders such as Netanyahu, just for the reasons of political convenience, risk undermining the credibility of a system designed to be impartial and universal.

This tension also exposes a deeper inconsistency in the Liberal Party's rhetoric. By selectively opposing ICC actions, critics appear to condone a double standard: one set of rules for Western-aligned states and another for less powerful nations. This selective application of justice parallels historical attitudes where marginalised groups and weaker states are subjected to the full force of law, while powerful nations or their allies are shielded from scrutiny.

In the unlikely event that Australia did withdraw from the ICC, it risks diminishing its influence in shaping global norms of justice and accountability. Such a withdrawal would align Australia with nations that reject the ICC's authority, often for reasons rooted in their own leaders' potential culpability for crimes against humanity.

Netanyahu's position as Israel's leader is itself precarious. The ICC's warrant adds to the mounting pressures he faces domestically and internationally. His political survival increasingly hinges on maintaining power, as stepping down could expose him to a wide range of legal consequences. This fragility reflects a broader crisis for Israel as a state dealing with its atrocious policies toward Palestinians, its strained relationships with neighbouring countries, and its dependence on diminishing American support.

NETANYAHU'S TIRED OLD TROPE OF ANTI-SEMITISM

Netanyahu's framing of the ICC's arrest warrant as an 'anti-Semitic' conspiracy follows a well-trodden path of deflection and politicisation. His claim that the court's actions constitute a "modern Dreyfus trial" not only misrepresents the principles of international law but also weaponises historical anti-Semitism to shield himself from accountability, a narrative which exploits the legitimate sensitivities surrounding Jewish history and identity while ignoring the substantive legal basis of the charges against him.

At its core, the ICC's decision is not about Israel's identity as a Jewish state but about the actions of its leadership, particularly Netanyahu's alleged role in policies and military operations that have led to widespread civilian deaths and suffering in Gaza. Over 45,000 Palestinians, two-thirds of them women and children, have lost their lives in conflicts where Israeli military strategies have been criticised—and documented—for their disproportionality, the targeting of civilian infrastructure, and the enforcement of a blockade that amounts to collective punishment. These actions are not protected under international law, nor are they beyond scrutiny simply because they are carried out by a allied nation-state.

Netanyahu's characterisation of the ICC as biased or 'rogue' fails when examined alongside the court's broader record. The ICC has a history of prosecuting leaders and military figures from diverse backgrounds, including those from African nations and the former Yugoslavia. These cases were not dismissed as discriminatory by the international community; they were widely seen as necessary steps in holding individuals accountable for crimes against humanity. The same standard *must* apply to Netanyahu, whose actions as a head of state do not grant him immunity from international law.

Netanyahu's refusal to engage with the ICC also shows his lack of confidence in his own defence: if he *truly* believes in his innocence, as he has repeatedly asserted, the appropriate course of action would be to appear before the court, present evidence, and allow an impartial legal process to determine the truth. The fact that he has chosen to attack the court's legitimacy suggests *guilt* rather than *innocence*, and it also speaks to the overwhelming evidence that has been documented, not only by independent investigations but also by members of the Israeli Defense Forces themselves, whose actions have been recorded and disseminated globally.

The argument that the ICC has suddenly become biased is particularly disingenuous given its previous broad acceptance. There were no significant objections when the court pursued cases against African leaders or officials in former Yugoslavia—Slobodan Milosević, Ratko Mladić and Radovan Karadžić—nor when it issued arrest warrants for Russian figures such as Vladimir Putin. The principle of universal accountability is the foundation of the ICC's legitimacy, and to abandon this principle now, in the face of highly credible allegations against Netanyahu, is to render that legitimacy meaningless.

GLOBAL PRESSURE WILL LEAD TO A RAPID TRANSFORMATION IN PALESTINE

The trajectory of Israel–Palestine relations, long characterised by stagnation and regression—while it might not seem evident at this stage—now appears poised on the edge of transformative change. While the situation in Palestine has been marked by decades of entrenched oppression, there is reason to believe that the international and economic pressures bearing down on Israel may finally bring about a long-overdue and positive change.

This arrest warrant for Netanyahu is emblematic of this growing pressure. It signals a shift in global attitudes and a willingness to hold Israel accountable for its actions, actions that have increasingly defined it as a pariah state. The comparison to apartheid-era South Africa is not hyperbolic; Israel's policies in the Occupied Palestinian Territories—ranging from blockades and forced displacements to a system of *de facto* segregation—mirror the systemic injustices that South Africa once institutionalised. The parallels are not lost on the global community, which is beginning to coalesce around the necessity of change.

This momentum has been bolstered by diplomatic shifts, such as Australia's recent vote at the United Nations to demand an end to Israel's unlawful presence in the Occupied Territories. For the first time in over two decades, Australia has aligned itself with 156 other countries in supporting a resolution that unequivocally calls for justice and peace. This is a significant departure from its historically cautious stance, particularly given the influence of Israel's staunchest ally, the United States, and reflects a growing recognition that Australia has a responsibility to support international efforts toward ending the cycle of violence and advancing the two-state solution, efforts which have, so far, been lacking and highly supportive of the actions of Israel.

Economic factors further amplify these pressures. Just like apartheid South Africa and the Eastern Bloc, Israel faces mounting economic vulnerabilities exacerbated by its prolonged occupation and military aggressions. While it does seem that the state of Israel has an endless supply of military and financial support from the United States, the financial toll of maintaining such policies, coupled with increasing isolation from significant segments of the international community, threatens to undermine its economic stability. As history has shown, economic collapse often serves as a catalyst for political change, forcing regimes to confront their untenable positions.

Netanyahu himself symbolises the fragility of Israel's current trajectory. His political survival hinges on maintaining power, not merely to enforce his hardline policies but to evade the legal consequences that await him. His indictment by the ICC serves as both a personal and political crisis, further destabilising a leadership already on precarious ground, and a leadership that is not worth supporting. As with other historical figures whose tenure ended in ignominy, Netanyahu's eventual departure will become a turning point for Israel, paving the way for a more just and equitable future.

However, the path to resolution remains fraught with challenges. Ceasefires, such as the one recently established between Israel and Lebanon, offer a temporary reprieve but fail to address the deeper, systemic injustices that fuel the conflict. The situation in Palestine, where millions endure daily violations of their human rights, remains the most pressing and unresolved issue. While international consensus is increasingly aligned against Israel's policies, meaningful change will require sustained pressure, coordinated diplomacy, and a genuine commitment to justice.

Australia's renewed engagement at the United Nations on Palestine—although we're yet to understand how long this will continue for—highlights the importance of collective action. While Australia alone cannot significantly influence the Middle East, its willingness to vote for resolutions that contribute to peace reflects a shift in priorities and an acknowledgment of the broader moral and political stakes.

History teaches us that when change does come, it is often swift and unexpected, although in hindsight, it always appeared inevitable. The end of apartheid in South Africa, once considered improbable, came rapidly after decades of international isolation and internal resistance. The fall of the Berlin Wall in 1989 and the collapse of communism in Eastern Europe were similarly unforeseen, yet they reshaped the world in profound ways. Israel and Palestine, though mired in decades of conflict, could likewise experience a dramatic and positive transformation. This is not naïve idealism or foolish speculation: when that moment arrives, it will be the result of years of sustained pressure, growing international condemnation, and the undeniable reality that the current status quo is unsustainable.

The mechanisms for change—economic instability, legal accountability, and international moral clarity—are already in motion. While the timeline remains uncertain, the inevitability of change is clear. For Israel to survive as a legitimate and democratic state, and for Palestine to achieve its rightful independence, autonomy and justice, the world must continue to press forward, united in purpose and unwavering in the pursuit of peace and justice.

***

2025

CEASEFIRE: GLOBAL FAILURES, AND THE UNCERTAIN ROAD AHEAD

20 January 2025

The ceasefire in Palestine has offered a reprieve from the violence and destruction that has been inflicted upon Gaza since October 2023 but a deeper historical and political analysis shows a continuing pattern of oppression, resistance, and repeated failures by the international community to address the main issues.

These hostilities are not isolated recent events but are deeply entrenched in the history of occupation, and it is important to remember how we have arrived at this point. The roots of this occupation go back to the Nakba in 1948, where hundreds of thousands of Palestinians were forcibly displaced from their homes to make way for the creation of the state of Israel, a state that was forced through by the British government, under the arrangements of the Balfour Agreement. This initial act of dispossession and the ongoing illegal military occupation of Palestinian territories has defined the relationship between Israelis and Palestinians for decades.

Palestinians living in the occupied territories have faced land confiscations, home demolitions, restricted movement, and the blockade of Gaza. In Gaza, 2.2 million people have lived under severe restrictions, unable to rebuild their lives or access basic resources and this cycle of blockade, violence, and destruction has perpetuated conditions of extreme poverty and despair.

The Hamas-led attack on 7 October 2023, marked a turning point in the ongoing struggle. While Hamas justified the operation as a response to the years of occupation and another attempt to bring global attention to Palestinian suffering, the attack and the subsequent retaliation by Israel unleashed a level of devastation not seen in many years. The Netanyahu government subsequently declared war, aiming to dismantle Hamas and recover Israeli hostages: however, the scale of Israel's military response—targeting civilian infrastructure, refugee camps, and essential services in Gaza—has highlighted the highly disproportionate nature of the conflict.

Statements such as former Defense Minister Yoav Gallant's declaration of a "complete siege" and the depiction of Palestinians as "human animals" also revealed the Israeli government's broader objectives, which targeted not just Hamas but the Palestinian population as a whole. The death toll, now estimated at over 46,000 Palestinians—according to the medical journal *Lancet*, it could be over 186,000—including thousands of children, and the mass displacement of civilians, have shown the consequences of these policies.

International efforts to end the conflict have been woefully inadequate. The paralysis of the UN Security Council, mainly due to the repeated use of U.S. vetoes to shield Israel from condemnation, has shown how limited international diplomacy has been. World leaders' tepid condemnations of violence have often failed to translate into meaningful action, leaving Palestinians to endure unimaginable suffering while the underlying causes of the conflict have remained unaddressed.

Of course, as the ceasefire takes effect, it should bring a moment of hope, but it also raises questions about what lies ahead. The international community has done little to acknowledge what has been happening to Palestinians, not just since October 2023 but going back all the way to 1948, and has done everything to support the actions of Israel; why would post-ceasefire arrangements be any different?

Palestinians are now returning to destroyed homes, schools and hospitals, and face an uncertain future—the international community's repeated failures to hold Israel accountable or to enforce resolutions that could lead to a just and lasting peace will also raise significant questions about progress after Stage 3 of the ceasefire is completed. For Palestinians, a return to pre-October 2023 conditions—systemic apartheid, an illegal occupation of their lands, and brutal dispossession—is totally unacceptable.

This fragile ceasefire is compounded by historical precedents where ceasefires have been frequently broken by Israel or exploited as opportunities for them to regroup militarily. The question of accountability also remains: what mechanisms, if any, exist to prevent a return to violence? Without addressing the structural inequalities and injustices that have been a feature of this deliberately intractable conflict, any pause in hostilities at this stage will just be a temporary measure, and not a long-term solution.

SELECTIVE JUSTICE AND THE EROSION OF INTERNATIONAL LAW

Israel's actions in Gaza and the broader lack of international support for Palestine highlights the selective application of justice and international law. The assassination of senior Hamas negotiators by Israel in 2024 amid discussions of a possible ceasefire are examples of the deliberate sabotage of diplomatic efforts, and far from being isolated incidents, this reflects a broader Israeli strategy of prioritising military action over meaningful conflict resolution.

Despite the clarity of international law and conventions outlining the protection of civilian populations and the prohibition of collective punishment, Israel has defied these principles with impunity. The starvation, mass killings, and forced displacement of Palestinians constitute acts that experts and international bodies have increasingly identified as genocidal, yet the response from the international community, particularly from powerful states such as the United States and Germany, has been characterised by double standards, inaction and hypocrisy.

The United States, Israel's staunchest ally, has consistently shielded it from accountability. By vetoing critical United Nations Security Council resolutions, the U.S. has ensured that Israel faces no meaningful consequences for its actions. At the same time, billions of dollars in military aid and weaponry have flowed into Israel, facilitating its military campaigns against Gaza. This unquestioning support has emboldened Israel to escalate its actions, knowing that it will face no significant repercussions—and, so far, it hasn't.

Germany has also maintained arms trade agreements with Israel while publicly condemning violence in abstract or weak terms. These actions undermine Germany's professed commitment to human rights and international law, exposing a willingness to prioritise political alliances over the lives of vulnerable populations.

In contrast, a small number of Western nations have sought to challenge this: Spain, Ireland, and Norway have demonstrated political courage by recognising Palestine and ceasing arms sales to Israel. South Africa's decision to bring a case against Israel to the International Court of Justice was a significant step toward holding Israel accountable for its actions. The Court's findings, which recognised the likelihood of genocide and called for an immediate cessation of such acts, reflect the severity of the situation.

The International Criminal Court also took decisive action by issuing arrest warrants for Israeli leaders, including Netanyahu and Gallant, and these developments signal an increasing willingness among *some* players within the international system—not all—to confront the Israeli government. However, these efforts have been met with fierce resistance, particularly from the United States, including threats of sanctions by U.S. Senators against nations that attempt to enforce the Court's arrest warrants.

This pattern of selective enforcement of international law not only perpetuates the suffering of Palestinians but also undermines the credibility of global institutions, and the message sent to oppressed populations worldwide is that justice is contingent upon geopolitical considerations rather than universal principles.

ISRAEL HAS LOST THIS WAR AMID GLOBAL MORAL FAILURES

While there will be arguments about the role of Hamas and its actions on 7 October 2023, there is no question that this war was initiated by Israel and is mainly a continuation of its actions since 1948. Conflicts should never be a comparative contest but the comparisons will be made: 1,195 Israeli's died on 7 October—including many killed by the Israel Defense Forces under the "Hannibal Directive"—and at least 46,000 in Palestine and 3,000 in Lebanon have been killed by Israel since that time. But by any measure at all, this has been a disproportionate response by Israel, even more disproportionate than any of its actions against Palestinian people since 1948.

However, despite the massive destruction inflicted by Israel, its ambitions have been mainly unfulfilled: Israel instigated this war, and it has lost. It targeted Hamas for total annihilation, yet the movement remains intact, and in some respects, is stronger today, at least numerically. Hamas retains its operational capacity, and its symbolic significance as a resistance movement has only grown, particularly as the devastation in Gaza has highlighted to the world the profound suffering of Palestinians caused by Israel. Tensions between Hamas and the Palestinian Authority may emerge, but the broader narrative is one of resilience amid destruction.

In addition to this, Israel's international standing has suffered catastrophic damage. Its status as a pariah state has been cemented by its actions, which have gone far beyond the constraints of international law. Once criticised as an apartheid state and brutal occupier—*as if that wasn't bad enough*—Israel's recent actions have added accusations of genocide, ethnic cleansing, and ecocide to its record. While its allies in the West have provided diplomatic cover, public sentiment globally has shifted significantly and the massive protests in capitals worldwide and growing condemnation of Israel's actions reveal a rising awareness of the atrocities committed.

The economic fallout for Israel is equally damaging. The war has cost the economy tens of billions of dollars, with long-term projections painting an even worse outcome—over $400 billion in lost revenues over the next decade. Declining investment, shrinking consumer confidence, and disrupted labor markets reflect the broader instability resulting from its militarised messianic policies. Even with its superior military and economic power, Israel emerges as the conflict's biggest loser, particularly as these events have only deepened internal political divisions and societal fractures.

The reconstruction of Gaza, however, presents its own challenges. With an estimated $80 billion required to rebuild, the question is who will bear the cost of this. While nations such as Qatar and Saudi Arabia have stepped forward in the past, the scale of destruction requires an unprecedented global effort. Yet, this reconstruction must come with guarantees that the rebuilt infrastructure and lives will not be destroyed again by Israel in future conflicts inflicted at the whim of Netanyahu, or whomever replaces him. Without accountability for Israel and strong international mechanisms to enforce peace, the cycle of destruction and rebuilding risks becoming endless.

The reputations of Western nations have also been seriously tarnished. The unwavering support for Israel from leaders such as Joe Biden, Anthony Blinken, Keir Starmer, and others has rightfully drawn criticism. Their refusal to hold Israel accountable, the continued sale of arms, and their rhetoric about Israel's "right to defend itself" have shown a deep hypocrisy. Biden could have demanded an end to hostilities in October 2023: why did he wait until his final days in office before engaging in any form of meaningful action? The rights of Palestinians have been consistently ignored, as have their pleas for justice and the indifference shown by these leaders during Gaza's livestreamed genocide will become a moral indictment that history will not forgive, or forget. And nor should it.

In the future, political leaders will be haunted by these questions: where were you when Gaza was subjected to genocide? Why did you enable mass suffering rather than working to end it? The complicity of Western governments in this tragedy will be a stain on their legacies, as will events such as the standing ovation for Netanyahu in the U.S. Congress—a moment that epitomised the moral failure of the global political establishment: Gaza was being destroyed, yet the man who inflicted this reign of terror upon the peoples of Palestine was applauded and encouraged to go even further. How can this ever be forgiven?

Palestine faces a long road to recovery, but there is no doubt that it will recover, as it always does and irrespective of how long it takes. But the moral and reputational damage to the West and its many leaders who supported Israel is this way, is unrepairable. The conflict has exposed not only the brutality of Israeli policies but also the structural failures of an international community unwilling or unable to uphold its own standards. And it may never recover from these failures.

***

ABC SACKING EXPOSES THE ACTIONS OF THE ISRAEL LOBBY

8 February 2025

How far will the ABC go to protect the interests of the Israel lobby? That's the key question in a legal case that exposes all the elements of political influence, media independence, and corporate misconduct. The case centres on the journalist Antoinette Lattouf and her unfair dismissal from the ABC—the catalyst for this case was a social media repost concerning allegations made by Human Rights Watch that the Israeli government was using starvation as a method of warfare in Gaza and in her repost, Lattouf referenced the organisation's work, adding the words "HRW reporting starvation as a tool of war".

Human Rights Watch is a globally recognised organisation that employs researchers, legal experts, journalists, and investigators across 70 nationalities, and received the Nobel Peace Prize in 1997 for its role in the banning of land mines. Despite its reputation as a credible source, the ABC chose to respond to pressure from the Israel lobby by terminating Lattouf's employment—which was a short five-day contract anyway—rather than addressing the substance of what she had shared.

The manner in which Lattouf was dismissed has become the focus of her unlawful termination lawsuit against the

ABC, raising key issues about editorial freedom, legal ethics, and the power applied by interest groups—in this case, the Israel lobby—over national broadcasters and other media enterprises. And, in this case, if the ABC had resisted external pressure and supported its journalist for reposting a fact-based statement from a credible human rights organisation, there wouldn't have been any controversy. None. Instead, the abrupt dismissal drew even more attention to Lattouf's work and questions about how the ABC handles its responsibility to maintain independent reporting.

In its haste to remove Lattouf, the ABC also contended that sacking her could not have been racially motivated because they refused to acknowledge that the Lebanese race exists. These details, which are surfacing as part of the ongoing legal case, reflect both confusion within the ABC's internal processes and flawed legal justifications for the dismissal, as well as confirming the position of the ABC as a white-bread organisation that, instead of stamping out racism, simply applies more of it to appease certain interest groups.

In addition, the *Lattouf v ABC* case has highlighted the double standards in how the ABC applies its own policies over the use of social media. Several high-profile ABC personalities regularly repost seemingly controversial material without being asked to offer a "counterbalancing" piece or present competing perspectives. Lattouf's single repost has triggered a disproportionate reaction.

This discrepancy shows an environment where editorial guidelines are inconsistently applied or easily influenced by powerful interests, such as the Israel lobby. This case could have far-reaching implications, not just for Lattouf's professional future but also for how the ABC, as a public broadcaster, shows its commitment to journalistic independence and freedom. ABC management has allowed interference to come in from one lobbying group and, because of this, the impartiality and integrity that the public should expect from a publicly funded broadcaster has been severely compromised.

THE EROSION OF DEMOCRATIC DEBATE IN AUSTRALIA

The capacity of Israel lobby groups to extract swift and unquestioning compliance from media outlets and political figures shows weaknesses in how power is wielded in Australia. It is not uncommon for influential individuals tied to the Israel lobby to make direct calls to editors and senior executives at mainstream media organisations, including the ABC and major newspapers, calling for particular actions to be taken that serve their interests.

The urgency and success of these demands brings about a culture of fear in which journalists, producers and board members find themselves scrambling to avoid a backlash. This leads to abrupt dismissals and retractions that ironically amplify the very issues these lobbyists seek to bury—the disproportionate response around the keffiyeh controversy at the Sydney Theatre Company in 2023 is a clear example of this. Rather than allowing a minor element after the end of the performance to pass unnoticed—the cast wearing keffiyehs on stage to show their support for the people of Gaza—the loud objections and funding threats turned a small, local matter into national news over several months.

The influence that flows from such well-connected minority groups is neither universal nor reflective of entire communities; many within the broader Australian Jewish community *do not* support these heavy-handed tactics. Instead, they see this kind of clampdown on discussion and criticism of Israeli government policy as counterproductive and damaging to the community's reputation.

However, the response from these people within the Israel lobby has been to double down, and even attack other members from the Jewish community with whom they disagree with, as shown by the recent commentary from prominent Zionist lobbyist Mark Leibler, where he claimed that "nothing is worse than those Jews who level totally unfounded allegations of genocide and ethnic cleansing against the State of Israel. They are repulsive and revolting human beings... they are vicious antisemites".

The broader outcome is the disastrous effect on journalism, where editors and reporters grow uneasy about even the most factual commentary related to Israel or its policies. In the case of Lattouf, the abrupt manner in which she was removed—before even completing her week-long shift—reflects how immediate and intense the lobbying efforts can be, and how swiftly corporate entities can fold under that pressure.

This environment of excessive sensitivity is made even more complicated by the fact that legitimate criticism of any government—Israeli or otherwise—can be conflated with anti-Semitism if those protesting the criticism choose to label it as such. Most observers strongly condemn genuine anti-Semitism, and no one should be singled out or vilified purely for their ethnic or religious background. Yet criticism of policy decisions and human rights records is integral to a functioning democracy. The capacity to examine the actions of governments is considered a core right, and to suppress that right risks eroding the very democratic principles it aims to protect. Exaggerating claims of fear or "being triggered" can also backfire, as it invites skepticism about the genuineness of those concerns, creating a situation where all expressions of genuine alarm risk being dismissed.

The ABC's choice to remove Lattouf immediately—and, it seems, *unlawfully*—has led to costly legal proceedings, and these outcomes cannot be dismissed as inconsequential, as they show a mismanagement of both public trust and public funding. At the same time, this debacle—which could have been easily avoided if senior managers had some backbone and credibility—has chipped away at the ABC's reputation for independence and integrity; when a publicly funded broadcaster caters to one narrow interest group instead of defending staff who are simply relaying credible information, audiences see a loss of editorial courage and it raises the questions about how easily supposed fundamentals of a liberal democracy can be eroded.

Although nearly all mainstream politicians publicly condemn anti-Semitism, few appear willing to address the merging of legitimate critique with hate speech, avoiding the risk of being targeted themselves. Over time, this removes robust discussion from public debate, replacing it with self-censorship—which is what the Israel lobby wants to achieve. This weakens democracy from within, discouraging the free exchange of ideas and relegating important conflicts—where it's domestic or international—down to whispered conversations, rather than open debate.

The unease reflects a more global phenomenon within the Western world, especially in the United States, where fear, partisanship, and systematic attacks on media outlets have contributed to more fragile institutions. Although the context for Australia is different, these signs are similar to those in other countries where the constant pressure from lobby groups chips away at journalistic independence and the capacity for transparent public dialogue.

SILENCING POLITICAL VIEWS

There is a pattern of incidents involving the dismissal of media figures for views and perspectives that are different to those of specific vested interests: the journalist Mike Carlton was suspended over incidents relating to an article he published about Gaza in 2014, and the cartoonist Glen le Lievre was reprimanded by the *Sydney Morning Herald* after depicting an Israeli man casually observing the bombing of

Gaza from a loungeroom couch. Neither were disseminating hateful material; instead, they were reflecting on events unfolding at that time.

The fact that such commentary could prompt intense pushback from the Israel lobby—enough to cost individuals their jobs—shows the fragility of free expression where certain topics are raised. More recently, the abrupt sacking of the cricket commentator Peter Lalor shows how far-reaching these pressures can be: he posted about Gaza on his personal social media, and before long, objections were voiced to his employer, SEN Radio that, somehow, hearing Lalor's voice over the radio and commentating on test cricket from Sri Lanka was "triggering".

Discomfort or disagreement over someone's views is neither unusual nor inherently dangerous in a pluralistic society. Far more concerning is the perception that a handful of influential figures can force employers, editors, or broadcasters to fire individuals whose opinions stray beyond narrow parameters. Despite the obvious disconnect between Lalor's tweets about Gaza and his capacity to offer cricket commentary, the chain of events suggests that even *minor* social media activity—totally unrelated to the job itself—can lead to immediate action if enough pressure is applied. This approach does not align with values of open debate and diversity of opinion; it instead entrenches a system in which certain ideas can be suppressed with little due process.

It also brings up questions about other journalists who have similarly been "disappeared": the contracts for the ABC's Sarah Macdonald and Simon Marnie were inexplicably not extended in December 2024, even though both had been successful journalists at the ABC for many years and, in the case of Macdonald, a high-rating and popular presenter of the *Morning* program on Sydney radio. Is there anything in their social media accounts or public engagements that was perceived to have been offensive to the Israel lobby—*real or imagined*—and were there any harassing phone calls made to ABC management at the time to remove these journalists? This is an issue that would be worth investigating because nothing else seems to make sense.

Some defenders of these decisions claim that particular forms of speech constitute a genuine threat, invoking anti-Semitism or other forms of bigotry. While it is critical to condemn actual hatred toward any minority—at *every* occasion—it is also critical to recognise that critique of the actions of a government—in this case, Israel—and calls to end violence do not constitute hate speech or anti-Semitism. They are part of legitimate, if uncomfortable, public discourse. When the label of anti-Semitism is overused or misapplied, it loses its potency in confronting real prejudice. And at the same time, the conflation of all criticism of Israel with anti-Semitism has become a powerful tool to silence journalists, commentators, and others who might otherwise raise credible objections to Israel's policies and actions in the Middle East.

The public expects that journalists, commentators, and political figures can express their perspectives without fear of a sudden, career-ending phone call to their employer and it is vital to recognise the difference between expressing strong positions on international affairs and inciting genuine harm. While genuine incitement requires intervention, routine expression of political or humanitarian concerns should not. By turning so swiftly to sackings and public condemnations, media institutions allow vocal lobbies to skew public discourse in ways that favours secrecy and compliance over truthful, in-depth reporting.

If the numerous dismissals of respected professionals illustrates anything, it is that capitulating to demands premised on "triggered" or offended individuals, without regard for the actual substance or impact of the speech, erodes trust in *all* media platforms. Many Australians—whether they share the same political beliefs or not—recognise that a true exchange of ideas will inevitably feature disagreements, and only in extreme cases should there be calls for someone's removal.

What has happened to these journalists and commentators shows how perilously close newsrooms and broadcasters have become to giving up fundamental freedoms when confronted by small but persistent and secretive voices, such as the Israel lobby. Once it becomes easier to sack commentators than to accept challenging viewpoints, society has lost sight of a key part of democracy—the capacity to engage in dialogue and hold power to account, even when the truth hurts.

***

THE MEDIA'S ALLIANCE WITH ZIONIST PROVOCATEURS

22 February 2025

A recent incident in Sydney's Inner West has raised many questions about the manipulation and creation of anti-Semitic incidents in Australia by right-wing extremists and agitators. Ofir Birenbaum, a prominent member of the controversial Australian Jewish Association and a known Zionist provocateur, attempted to manufacture an incident at the Cairo Takeaway cafe in Newtown where, wearing a Star of David cap, he tried to provoke a hostile or anti-Semitic reaction that could be captured by *Daily Telegraph* reporters waiting outside.

The goal was to create a sensational story about rampant anti-Semitism in Australia, push a narrative of an under-protected Jewish community and, in turn, continue to launch political attacks against the Labor government. Yet in Newtown—a suburb well-known for its diversity and inclusive culture—the provocation didn't succeed: Birenbaum's actions were met with disinterest, and a *best to leave this dickhead alone* approach. No matter what he tried, staff and patrons at the cafe simply went about their day. Consequently, not only did the *Daily Telegraph* fail to get the inflammatory story they were after, it also exposed the larger dynamics between right-wing media outlets and extremist pro-Israel activists who collaborate to manipulate public sentiment.

The issue goes beyond this one incident: Rupert Murdoch's media empire has a long record of backing pro-Israel positions and narratives, with coverage that is often supportive of the Israel's government and policies, leaving no room for more nuanced or critical perspectives. Such one-sided messaging deepens community tensions, stirs up Islamophobia, and delegitimises anyone critical of Israel's policies by painting them as prejudiced or anti-Semitic.

In many cases, it works because they exploit the fear of anti-Semitism—which, of course, is a very real phenomenon—and exaggerate or manufacture incidents to heighten public anxiety. This approach not only fuels prejudice toward other communities, particularly Muslim and Middle Eastern Australians, but it also distracts from legitimate discussions about the Israeli government's controversial policies, such as settlement expansion in the West Bank, the unresolved status of the occupied territories, or the attempts of genocide in Gaza.

Birenbaum's failed attempt to manufacture outrage reveals how much of a miscalculation it can be to try such a stunt in an area like Newtown, where cultural diversity is part of everyday life. Here, anyone is generally free to dress and express themselves as they please, religious symbols included. Ironically, his actions inadvertently shone a light on exactly how certain factions are trying to foment hatred, and strengthened the resolve to reject such divisive tactics in the process.

Beyond this incident, there is a concern about a wider pattern of racially motivated violence and intimidation. Recent incidents, such as two women being assaulted in Epping in Melbourne—one of them pregnant and choked with her own hijab—remind us that hate crimes and racism of all types must be taken seriously. The police response to these cases was relatively slow, which raises other questions about biases in law enforcement.

What emerges from all of this is how particular media operators and ideologically driven individuals can collude to manufacture controversies for political advantage. Broader debates about Israel—whether it pertains to its establishment, the 1948 or 1967 borders, the ongoing violent settlement and policies, or genocide in Gaza—need to occur in an environment where all voices can be heard, without fear of being automatically labeled as hostile to an entire group of people.

ONE-SIDED POLITICAL RESPONSES HAVE AIDED THE OUTRAGE

Australia's political leaders often position themselves as staunch opponents of racial or religious hatred, yet their actions frequently reveal a very different story. In the aftermath of this failed provocation in Newtown, the conspicuous silence from key figures, including the Prime Minister, Anthony Albanese, shows how officials can shrink from manipulative media narratives—especially when they originate from powerful outlets.

The fact that this incident took place in Albanese's own electorate of Grayndler without so much as a public statement of support for the workers at the Cairo Takeaway cafe speaks volumes. Political leaders are busy people, but they often find the time to comment on a range of local matters, and it would not have been unreasonable for the Prime Minister or even the NSW Premier to express concern or, at the very least, check on the concerns of a business drawn into a media stunt. That nothing of the sort happened fuels the double standard, where criticism or scrutiny of certain individuals or groups is all but off-limits and the political class mostly looks away.

It seems that nobody in government wants to risk the wrath of a media apparatus that holds the power to amplify or dampen political fortunes. As a result, the government's message to the public is one of tacit acceptance, suggesting that if powerful media barons or well-connected interest groups orchestrate disinformation, officials will quietly stand aside.

The weakness of political leadership is also apparent when sensational, potentially harmful media stories go unchallenged. An example of this is the *Sydney Morning Herald*'s report about a caravan allegedly loaded with explosives on the outskirts of Sydney and a supposed list of Jewish targets. Their alarmist headlines—which were then magnified in other media outlets—implied Australia was on the verge of a serious terrorist plot, but the follow-up revealed that the explosives were decades old, likely to be inactive, and that the "list" of targets just simply didn't exist. Someone had just made the story up.

Despite the story's debunking, there was no *mea culpa* from either the newspaper or public officials who might have questioned the narrative's origins. Instead, the correction was buried, and the fleeting panic it caused lingered in the public consciousness. Such episodes show how easy it is for the media to manufacture panic that benefits specific agendas, with little pushback from political leaders who ought to defend the public's right to fair and accurate information.

By tolerating these fabrications, or at least failing to challenge them, political leaders are enabling a climate of mounting tension. When false or exaggerated stories about anti-Semitic plots are circulated, it leads to inflated fears within Jewish communities. Meanwhile, some in the broader public grow cynical, feeling that accusations of bigotry and hatred are wielded more like political tools than genuine concerns—which then dilutes the seriousness of real incidents of anti-Semitism.

This same dynamic spills over into other forms of prejudice, including Islamophobia, contributing to an atmosphere where the term "hate crime" can be weaponised for political point-scoring rather than addressing actual offenses. Ultimately, those who face genuine discrimination, whether they be Jewish, Muslim, or any other group—are left in a precarious position, unprotected by political leaders who are more interested in appeasement rather than principled leadership.

The real tragedy here is that such timid political responses harm both majority and minority communities. They allow extremist viewpoints—those that genuinely do advocate racist or hateful ideologies, such as News Corporation—to flourish amid the loud noises of manufactured outrage. By not calling out hoaxes out with the same force used against legitimate cases of discrimination, the government places all of these incidents on the same level, fostering public confusion and weakening the seriousness of legitimate concerns. This environment emboldens individuals who truly harbor anti-Semitic or Islamophobic sentiments, giving them more credibility than they should ever have. It also undermines the possibility of critical debate about foreign and domestic policy related to Israel, Palestine, and other contentious issues.

What is needed is simple yet it remains elusive: principled leadership willing to hold media organisations accountable, regardless of the political risk, combined with a commitment to confronting bigotry in all its forms. When politicians refuse to waver in the face of powerful media proprietors, they send a clear message that weaponising hatred for clicks, sales, or political favour will not be tolerated. Conversely, by not doing anything about these issues, it suggests that these political leaders either condone the behaviour, or are simply too weak and lack the courage to call out these manipulations, regardless of the source.

THE SILENT STRINGS: HOW THE ISRAEL LOBBY MUTES CRITICISM

One of the other parts of the ongoing manipulation in Australia's public debate is the growing list of individuals who find their voices muzzled the moment they challenge or question Israel's policies. From the journalist Antoinette Lattouf to the academic Tim Anderson, and now the artist Khaled Sabsabi, whose commission at the 2026 Venice Biennale was withdrawn by Creative Australia, each example shows a pattern of swift and disproportionate retaliation. Instead of open dialogue or genuine engagement with the substance of their critiques, these people have faced professional setbacks, terminations, and erasure from cultural and academic institutions.

The rationale is almost always vague—somehow "offensive" work or "controversial" statements—while the real story, as many suspect, is that a small, well-connected lobby has exerted influence behind the scenes, usually through threats of withdrawing funding or other retaliations. When art containing images of the Palestinian flag is quietly censored—the National Art Gallery in Canberra censored the tapestry created by the art collective SaVĀge K'lub—or individuals are dropped from high-profile exhibitions without transparent explanations, it's obvious that the criticism of Israel is being relegated to the margins in a supposedly free society.

What makes this trend unacceptable is that it dismantles the very principles that Australian democracy claims to hold dear. The nature of academic inquiry is supposed to be rigorous, involving a contest of ideas tested against facts and peer review. If a professor calls Israel an apartheid state—as

Tim Anderson did in 2018—a proper response should emerge through research and debate rather than abrupt dismissal.

The same principle applies to the arts; creative expression often provokes discomfort or controversy, and that is precisely its job. By punishing artists who reflect on real-world conflicts, cultural institutions abandon their commitment to diverse perspectives. In these acts of censorship or "quiet removals", officials are placating a tiny but influential lobby, stifling conversation on issues that deeply affect Australia's multicultural population. Meanwhile, the broader public is left wondering why certain topics are off-limits and who decides that some viewpoints must vanish without explanation.

This climate is evolving into a modern-day McCarthyism, in which the smallest suspicion of being "too critical" of Israel triggers punitive measures. For those who stand up for Palestinians, it can feel like a precarious balancing act. Rather than fostering a safe environment for legitimate dissent, Australia's institutions are sending a message: *speak out and you will be removed*. The result inhibits not only controversial or provocative voices but also anyone who might support them. Eventually, public debate becomes sterile, absent of the kind of fearless, critical thought that marks a robust and healthy democracy. And this, ultimately, is not good for *any* democracy.

Yet this level of censorship, even if it might be effective in the short term, rarely silences an idea *forever*. The anger it generates often leads to stronger, more unified calls for change. As more people notice the removal of dissenting voices, they begin to question the motives and the power structures behind such decisions. Although censorship on behalf of the state of Israel may not be on the scale of the United States, where media consolidation and lobbying are furiously ridiculous, bordering on fascism, the echoes in Australia are loud enough to raise alarm.

It's unlikely to happen, but this is the moment that demands courage from those who occupy positions of influence, whether in government, media, academia, or the arts. People who promote free speech and the right to critique power must be willing to protect those who offer inconvenient truths or unpopular perspectives. The irony is that open debate would likely strengthen Australia's institutions; it would give communities—Jewish, Muslim, or otherwise—more confidence that concerns and criticisms can be aired without fear of reprisal and the refusal to engage openly simply breeds more mistrust.

No matter how strong the attempt to silence critics, the fundamental issues remain: the complex reality of the Israel–Palestine conflict, the consequences of foreign policy decisions, and the moral questions raised by longstanding military occupations, genocide and human rights abuses. Suppressing discussion about these matters only heightens divisions, disenfranchises the marginalised, and allows genuine extremism to grow in the shadows, such as the extremism that is promoted by News Corporation.

Australia's best defence against imported hatred and internal strife is a forthright commitment to democratic values—ones that do not kotow to pressure from any lobby, no matter how well-funded or influential. It doesn't require additional protection, just application of the laws *as they exist*: protecting those who challenge entrenched power structures, insisting on transparency in decision-making, and standing up for the free flow of ideas—even when doing this poses a risk. Only then can a functional, pluralistic Australia thrive, unburdened by the question of whose voices are being silenced, and why.

***

MANUFACTURING FEAR: FAKE TERROR AS A POLITICAL WEAPON

15 March 2025

There was a new development during the week in the widely-reported terrorist caravan plot and threat from January—it didn't actually exist. The fabricated nature of this alleged attack—a caravan was found on the outskirts of Sydney supposedly filled with *live* explosives to be used against synagogues—was clear to those who were willing to scrutinise this incident and ask the right questions. Yet, raising these doubts at the time was met with accusations of anti-Semitism, which provided a convenient deflection from the larger question: *who* orchestrated fabrication, and *why*?

Who knew that the plot was likely a hoax, and when did they know? It seems that the leader of the opposition, Peter Dutton, *did know* but either deliberately avoided a security briefing in January or has denied receiving a briefing when he actually *did*. The Australian Federal Police were aware at the time that the incident was highly likely to be a hoax but kept this information under wraps to avoid jeopardising their investigation into the origins of the threat which, on face value, seems to be a reasonable proposition. But if Dutton was aware early on that the incident was not real, why did he persist in pushing the narrative of a terror threat for political gain?

MANUFACTURING FEAR: FAKE TERROR AS A POLITICAL WEAPON

Throughout February, Dutton continued to exploit this "attack" to fuel anxiety within the Jewish community and amplify a rising tide of anti-Semitic behaviour. He repeatedly raised his alarmist rhetoric in Parliament and scored political points by constantly framing the government as *weak on security*, attempting to boost the Liberal Party's 'tough on crime and terror' position while pushing the message that the Albanese government is incompetent in handling national security matters.

Despite the confirmation from the shadow Home Affairs Minister, Senator James Paterson, that the Liberal Party *had* received a security briefing, Dutton continues to deny any personal knowledge of the hoax at the time. It stretches credibility to believe that the party leader would be left out of such a crucial briefing on national security and if Dutton was truly uninformed, it then raises questions about why his own party failed to update him. More likely, he *was* well aware but saw an opportunity for political exploitation.

The complicity in this deception extends beyond federal politics. NSW Premier Chris Minns was also privy to the information that this incident was a hoax, yet his government proceeded to fast-track draconian anti-Semitism legislation in response. While combating anti-Semitism is, without question, and issue that needs to be stamped out, Australia already has robust legal frameworks at both state and federal levels to address racism and hate speech. The speed with which these new laws were introduced raises another question: was it forced by political agendas rather than a genuine concern for Jewish communities?

Even more troubling is the sphere of influence held by extremist Zionist organisations and Israel lobby groups in Australia, who have long pushed for increased criminalisation of criticism against the state of Israel. If this legal path continues, even journalists and commentators discussing these developments—let alone questioning them or discussing the issues of concern in an article such as this one—may soon find themselves at risk of prosecution. The effect on free speech is not speculative paranoia; it's a clear direction in which legal frameworks are shifting.

The question of who ultimately benefits from these legislative changes and heightened public fear is critical. If the fabricated plot had instead targeted a mosque, a church, a Hindu temple, or any other religious institution, the political response would have been vastly different—we've seen that happen time and time again. The selective outrage and opportunistic exploitation of this event reflects a broader strategy: the manipulation of public fear for political and ideological gain.

HOW NSW'S REACTIVE LAWS THREATEN CIVIL LIBERTIES

The consequences of knee-jerk legislation extend far beyond the immediate moment of the political environment in which they were introduced. The NSW government's rapid introduction of these new laws not only have troubling implications—they are damaging to the basic principles of democracy, free speech and civil liberties. These laws were passed, even though Minns knew the threat was a fabrication, raising concerns about the motivations behind them and the longer-term ramifications.

Once a government introduces these kinds of security measures, they are *never* rolled back. Even when such measures are later revealed to have been unnecessary or disproportionate, the act of attempting to repeal them would become a political minefield. Any future government that attempts to amend or remove these laws will inevitably face accusations of enabling anti-Semitism, even if their only goal is to restore civil liberties eroded under false pretences. This is the insidious trap of reactive policymaking: once embedded, these laws become entrenched, unchallengeable, gradually normalised, and weaponised by groups such as the Israel lobby.

The deeper issue here is that laws passed in response to hysteria or political pressure are rarely about protecting the public at large. Instead, they serve as tools of political leverage for interest groups with a vested stake in controlling public discourse. The new NSW laws effectively set a precedent that elevates one particular type of discrimination above all others, making it more difficult to critique specific political movements or international actions—particularly those related to Israel—without the risk of legal repercussions. This is not about addressing genuine hate crimes, which existing laws already cover, but about reshaping the limits of acceptable political discussion.

Once the state grants itself the power to criminalise certain opinions under the broad banner of "anti-Semitism", it's only a matter of time before these laws are used in ways that go far beyond their original intent. Activists who protest against the Israeli government's policies may soon find themselves legally silenced, as was the case with the unlawful arrest by U.S. Immigration and Customs Enforcement of the permanent resident and Palestinian student activist, Mahmoud Khalil. Academics engaging in legitimate historical analysis may be accused of incitement. Journalists who dare to investigate the political influence of foreign lobbies could be prosecuted under the very laws designed to combat extremism. This is the creeping authoritarianism that masquerades as moral righteousness, and it is precisely how democratic societies slide toward repression under the guise of protection.

The fact that these laws were introduced following a fabricated event makes the situation more unacceptable. It also raises the question: if laws can be passed based on an event that never actually happened, what else can be legislated into existence? If politicians and lobby groups can manufacture a crisis, weaponise it for political gain, and then cement their advantage through law, the danger is not just restricted to one particular issue—it is to the entire framework of democratic governance.

The broader problem with legislating based on fear is that it plays into the hands of those who thrive on division and control. The Israel lobby, like any powerful political entity, understands the value of creating an atmosphere of perpetual crisis. When the perception of threat is constant, the justification for ever-expanding state powers never disappears. Governments, in turn, benefit from having new tools to suppress dissent, regulate speech, and brand opposition as dangerous. This is why the trend of enacting hyper-specific legislation in response to politically sensitive events is so dangerous—it is not about solving a problem, but about shifting the power dynamics of public discourse in a way that is near impossible to reverse.

The NSW government has set a precedent that will be difficult to undo. Today, the laws are framed around anti-Semitism; tomorrow, they could be expanded to other forms of political speech. Once you establish the principle that certain criticisms are off-limits under threat of legal action, the logical next step is to broaden the scope. Could criticism of U.S. foreign policy be labeled as "anti-Americanism" and subject to the same restrictions? Could protests against military interventions be categorised as "undermining national security" and shut down? The possibilities are endless once the principle is accepted.

The most glaring irony in all of this is that far from preventing hate speech, laws like these often create the conditions for more resentment and division. When the government is seen as selectively protecting one group's interests over the broader community, it fuels the very animosity it claims to be fighting. The public, sensing that they are being manipulated, becomes increasingly distrustful of official narratives and far from reducing tensions, such measures can push discourse underground, creating a breeding ground for genuine extremism that festers outside of public scrutiny.

AUSTRALIA PLACATES THE ISRAEL LOBBY WHILE NEGLECTING ISLAMIC COMMUNITIES

The political establishment in Australia has made its allegiances clear. When it comes to support, advocacy, and policy decisions, the Israel lobby enjoys unwavering quick and bipartisan backing, while Palestinian and Islamic communities are usually met with silence, neglect, or outright hostility. From funding allocations to legislative changes, there is a massive imbalance in how these communities are treated and this situation exposes a deeper political reality: Australia's ruling class is willing to serve the interests of Israel and its allies, even at the expense of its own social cohesion.

A Home Affairs report from November 2023 confirmed what many in the Palestinian and Islamic communities had already been feeling for years—there is no place for them in mainstream political discourse. That report warned that the one-sided political support for Israel was creating divisions in Australian society yet, instead of attempting to bridge these divides, both the government and the opposition doubled down, choosing to amplify their commitment to Israel rather than acknowledge or mitigate the social exclusion of Palestinian and Muslim Australians.

The clearest evidence of this bias is the financial support directed toward different communities. Following the 7 October attacks and the subsequent Israeli assault on Gaza, the Australian government provided $7 million to SBS and AAP to "combat misinformation" about Islamic and

Palestinian communities. But instead of directing any of that funding to the very communities affected—to organisations on the ground, to Muslim or Palestinian advocacy groups, or to civil society organisations that could offer direct assistance—every cent went into government-approved media narratives. In contrast, $25 million was provided directly to the Executive Council of Australian Jewry, an organisation that actively lobbies for pro-Israel policies in Australia. The message from government could not be clearer: one community is entitled to state-backed advocacy, while the other is deemed a public relations problem to be managed.

This isn't just about money; it's about the broader institutional landscape. Jewish community groups have the full weight of government support behind them, from new anti-Semitism laws to enhanced security measures, even when the threats they claim to face turn out to be fabricated. Meanwhile, documented Islamophobic attacks have doubled since 2023, and yet there has been no comparable response—no task force, no emergency funding, no high-profile government statements condemning these acts in Parliament.

Why is this happening? The Israel lobby is politically well-organised, well-funded and well-connected to both major political parties, enjoying direct ties to influential figures in media, business and government. And it has the *confidence* and the *swagger* to exploit these relationships. In a recent video exchange, David Adler from the reactionary and aggressive Zionist agitator, Australian Jewish Association, bragged to the Liberal MP, Julian Leeser, that he had compiled a dossier of the "hostile acts by the foreign minister [Penny Wong] and Labor" against Israel and the Jewish community and sent it off to the Israeli Knesset.

In contrast, Palestinian and Muslim advocacy groups have nowhere near the same level of institutional influence and their concerns are routinely dismissed as fringe or inconvenient.

Even the most basic acts of solidarity—such as calling for a ceasefire in Gaza—have been met with political cowardice from Labor and outright hostility from the Liberal–National Coalition.

Even when Israel launched one of the most brutal military assaults in recent history, killing at least 46,000 Palestinians, including thousands of children, Australia's political class refused to shift its stance. Instead, it issued weak statements about Israel's *right to defend itself* and repeatedly blocked even symbolic measures of support for Palestinian civilians. This unwavering support continued even as international legal bodies began investigating Israel for war crimes. No such hesitation would have existed if the situation were reversed— if an Arab state were inflicting such mass atrocities, Australia would have been at the forefront of diplomatic condemnations and sanctions.

This is not just an issue of fairness; it is an issue of democracy. A society that selectively protects one group while neglecting or demonising another is not a free society. A government that aligns itself with a powerful foreign-backed lobby at the expense of its own citizens is not acting in the national interest. And a political class that criminalises legitimate criticism while allowing real discrimination to go unaddressed is failing in its most basic responsibilities.

The reality is that this dynamic will not change by itself. The entrenched power of the Israel lobby in Australia ensures that political and media institutions will continue to serve its interests unless a serious challenge to this dominance emerges. This challenge will not come from within the political class— it will have to come from the public, from activists, from independent media, and from the communities that have been abandoned by those who claim to represent them.

Until this changes, the message remains clear: in the eyes of Australia's political establishment, some communities are worth protecting, and others are expendable. The growing anger, frustration, and disillusionment among neglected communities will not simply disappear—it will continue to build, and when it reaches a breaking point, the political class will have no one to blame but itself.

***

SILENCE AT THE BALLOT BOX

12 April 2025

The recent killings in Gaza of fifteen medics and rescue workers by the Israel Defense Forces was one of the most horrifying developments that we've seen, in a spate of massacres that has long crossed the boundaries of legality, morality, and humanity. All available evidence doesn't suggest accidental crossfire or collateral damage, but targeted killings—executions in the service of a slow, methodical ethnic cleansing campaign by the state of Israel. It is a campaign which has, over the past two months, claimed the lives of women, children, aid workers, journalists, and civilians of all types. The pretext, endlessly repeated by Israel and parroted by its international allies, is *Hamas* on all occasions, but the nature of these victims—their roles, ages, and identities—tells another completely different story. Medics are not militants. Babies are not insurgents. And yet, this indiscriminate slaughter continues, cheered on by the state of Israel and met with complicity, cowardice, and silence from much of the international community—including Australia.

In any democracy on morality and the rule of law, a moment like this—when the world is witnessing a slow genocide, broadcast in real time—should provoke urgent political debate. But in the middle of Australia's federal election campaign, there is a glaring absence. Labor is not talking about Gaza. The Coalition is not talking about Gaza—except to score points on anti-Semitism—and the mainstream press, with a few notable exceptions, is hardly questioning them at all. It's as though the issue of Gaza—one that has moved hundreds of thousands of Australians to protest, to grieve, and to question their own government's international allegiances—simply doesn't exist within the official campaign narrative, as though the conflict has never happened and doesn't even exist. And this is all by design.

Labor, under Prime Minister Albanese, is aware that any criticism of Israel can and will be quickly weaponised as an accusation of anti-Semitism—a smear that has already crippled political debate in Britain, the United States, and many other countries in the Western world. Rather than confront this risk head-on, the party appears to have opted for *evasion*: relying on vague talking points, offering sterile platitudes, and hope the issue just doesn't appear in the public view before election day. When Foreign Minister Penny Wong was asked about the killing of those fifteen medics, she responded not with outrage or condemnation but with bureaucratic diplomacy. There must be a "full and thorough investigation," she said, and the need for protection of humanitarian workers under international law, suggesting that Australia was working with other countries on a "declaration" to that effect. A 'declaration' is the only thing Australia can offer at the moment? On parchment, or sent via e-mail? Or perhaps a post on Twitter. A declaration of *cowardice*, that's all it was.

This is the language of delay, of ambiguity, and of passive complicity. It's not designed to call out war crimes, or hold power to account, or provide moral clarity. It is designed to *appease*, and to downplay any public debate. Labor has taken refuge in the bland language of 'international humanitarian law,' knowing that these mechanisms are slow, ineffective, and easily bypassed by powerful vassal states such as Israel.

A 'declaration' won't stop bombs. A statement about the importance of 'every innocent life' won't bring back the dead. And a generic call for a ceasefire, without demanding accountability from those committing the crimes, is not a political position—it's just an abdication of responsibility.

The Prime Minister, too, has offered little of substance. Albanese has acknowledged the trauma felt by Australians with families in Gaza, Israel, or Lebanon, but quickly moved back to cautious generalities. *Every innocent life matters*, he said. *We want a ceasefire* and *we want hostages released*. And then came the inevitable cliché of the 'two-state solution'—a phrase that nobody understands the meaning of anymore, and in the context of Israel's ongoing settlement expansion, military occupation, and *de facto* annexation, has become little more than a diplomatic ghost. It's a slogan with no plan behind it, no timeline, no enforcement, and no credibility. And it's used because it allows politicians to appear principled while doing nothing about the issue.

If the Labor government cannot speak clearly about such an issue during an election campaign—and on an issue that is so clearly defined within the Labor Platform—if it cannot defend the rights of journalists, doctors, and children not to be bombed into oblivion, then what does it stand for? How many more headless children does it need to see being held by grieving parents before it can go beyond the stage of offering meaningless platitudes and gratuitous declarations?

There is still time in this election campaign for these issues to be confronted. But at the moment, the silence from both major parties, in the face of genocide, is not neutrality. It's just complicity.

THE GREENS ARE SPEAKING UP ON GAZA

While the major parties bury their heads in the diplomatic sand, one political force in Australia has consistently refused to look away. The Australian Greens have emerged as the only parliamentary party willing to speak with moral clarity about what is happening in Gaza, and calling it what it is: *genocide*. While Labor and the Coalition tiptoe around the truth, desperate to avoid offending powerful lobbyists or inviting bad-faith accusations of anti-Semitism, the Greens are campaigning unapologetically on a platform grounded in international law, human rights, and humanitarian principles.

The leader of the Greens, Adam Bandt, hasn't minced his words: "Tens of thousands of children have been killed," he said during the week, "a health care system has been destroyed... people's homes have been reduced to rubble". Bandt also pointed out that this is not a radical opinion but a matter of public record, supported by reports from organisations such as Amnesty International and corroborated by the International Criminal Court, which has issued arrest warrants for Israeli Prime Minister Benjamin Netanyahu. In an age where truth is filtered, managed, and spun into silence, the Greens have opted for confrontation—willing to challenge the orthodoxy of Australia's outdated foreign policy influenced by Israel and the U.S., and are risking a political backlash to stand on the side of justice.

This is not a fringe opinion. As the death toll in Gaza climbs and images of mass graves, bombed-out hospitals, and murdered medics circulate globally, more Australians are beginning to demand that their government takes a stand. But it is only the Greens—and a few independents in electorates with high Muslim populations—who are prepared to call out the obvious: a genocide is being perpetrated by Israel, and the Western world is watching on and aiding this genocide, including Australia.

While Gaza issue might not reshape the entire election outcome, it will influence thousands of votes. In tightly contested seats—such as those in inner Melbourne—those votes will matter. For many Australians, particularly younger and ethnically diverse voters who see the situation with a sense of moral urgency, Labor's timidity is seen as a betrayal. These voters are not confused by the talking points about 'balance' and 'both side-ism'—they see a state with overwhelming military power crushing a besieged population—and a Western-backed government too cowardly to call it for what it is.

That cowardice is further exposed when comparing the Greens' straightforward language with Labor's evasive rhetoric. Where Senator Wong hides behind procedural jargon and vague diplomatic gestures, Bandt confronts the brutal reality of a military occupation, settler violence, and the long-standing refusal of Israel to recognise Palestinian sovereignty. He links peace to justice; he ties any resolution to the fundamental requirement of ending the occupation. And most importantly, he points the finger at Australia's complicity: the military contracts, the diplomatic cover, the deference to Israeli lobby groups who shape domestic narratives through fear and misinformation.

Even the most recent atrocity—where Israeli forces bombed clearly marked ambulances belonging to the Red Crescent—has failed to stir outrage from the government. First, Israel lied: it claimed the vehicles weren't identifiable. Then, as footage emerged showing sirens blazing and markings visible in plain sight, the truth was undeniable. And yet again, silence from the Australian government: no condemnation; no consequences; no re-evaluation of diplomatic or military ties. Just the same mealy-mouthed statements about implementing more ceasefires that Israel doesn't abide by, and platitudes about 'balanced positions'. The facts are there for all to see, but those in power prefer the politics of evasion.

THE BLOWBACK IN MULTICULTURAL AREAS

The Albanese government's silence and indifference on Gaza won't be without some electoral consequences. While there are certain seats in western Sydney that might feel some of that heat—Watson and Blaxland—the more likely electoral blowback will occur in Melbourne, which is placing Labor under increasing strain in seats where multicultural identity, foreign policy, and local politics are strongly mixed. Two electorates in inner Melbourne—Wills and Macnamara—will offer a clear test for whether Labor can hold together a fragile coalition of support amid an international crisis it refuses to confront honestly.

The seat of Macnamara is probably the more tenuous out of the two, and is home to one of Australia's most politically active and tightly knit Jewish communities, where the sitting Labor MP Josh Burns—a staunch supporter of Israel—finds himself politically exposed and under criticism from both sides: pro-Israel groups see Labor's statements as weak and insufficiently supportive of Israel's military actions, while pro-Palestinian activists condemn the government's refusal to call out Israeli war crimes or to demand an end to the occupation.

Despite the debate around Israel and Gaza, cost-of-living concerns and other issues will ultimately swing the vote in this seat, which will be a close and genuine three-way contest between Labor, the Greens and the Liberal Party. There were under 3,000 primary votes between Labor (29,552), Green (27,587) and Liberal (26,976) at the 2022 federal election and preference flows will, again, decide the winner. Of course, there won't be the one overriding issue that will determine the ultimate result, but it will be the combination of different issues and how they influence different parts of the community, with Gaza being one of those issues.

But how much will Gaza affect the final result? No-one really knows. Voters are dealing with soaring rents, housing shortages, and climate change, and these are the bread-and-butter issues that every candidate must address. But the genocide committed by Israel in Gaza hovers in the background—not as a distraction, but as a test of political and moral integrity, and not just in Melbourne or in western Sydney. It has become a proxy for whether candidates truly represent the values of their constituents or just echo the empty rhetoric of the Labor–Liberal foreign policy consensus.

Labor is in a difficult electoral position, but it's all of its own making. In trying to be all things to all people—offering strong support to the Jewish community and tepid words to Islamic communities, but avoiding hard truths—it is alienating both. In the one electorate—and it's just in these electorates in Melbourne—it's losing trust for not being supportive enough of Israel; in another, for refusing to hold Israel to account. This double bind reflects the broader crisis of moral leadership that haunts the Albanese government's foreign policy posture. The party's refusal to confront the reality of Gaza, to speak with clarity and principle, is not just eroding its moral standing—it may cost it seats.

As preference flows and final rankings become decisive, the Gaza conflict may yet leave a mark on this election in ways few anticipated. Not with sweeping national swings, but through precise, community-driven acts of electoral defiance in places where silence feels like betrayal and inaction feels like complicity. The lesson for the Labor Party is clear: in an era where the *personal* is *political* and the *global* is *local*, foreign policy silence and trying to appease one group over another, might not be a safe political strategy anymore.

***

THE ONGOING COWARDICE FROM THE AUSTRALIAN GOVERNMENT

23 May 2025

If there were any doubts about how the Labor government would respond to Israel's continuing actions in Gaza and the broader question of Palestine, those doubts have been removed: *it just doesn't care.* The government's re-election on 3 May came without very much engagement on the Gaza crisis, and the weeks since have only confirmed the reality of this domestic situation: the Labor government has remained indifferent to what is one of the biggest humanitarian catastrophes of this generation. Despite international outcry and the overwhelming civilian death toll—over 55,000 killed, the majority of them women and children—the Australian government has taken no meaningful steps to condemn, confront, or even question Israel's ongoing campaign in Gaza.

Initially—and to give the Labor Party just the *small* and *slightest* benefit of the doubt—their silence since 2023 could have been interpreted as a calculated wait-and-see approach—another flashpoint in the long, brutal history of Gaza since 1948 that might briefly dominate the news cycle, then dissipate from the public view. This tactic of performative indifference relied on well-worn scripts: Israel's *right to defend itself* (but not for Palestine), expressions of *concern* for civilian lives, calls for *restraint*—while avoiding the language that might antagonise pro-Israel voices in Australia. That might have been the case in the past brutal actions by Israel against Palestine but this time, the conflict didn't end in just a matter of weeks. It dragged on and on, and so, it has continued for nineteen months. The bloodshed continued, and still, the Labor government remained silent for most of that time, occasionally offering flaccid words and platitudes.

As the months wore on and the federal election go closer, the platitudes took on another political step: *avoidance*. The government, perhaps correctly *on the politics*, calculated that any serious engagement with the Gaza issue would open it to attacks from the media and the right, particularly from Peter Dutton's Coalition, which was already weaponising anti-Semitism for political gain, as well as from Israel lobbyists and Zionist groups. In this light, Prime Minister Anthony Albanese's decision to steer clear of the issue became not just an act of cowardice but a strategic suppression—Gaza was a powder keg best left untouched until after the votes were counted. While this might have been the best *political* decision at the time, it was the *morally* repugnant decision.

In this context, the government's courting and appeasement of pro-Israel lobby groups—including the Zionist Federation of Australia, the Australian Jewish Association, and other influential players—can be seen as a hard and cold political calculation. Albanese, the foreign minister Senator Penny Wong, and the broader Cabinet went out of their way to placate these groups, while offering only the most lukewarm and weak acknowledgement of the Palestinian cause. The Palestinian and broader Islamic communities, so often ignored or marginalised in Australian politics, were again pushed to the fringes. Politically, it was a risk-averse and morally inept government clearly acting in its own interests.

The strategy paid off, *politically*. The Labor Party not only avoided any electoral blowback—it achieved a historic win, securing 94 seats. In electorates in western Sydney, where the Muslim communities are large in number and politically engaged—in the seat of Blaxland, the Islamic community makes up around 30 per cent of the electorate—candidates running under the Muslim Vote banner made an impact on primary votes, but not enough to change the outcome. Labor held these seats in Blaxland and Watson, and even increased its two-party preferred margins. Meanwhile, in the inner-Melbourne seat of Macnamara—with a significant Jewish population—the sitting Labor MP, Josh Burns increased his vote. The much-anticipated backlash from both Islamic and Jewish constituencies failed to materialise.

And this what lies at the heart of Australia's Gaza dilemma—silence, as it turned out, is electorally safe: the government didn't suffer for its inaction and weasel words on Palestine. The Liberal Party, which tried to elevate the issue with inflammatory rhetoric and culture war tactics, was comprehensive rejected, losing fifteen seats. The message received by Labor was not one of moral urgency, but of political vindication: voters didn't punish them for their indifference, and it's evident that not enough people in the electorate felt that Gaza and Palestine are significant issues. But that's not really the point.

With a commanding parliamentary majority—38 seats—and no immediate electoral threat from a hopelessly splintered Liberal and National parties, the Labor government has no excuses left to just *do the right thing* about Palestine. And yet, it still chooses inaction. The genocide continues, and the Australia government remains silent. The question now is no longer about *why* they stayed silent before the election; it's about what will it take to finally break that silence.

SELECTIVE OUTRAGE AND THE POLITICS OF MORAL EVASION

While the Labor government might have been hesitant about how the Israel–Gaza conflict and genocide might influence the outcome of the election, that caution isn't just now unnecessary, it's morally indefensible. The political risk for Labor to have a stronger voice during the election turned out to be negligible. The moral consequences, however, are profound. For well over a year, the world has watched the livestreamed horrors from Gaza: emaciated children starved to death; hospitals bombed into rubble; doctors, nurses and journalists executed in the streets, and families burned alive in tents. These are not ambiguous tragedies, they're crimes against humanity, visible to anyone with a screen and half-a-brain, and undeniable to anyone with a conscience.

Yet since securing one of the most decisive electoral victories in Australian history, the Labor government has doubled-down and put out even more words of diplomatic irrelevance. Senator Wong, once framed herself as a principled and thoughtful voice in international affairs but on Gaza, her responses have grown increasingly detached, bureaucratic, and hollow—a piss-weak tactic that says nothing, evades accountability and obscures human morality.

When Israel blocked vital humanitarian aid from getting into Gaza, causing further death by starvation and dehydration, Wong's response on May 20 was the perfunctory impersonal appeal for procedural normality:

"Australia is part of the international call on Israel to allow the full and immediate resumption of aid into Gaza. Israel must enable UN and humanitarian organisations to do their life saving work. We urge all parties to return to a ceasefire and hostage deal."

It's like a Year 6 school assignment or an inane comment at a beauty pageant hoping for world peace: what does it actually mean? There's no condemnation. No urgency. Just a held-back appeal to *all parties*—as though both sides equally share blame for mass famine, displacement, and the deliberate targeting of aid workers. How would Wong feel if she was watching the images of her own children decapitated by the rogue and out-of-control Israel Defence Forces? Maybe then she might change her tune?

Contrast this with her response following the killing of two Israeli Embassy staff in Washington DC on May 22, where Wong issued an immediate and emotionally charged statement:

> "The Australian Government is shocked and appalled by the killing of two Israeli Embassy staff in Washington DC. Our thoughts go out to their families, loved ones, and colleagues. There is no place for antisemitism in the world. It must be denounced and condemned."

There was no hedging, no ambiguity, no calls for calm from "all parties." Just swift, decisive moral judgement. Certainly, the actions of Elias Rodriguez—the perpetrator of the killing of Yaron Lischinsky and Sarah Lynn Milgrim in Washington DC—are reprehensible and must be called out and condemned.

Wong was right to harshly condemn these actions but it's not the expression of sympathy that is troubling. *All* innocent life deserves defence, and *all* acts of violence demand scrutiny. But there's an obvious discrepancy: why is Wong so quick to condemn violence against Israeli citizens—but struggles to denounce the far more systematic and large-scale extermination of Palestinians? Why is clarity possible when it involves Washington, but not when it involves the Palestinian cities of Rafah, Khan Younis or Jabalia?

Wong has previously justified her soft handling of Gaza by saying that "it's always very difficult from over here to make judgements", but Washington is thousands of kilometres further from Canberra than Gaza is. Distance, clearly, is not the issue and it never was.

This selective outrage is a failure in Australian foreign policy to uphold consistent principles, and a willingness to swap moral clarity for political comfort. When atrocities are met with euphemisms and when genocidal violence is framed as a matter of 'restraint' or 'urgency' rather than condemnation and calling for strong action, Australia doesn't just lose credibility, it loses a part of its humanity.

WHAT WILL IT TAKE?

So, how to explain the enduring silence and weakness from the Australian government on Palestine? The election is over, and Labor has achieved a historic majority. The government is free of the usual constraints—political, electoral and even diplomatic shackles—that might once have justified caution. The Israel–Palestine conflict, for all its moral weight, has proven electorally irrelevant in Australia, and the candidates who openly aligned with the Palestinian cause made some gains, but they didn't swing any seats. The pro-Israel lobby in Australia, while loud, has shown itself to be politically ineffective, the smallest of paper tigers. So, with the path clear, why does the Albanese government still refuse to act? What is it so afraid of? A fear of losing donations from Israeli interests in Australia? A fear of losing the 2028 election? Afraid of Mossad? *What is it?*

The facts clearly favour any actions the Australian government would like to take against the state of Israel. The International Court of Justice has found Israel's occupation of Palestinian territories to be *unlawful*, its settlements in the West Bank are in violation of international law and has acknowledged that the racial segregation and systemic discrimination is a policy of apartheid. In a 2024 advisory opinion, the Court also reaffirmed the illegality of Israel's continued presence in the Occupied Palestinian Territories and the pattern of conduct that disregards international law.

Israel has also been formally accused by credible international bodies and human rights organisations of using starvation as a weapon of war. The Palestinian Ministry of Foreign Affairs, Human Rights Watch, Physicians for Human Rights–Israel, Plan International, and even senior UN officials have all condemned Israel's blockade and manipulation of humanitarian aid as a tactic of war. This consensus is pretty obvious: these are *war crimes*. It's not the vague language or the usual diplomatic ambiguity that comes from these kinds of bodies: these are legal determinations, supported by mounting evidence and affirmed by global institutions.

In November 2024, the International Criminal Court also issued arrest warrants for Israeli Prime Minister Benjamin Netanyahu and former Defence Minister Yoav Gallant, holding them personally accountable for war crimes, including the use of starvation as a weapon of war and the deliberate targeting of civilian infrastructure.

Still, Australia has nothing to way.

What can Australian actually do? It's a question many people in Australia ask, especially in the context of Palestine— in the words of Senator Wong—being too far way "to make judgements". But South Africa was also *too far away* to make judgements, but the Australian government lead by Malcolm Fraser in the 1980s *did* make judgements about the behaviour of that country and pushed for actions and sanctions under the Gleneagles Agreement in 1977. Thirteen years later in 1990, apartheid ended in South Africa: Palestine can't wait another thirteen years, but firm action does have to start somewhere.

Like it did on South Africa, the Australian government can actually do a great deal, if it *chooses to act*. It could begin by expelling the Israeli ambassador and recalling its own from Tel Aviv. It could review trade and military agreements, as some European states have begun to do. It could impose, or even threaten, targeted sanctions—economic, diplomatic, or travel-based—on senior Israeli officials. It could cancel cultural exchanges with the state of Israel. None of these measures are radical or unprecedented: they're actively being discussed or implemented by allies such as the U.K., France, and Canada. Australia is not an outlier in *taking* action—it is an outlier in *failing* to do so.

The question is not about how to implement these actions, but getting the will to do it. Israel is behaving like an unhinged psychopathic state—not just in its military conduct, but in its defiance of international law, its disregard for human life in Palestine, and its impunity in the face of global criticism. And like all tin-pot rogue states, it will continue to behave in this way and continue with the genocide in Gaza until it's confronted not just with niceties of diplomacy, but with real, serious and long-lasting consequences.

What will it take for Australia to stop looking away? How many more babies and young children need to starve or lose limbs, how many more hospitals and intensive care units need to be turned into smouldering ruins and dust; how many more entire families need to be buried beneath the rubble before Canberra finally admits that something is seriously wrong with the state of Israel and its leadership?

This isn't just about the present genocide in Gaza, it's also about what happens next. Starvation, displacement, the trauma of war—these leave scars on children that linger for decades. Children who survive today might end up dying from the medical trauma tomorrow. The damage being done is not just physical—it's generational.

And still, Australia does nothing. It's just so sickening that the best the Australian government can do is offer up weasel words, even at a time when it doesn't have anything to lose politically or electorally. It's outright *cowardice*—there's just no other word for it. Pusillanimity, weakness, timidity, patheticness—all of these terms could apply as well, but *cowardice* will do for the time being: *moral cowardice* disguised in the whimpy language of diplomacy. It's a refusal to risk even a fraction of carefully banked-up political capital in order to stand for something greater than re-election; a fear of offending Israeli lobbyists and Zionist interests in Australia, while entire communities in Palestine are being erased.

So again: *what will it take?* That's the only question that remains. Perhaps 100,000 deaths? Will that be the red line, the threshold for action by the Australian government? How many more emaciated children does the government need to see before it can say enough is enough? Or will they wait until it's too late—until Israel has removed all Palestinian people from Gaza and the West Bank—before finally condemning and acting against these atrocities? Is that what it will take?

And with each day that goes on without an answer, the blood is not just on Israel's hands. The Australia government, through its silence and inaction, is becoming increasingly complicit in the suffering of Gaza. And why it has decided to do this will also take a long time to answer.

***

AUSTRALIA'S SHIFT ON ISRAEL: TOO LITTLE, TOO LATE?

28 May 2025

Prime Minister Anthony Albanese has finally found the courage to speak out against Israel's relentless campaign of violence and destruction in Gaza, condemning its restrictions on humanitarian aid as "completely unacceptable and an outrage". For a government that has for nineteen months maintained a position of cautious neutrality—and, to be honest, one that often sounded like tacit support for Israel's actions—this marks the strongest public rebuke of Israel's actions from the Prime Minister since this genocide began in October 2023. And while these words are always to be welcomed, they have arrived far too late, and come in the context of political calculations that were made to downplay the issue in the lead up to the 2025 federal election.

Albanese's comments, made *after* the election, reflect the reality of Australian politics: the issue of Palestine will never be treated as a matter of urgency or international justice, but as a political inconvenience to be carefully managed out of sight. Before the election, the government's unwavering support for Israel—expressed through votes at the United Nations, public statements that were always downplayed, and a refusal to call out even the most egregious of war crimes— was a politically cautious strategy: immoral, *absolutely*, but *politically* correct. It was about managing perceived risks: the fear of backlash from pro-Israel lobby groups, the influence of media outlets that routinely suppress or distort coverage of Palestine, and the anxiety over alienating sections of the electorate, especially within Sydney and Melbourne's Jewish communities. That doesn't make it acceptable, but it can be seen why the government would follow this political course.

Yet, the election result has revealed the moral bankruptcy of these assumptions. Labor's resounding victory demonstrated that the issue of Palestine, while morally significant, did not materially affect the outcome of the campaign. The fear that Palestine would be a political liability—one way or another—was, in the end, not supported by the facts. The Israel lobby—a loose coalition of pro-Israel advocacy groups, think tanks, media gatekeepers, and well-connected individuals who have long sought to intimidate politicians, censor public debate, and block pro-Palestinian voices in the arts, academia, and public life—has been exposed as a paper tiger. It's a noisy, aggressive minority that has successfully cowed successive governments into silence, but doesn't reflect the views or priorities of the broader Australian public.

The Prime Minister's comments are now a big test: will the government begin to act in line with international law, human rights principles, and the overwhelming evidence of Israel's war crimes? Or will this be yet another brief moment of posturing, quickly retracted under pressure from the usual lobby groups? The Israel lobby has a bank of people who spend their time monitoring the media and will interfere wherever possible—the phone calls will come, as they always do—pressure will be applied, threats will be made, warnings whispered into the ears of ministers and advisers. There will be the accusations of anti-Semitism, of the *bias* that no-one else seems to be able to find, and the talk of undermining Australia's 'strategic alliances'—all the familiar tactics designed to maintain the culture of fear and self-censorship that has long manipulated Australia's foreign policy on Palestine.

But this election result has cleared the decks. The Labor government won 94 seats and that's 94 reasons for why it now needs to take stronger action—Labor governs with a clear mandate, and Albanese has an opportunity—if he has the courage to take it—to break from the past, to dismantle the false consensus that has protected Israel from accountability, and to stand on the side of justice.

It's not enough for the Prime Minister to condemn Israel's actions in a single speech and then go and retreat under pressure. The moral obligation for Australia is very clear: for nineteen months, the government has chosen complicity—by omission, by silence, by deferring to U.S. foreign policy, and by shielding Israel from meaningful criticism. Every day of inaction has been a day in which Australia contributes to the machinery of genocide—by failing to speak out, by failing to act, and by failing to represent the values of justice and equality that it claims to uphold on the international stage.

THE PATH IS CLEAR FOR THE POLITICAL WILL TO FOLLOW

This belated condemnation of Israel's actions comes at a time when other Western democracies are beginning to take stronger stands. The United Kingdom, France, and Canada—none of which are known for their radical stances on Middle East issues, especially the U.K.—have issued strong criticisms of Israel's conduct in Gaza. Some of these countries are even discussing the possibility of sanctions, a move long considered politically impossible. Australia won't be a leader on this issue—by choice—like it was during the moves to end apartheid in South Africa, that should be obvious by now, but the path has been cleared. There is now a *precedent* provided by others, the election is over, and there is a politically safe process for Australia to follow.

If the government had been waiting for cover, for reassurance that taking a stronger stance against Israel would not isolate it from its allies, then that excuse is now over. The international mood has shifted, which tends to happen when an ally behaves so horribly and consistently. The world is no longer willing to accept Israel's impunity in the face of overwhelming evidence of war crimes, including the mass killing of civilians, the deliberate starvation of populations in battery-chicken pens, and the destruction of Gaza's critical infrastructure.

Within the Labor Party, the growing discomfort is becoming more public. Ed Husic, recently dumped from Cabinet as part of factional realignments, has publicly suggested that his position on Gaza played a role in his demotion. However, now that he's free from the constraints of collective Cabinet responsibility, Husic has become more outspoken—calling for serious action, including the recall of Australia's ambassador to Israel and the imposition of sanctions on those responsible for the atrocities in Gaza. Husic's position is a sign of what's possible if more MPs break rank from the rigid, pro-Israel orthodoxy that has dominated Australian foreign policy for decades. It also shows that even within Labor's ranks, there is a growing recognition that Australia cannot continue to ignore the reality of what is happening in Palestine.

Predictably, the pro-Israel lobby has responded with the usual fury. The Executive Council of Australian Jewry attacked Husic's remarks, accusing him of ignoring Hamas's role in the conflict and painting his call for accountability as biased and unfair. And of course they would, this is their playbook: every criticism of Israel, no matter how mild or how factually grounded, is met with immediate condemnation. The lobby works to distort the narrative, to present events through a rigid ideological lens that doesn't allow for any dissent at all.

It seeks to dominate the conversation, presenting its own version of reality as the only acceptable one, while smearing critics as dangerous, anti-Semitic, or misinformed.

This climate of fear and censorship from these lobby groups has poisoned public discourse in Australia for years. It discourages and shuts down open debate about Palestine, silences Palestinian voices, and suppresses cultural and artistic expression that dares to challenge Israel's actions. The lobby's influence is not just political—it extends into the media, into the arts, into the very language we are allowed to use when discussing Israel and Palestine. It is an extreme form of 'cancel culture' control that thrives on intimidation and distortion, shutting down any conversation that does not conform to its rigid, pro-Israel orthodoxy.

But despite this, the cracks in the façade are getting bigger and Husic's commentary shows that the wall of silence is no longer unbreakable. The international climate has changed. The old myths about the political risks of standing up to the Israel lobby have been exposed by the re-election of the Labor government. The Prime Minister's recent condemnation of Israel's actions, however cautious and belated, is part of this shift. But it needs to go *much* further.

The government needs to recall the ambassador from Tel Aviv, as a clear signal that Australia will not tolerate genocide. It needs to join the calls for sanctions on Israeli officials responsible for war crimes. It needs to restore funding to UNRWA, support the International Criminal Court's investigations, and stand with other countries calling for an immediate ceasefire. And it means resisting the relentless pressure of the lobby groups that will inevitably try to shut down this debate before it gains momentum.

BREAKING THE SILENCE

The pressure to conform to a pro-Israel narrative in Australia isn't just limited to the political class—it extends into the mainstream media and cultural institutions. The experience of Nasser Mashni, the President of the Australia Palestine Advocacy Network, is a reminder of how dissenting voices are silenced on this issue. In a rare moment of balance, the ABC aired an interview with Mashni, in which he echoed the Prime Minister's condemnation of Israel's actions—but went much further, calling out the genocide for what it is. Yet the interview was later removed from ABC's platforms, following pressure from Zionist groups. This is how the lobby operates: by suppressing views it deems unacceptable, by working behind the scenes to control what the public is allowed to hear, and by ensuring that Palestinian perspectives remain marginalised and erased from mainstream discourse. But it also brings on the *Streisand effect*, where by seeking to remove an issue from public debate, only highlights the issue even further.

In another example of Australia's own version of McCarthyism, the Indigenous author Karen Wyld had her $15,000 writing fellowship from the State Library of Queensland cancelled after intervention by the Queensland Arts Minister, John-Paul Langbroek, a decision which followed pressure from Zionist groups opposed to Wyld's support for Palestine. And there's just no transparency—no reasons given, no information about who complained, no due process, no appeal. It was the politics of the blacklist, an authoritarian exercise of power in a supposedly democratic country. Yet, it was another stain on Australia's cultural and intellectual life that needs to be addressed if the country is to have an honest conversation about Israel, Palestine, and the ongoing genocide in Gaza.

There is also hope in new voices emerging within Australia's political landscape. For the first time, a Palestinian–Australian, Basem Abdo, has won a federal Parliament for Labor, in the Melbourne seat of Calwell. He's not the first MP though—Joe Hockey was the first Palestinian–Australian to sit in the Parliament in 1996—but this offers the opportunity for a more balanced and representative debate in Australian politics.

There is a history of bipartisan support for Palestinian rights in Australia, though that has been conveniently forgotten in recent years. Albanese himself was once a member of the Parliamentary Friends of Palestine, as was Hockey. The current Liberal leader, Sussan Ley, and even the conservative MP, Ross Cameron, were also members.

But this is the time to break the silence and start remembering Palestine. Australia needs to reject the culture of censorship and intimidation that has distorted public debate for too long, and needs to ensure that all perspectives—including those of Palestinians—are heard.

This isn't just about Palestine—it's about the health of Australian democracy: a free society does not silence dissent. It does not blacklist artists. It does not erase inconvenient voices from the airwaves. And it does not allow a minority lobby to dictate national policy in defiance of justice and international law. The genocide in Gaza must end. Australia has a moral responsibility to speak up, to act, and to lead where it can. The time for silence is over. The time for action is *now*.

***

A GREAT AUSTRALIAN SILENCE

28 June 2025

S ometimes, it's the words that *are* not made that make the biggest impression, and Australia's great silence after the United States bombed Iran's nuclear facilities with stealth bombers last week gave the biggest indication of where the Australia–U.S. diplomatic relationship stands: it's *subservient* and guided by a lack of principles. When Prime Minister Anthony Albanese and Foreign Minister Penny Wong finally emerged from their 24-hour silence, their words just repeated Washington's talking points, framing the strike as unfortunate—but necessary—and an extension of obligations of the alliance. This pantomime felt familiar: in 1966 Harold Holt promised to go "all the way with LBJ", and in 1999, when John Howard first boasted that Australia would act as America's "deputy sheriff" in the region. Half a century on, the deference from Canberra remains: different players and different words, but the sentiment remains the same.

What makes this particularly offensive is the contrast with Australia's post-war record as a multilateral player and a force for positive change, being one of key voices in the creation of the United Nations, the Genocide Convention and the Non-Proliferation Treaty, the frameworks that were designed to prevent the types of military adventurism that we often see from the United States. And by supporting this

U.S. bombing, Albanese has sided with a unilateral action, rather than the "rules-based international order" that his government frequently talks about.

The official justification—that the attack stopped an imminent Iranian breakout of nuclear weapons—sits uncomfortably with the flood of facts coming out of Vienna and The Hague. International Atomic Energy Agency inspectors have not found fresh evidence of weaponisation, and Tehran's foreign ministry insists enrichment remained within thresholds of the Iran nuclear deal (JCPOA)—even though Wong is now claiming the opposite. Where did these alternative facts come from?

Meanwhile, U.S. officials privately concede that this operation was hastened by domestic politics: the survival strategy of Israel's Prime Minister, Benjamin Netanyahu, Donald Trump's mid-term election politics, and lucrative deals and contracts in the arms industry. Australia's endorsement risks entangling it in a conflict driven more by American primaries and Israeli politics than by any genuine threat to regional security, so why do it?

Domestically, the episode has also reignited the long-simmering debate over autonomous defence policy. Polling since the AUKUS deal was created in 2021 already shows a majority of Australians favour a more independent foreign strategy, and Labor's progressive base is openly asking why the government condemns violations of international law in Moscow or North Korea yet stays silent when they originate in Washington. Albanese's reluctance to criticise the United States has also undermined his own narrative of pursuing a "middle-power diplomacy" that should be placing human rights at heart of its actions.

For now, a fragile Iran–Israel ceasefire is holding, but Israeli defence spokespeople are already claiming a "broken truce"—without providing evidence—and hinting at the need fresh attacks on Tehran. The real question is whether Australia can still draw on the moral imagination it displayed in San Francisco in 1945—when H. V. Evatt insisted even great powers needed to be bound by law—or whether it will just settle for the quiet comfort of U.S. subservience.

THE ABC OF MANUFACTURING CONSENT

In the aftermath of the United States' bombing of Iranian nuclear facilities, Western media coverage quickly fell into its well-worn cliches and talking points: Israel and the U.S. were cast as defenders of peace and democracy; Iran was framed as the unpredictable villain and rogue. Of course, these tropes are not new, but their repetition in the wake of such a serious escalation reveals a Western information ecosystem that's more invested in narrative control than independent scrutiny. While many non-Western media outlets reported the strike as a violation of international norms and gave airtime to Iranian officials articulating the legal basis for self-defence, most of the Australian and U.S. mainstream media doubled down on their binary worldview, just like in a Hollywood action movie, where American power is always legitimate and on the *side of right*, and its enemies always irrational and on the *side of wrong*.

Iran's foreign minister Abbas Araghchi, in a sober and legally grounded statement, condemned the attack and invoked the UN Charter's provisions on self-defence. He was one of the few adult voices in a room increasingly dominated by partisan Western war rhetoric and military fanfare. Yet voices like his were almost entirely absent from Australian media coverage, replaced instead by recycled commentary from embedded Western correspondents and a handful of dubious "expert" guests—most of them with longstanding ties to the political establishment or the arms industry.

The ABC, Australia's national broadcaster, did itself no favours by inviting former Prime Minister Scott Morrison to offer his perspective on the bombing—without disclosing that he now has advisory roles with American Global Strategies and DYNE Maritime, major players in the arms manufacturing and defence industries. Morrison offered a predictable defence of the U.S. strike, painting it as reluctantly necessary, restrained, and justified. His commentary was more like a press release than real analysis, and while as a former Prime Minister, he's entitled to speak in public, the ABC's decision to platform him without even a passing reference to his role in the arms industry undermined its duty of transparency.

But it wasn't only Morrison: ABC viewers were also regaled through a lengthy interview with Mike Pezzullo, the former Home Affairs Secretary removed by the Labor government for political interference and leaking. That the ABC would prioritise a disgraced bureaucrat—as well as a disgraced former Prime Minister—over any number of available legal experts or seasoned foreign policy analysts is bewildering at best, and absolutely cynical at worst.

Australia is not short of foreign policy experts— international lawyers, retired diplomats, experienced journalists, and even former ministers could have offered context, insight, and critique. But these people were all bypassed in favour of Morrison and Pezzullo—two players with reputational baggage and clear conflicts of interest. This isn't a call to ban figures like this from public debate, but it is about presenting their words appropriately and offering audiences the disclosures they need to evaluate opinions critically.

Of course, the ABC is a complex institution. While it continues to produce standout investigative journalism and informed commentary in some areas, the rot of managerial confusion and political appeasement is quite obvious, and evident whenever issues do arise from the Middle East, and within Israel and Palestine. It's a 1980s-style broadcasting strategy, compromised by political obedience, that is ill-suited to the complex media landscape of 2025. The result is an uneven output: excellent at times, but increasingly riddled with soft propaganda and unexamined privilege.

Scott Morrison may eventually attempt to rewrite his legacy—as many failed leaders do—but the historical record is already very unkind. Robodebt alone should have sealed his fate as one of the least respected prime ministers in Australia's modern era, and attempts to resurrect his authority through appearances on the national broadcaster serve no one, least of all the Australian public.

During times of conflict, facts matter, and so do the voices that are coming out to discuss these conflicts. And right now, Australia's national conversation is being warped by the reappearance of discredited men in suits, whose past failures should disqualify them from setting the agenda of such difficult international discussions.

THE BROKEN WORLD ORDER

In 1945, "Doc" Evatt didn't just represent Australia at that San Francisco Conference—he fought to ensure that smaller nations had a voice equal in principle, if not power, as a counterbalance to the giants of the postwar world structure. Australia also played a founding role in shaping the International Monetary Fund and the Bretton Woods system—tools meant to rebuild and stabilise a devastated global economy and prevent future wars through economic interdependence and rules-based diplomacy.

Australia's legacy now lies in ruins.

Australia today is no longer provides a pathway for cooperative multilateralism. Instead, it has become a muted appendage to a crumbling hegemon in the U.S. With each American airstrike justified in the name of "self-defence" and each Israeli bombardment reframed as necessary "retaliation",

Canberra justs nods along. Penny Wong and Defence Minister Richard Marles just offer the words from a pre-packaged statement of alliance with the US, while Albanese seems to look the other way. The legacy of 1945 has given way to the politics of acquiescence.

Since October 2023, in the shadow of Israel's campaign in Gaza and now the U.S. strikes on Iran, Australia has failed to raise even the mildest public criticism of these Israel or the U.S. Instead, its silence is often coupled with an authoritarian response: protestors in the Australia are silenced and police are mobilised—as shown in the recent incident where former Australian Greens candidate Hannah Thomas suffered graphic injuries from police during a pro-Palestine protest in Sydney—cultural figures are hounded by Israeli lobby groups and forced into cancellation and submission.

The government that once championed the idea of a rules-based international order is now too timid—or too cynical—to defend its founding principles. When asked if the U.S. bombing of Iranian nuclear sites violated international conventions, Australia had no comment, perhaps because to comment would reveal an inconvenient truth: that the so-called rules-based order no longer exists, or at least not in any coherent or enforceable form.

The heart of the problem lies in the global system's cancerous and sclerotic architecture. The UN Security Council, designed in 1945 by the victors of a global war, has remained virtually untouched in the 80 years since. The world it was meant to manage just doesn't exist anymore. The United States is no longer the unchallenged superpower; the United Kingdom is now diminished in its post-Brexit shell; Russia is a declining, disruptive force locked in Cold War nostalgia; France does wield some cultural and diplomatic capital but has a limited strategic reach; and China has emerged as the only power with the capacity—and intent—to reshape global norms and, in the absence of true leadership provided by the U.S., probably will take on that role on international leadership. The Security Council today is like a diplomatic museum, and the permanent members are a snapshot of an era that ended decades ago.

Any proposal to modernise the Security Council—by bringing in countries such as Germany, India, Brazil, Nigeria, Japan and Indonesia—would be opposed by these entrenched interests, as the existing permanent members would never voluntarily surrender their veto rights or their prestige. And yet the logic for change is overwhelming.

A more relevant structure wouldn't just reflect the demographic and economic weight of many countries around the world, but provide for a new legitimate global structure. And while it might not resolve everything, it would at least reflect the times that we are living in.

Until this type of change takes place, the world just seems to be stuck in a system that was designed for the *real politik* at the end of World War II, and not for the realities of the twenty-first century. And it's not a system that offers justice on the world stage, provides no guarantees for action against abuse of power and, as we have just seen with the US, has nothing in place to stop a rogue superpower.

This is how major wars begin: through old alliances, outdated treaties, and institutional paralysis. World War I was launched under the weight of decaying empires acting on long-expired commitments—a century-old promise to protect Belgium from Napoleon provided the catalyst for Britain to enter the war. World War II followed less than three decades later, fueled by the failures of a League of Nations which was unable to hold fascist powers to account.

We're repeating the pattern. An outdated international system that has once again lost control of the moment, and Australia—once a leader in building a new global order—

now appears too frightened to say so. If catastrophic war is to be avoided—in the Middle East or anywhere else— the world must not only confront the many failures of U.S. imperial overreach but also find the courage to reimagine the institutions that were meant to prevent exactly this kind of spiral. Australia can't afford to sit silent while history repeats itself.

***

THE WALK AWAY FROM PRINCIPLE FOR SENATOR PENNY WONG

28 June 2025

In 2022, Penny Wong entered government with a reputation for strong character and a parliamentarian based on principle: this was the Senator who sparred forensically in opposition, who then went on to be the foreign minister who strategically and carefully reset relationships with Beijing after they were severely damaged by the Morrison government, and the tirelessly worked to put Australia back into the centre of Pacific diplomacy.

This aura, however, has been dulled by the politics of Israel–Gaza and the wider Middle East region. As civilian casualties in Gaza have risen over the past 20 months, and as the Trump administration continues to override international law in Iran, amongst other places, Wong—normally unafraid of clear and tough language—began to speak in abstract and obtuse language. She would not label the unfolding catastrophe in Gaza as a *genocide*, nor would she accept that the United States had breached international law and protocols, or explain how Australian interests were served by silence on these key issues. In the space of eighteen months, one of Australia's most articulate foreign minister has drifted towards joining the "unprincipled greats" of Australian diplomacy.

Of course, unprincipled behaviour is not new in foreign affairs. Alexander Downer presided over the bugging of the East Timorese government in 2004, then defended the immoral invasion of Iraq in 2003 on the grounds that it might bring commercial rewards to Australian farmers. Gareth Evans toasted a Timor Gap oil deal with the corrupt Indonesian government in 1989 while their forces were brutalising East Timorese civilians and committing human rights abuses.

These incidents were morally bankrupt, yet at least they were framed as advancing Australia's strategic or economic interests, however tenuous and immoral this link might have been. With Wong, even that weak justification or sophisticated diplomatic language to deny the obvious is missing. When asked to outline the national benefit in not speaking out about Gaza or hedging on U.S. law-breaking actions, her answers fall into talking points about Israel's right to defend, Iran's enriched uranium stockpile and the sanctity of the non-proliferation regime: she always talks about *something else*. The disconnect between rhetoric and reality raises the more important question: whose interests are shaping Australian diplomatic policy?

This disappointment, of course, is magnified by Wong's earlier performances as foreign minister and before that in opposition when she was relentless—*tough* when toughness was required, *compassionate* when the circumstances needed it, but always diligently briefed. These qualities surely remain *somewhere*; what has changed is the willingness to deploy them. Something—maybe it's the weight of Five Eyes intelligence, the sell-out of Australian interests through Pine Gap, or the daily grind of needing to make compromises in Cabinet— which has moved the minister in a place where she doesn't want to go to. Unlike Downer, who never pretended to be morally scrupulous, or Evans, who wore his realism openly,

Wong seems to have trashed her own convictions, as she did with the marriage equality debate all those years ago.

Meanwhile, the Albanese government has begun to mimic its predecessor's secrecy on national security matters. Questions about Pine Gap's role in the U.S. bombing of Iran are met with the same bland lines that were frequently used by Scott Morrison. And it's the same garbage that's always served up: Labor is now copying the stonewalling that the Coalition frequently displayed in office. And the electorate is left with a political class locked in bipartisan two-party silence and protected like a steel trap, the public interest kept at arm's length, and a foreign minister whose moral compass appears to turn depending on who's asking the question.

Australia's core obligation abroad should be clear: protect its citizens and advance genuine national interests and not outsource its moral agency. Instead, the country moves toward the familiar pattern of buying more U.S. weapons, sending more military advisors over to the Pentagon, and accepting more strategic liabilities through AUKUS. Whatever has happened to Penny Wong, it has left a vacuum where principle once lived, and that absence is now existing in every carefully hedged press conference and every evasive departmental brief.

THE CANBERRA CULT OF SECRECY CONTINUES

The language is strangely familiar and we've all heard the words before. Where Scott Morrison once brushed aside awkward questions about asylum seekers with the standard phrase, *we don't comment on on-water matters*, Anthony Albanese now falls back on the equally obtuse, *we don't talk about intelligence*. It surfaced last week when the Canberra press gallery started asking whether the giant U.S.-run surveillance base at Pine Gap had assisted in Washington's sudden strike on Iranian nuclear facilities. The prime minister insisted his government was "always up-front," yet provided nothing beyond the admission that the attack was "unilateral action taken by the United States". A Labor government elected on promises of openness to differentiate itself from the Morrison years is copying the same culture of obfuscation that defined the Coalition era in government.

No one expects a leader to announce classified information or jeopardise operations in the field, but the Australian public is entitled to know whether their territory and technical assets are being leveraged for acts of war. Pine Gap isn't a weird abstraction in the middle of nowhere; it's on the edge of Alice Springs. It's the southern hemisphere's most important part of America's tools of global targeting, capable of feeding missile guidance data in near-real time. If Pine Gap is helping pinpoint Iranian targets or used to massacre civilians in Palestine, Australia isn't just an innocent bystander—it's an active participant.

This refusal also contradicts the government's own rhetoric. In opposition, Labor castigated the Morrison administration for the lack of transparency on the AUKUS submarine deal, yet when the system of secrecy suits it, the same "can't comment" shield of defence goes up. It is a sleight of hand that drains credibility from the promise of a *foreign policy for all Australians*, because the public can't judge what it's not allowed to see.

Penny Wong is at the centre of this contradiction. In the Senate, she goes on about the international rules-based order, but outside the doors of parliament, she deflects on Pine Gap, the targeting of Gaza, any information at all about how drone intelligence might be being used in Palestine. Every answer of deflection chips away at her own authority, and confirms that much of Australia's foreign policy is being outsourced to the U.S.

This should be a time when Australia projects the confidence of a middle power with a clear sense of its own interests. Instead, it behaves like a client state that just rubber stamps the decisions made somewhere else.

SHORT MEMORIES AND THE POLITICS OF TRANSPARENCY

When the United States launched that strike on Iran, the Australian government's response was delayed by almost 24 hours, for reasons that were never fully explained. And during this vacuum of information, Shadow Defence Minister Andrew Hastie stepped into the breach, and demanded more transparency over how the U.S. military is using Australian soil and intelligence facilities like Pine Gap. On the surface, this is reasonable demand: of course Australians deserve to know whether their country is playing an active role in military conflicts initiated by a foreign power. But a demand like this coming from Hastie, a key member of the Morrison-era of cover-up in defence and a time of a total lack of transparency, was a bit rich and hard to swallow.

This is the same Coalition government that negotiated the 2021 AUKUS submarine deal in near-total secrecy—a deal so secretive that even many Cabinet ministers were kept in the dark until it was announced. It blew a $5 billion hole in the federal budget through cancellation penalties to the French Naval Group, left diplomatic relations with France in tatters, and committed Australia to a murky 30-year defence arrangement with the United States and United Kingdom. We still have no clear delivery date for the nuclear-powered submarines—or even a concrete blueprint—and yet the Coalition delivered this agreement without public consultation, strategic debate, or parliamentary scrutiny. That is nowhere near the idea of transparency that Andrew Hastie is now demanding from others.

If Hastie and the Liberal Party are really committed to open government, they would have practised it when they had the chance. Their sudden concern for democratic oversight only highlights how little of it they were willing to tolerate while in office, and are now lecturing others about it from opposition, when they don't have a chance to practice this transparency that they never achieve when they're in government.

But the Coalition's hypocrisy doesn't make the failure of the Labor government on this issue any more acceptable. In fact, the great disappointment lies in the fact that Labor— particularly figures such as Penny Wong, once seen as principled and progressive—are repeating the same evasive behaviour. The government's reluctance to clarify Australia's strategic role in the Middle East, its silence on Pine Gap's function in the Iranian strike, and its deflections about intelligence matters all suggests an even deeper malaise: the bipartisan culture of secrecy. And if all the major parties are just taking turns at suppressing public scrutiny when they're in office, it's democracy that suffers the biggest blows.

It's easy to talk tough from the opposition benches and the true courage of political leaders is revealed by their actions when they hold power—this is when true political character comes to the fore, not when they're in exile. For example, Malcolm Turnbull, has found a new voice for bold progressive ideas since retiring from politics—but he rarely showed any of that courage when he was prime minister, when it would have mattered the most. The same can now be said of Labor: a party that promised decency and reform in opposition, is now happy to inherit Scott Morrison's practice of secretive behaviour.

Good governance isn't just a matter of rhetoric: it's a matter of the decisions made when you *can* do something about it— not just when it's safe to speak. And when hard questions arise—about war, surveillance, alliance obligations—the right answer is often the simplest one, and the one that we've always suggested: just *do the right thing*; and then everything else will fall into place. That is the test Penny Wong and Anthony Albanese now face. And so far, they're falling short.

***

CRIMINALISING PROTEST IN NEW SOUTH WALES

5 July 2025

The rain had barely cleared from Lakemba Street in Belmore when police descended on a peaceful protest outside SEC Plating, a modest factory that turns raw aluminium into the shiny finishes that are bolted on to Israeli F-35 fighter jets—which are then used to drop bombs over Gaza, killing innocent civilians, including children. This was meant to be a routine mid-week protest organised by Weapons Out of The West—a loose collective of teachers, students and shift workers who are furious that a secretive arms manufacturing network in the western Sydney region is exporting military parts to Israel and wanted to raise public awareness of this. Instead, it ended with Hannah Thomas, an activist and candidate for the Australian Greens at the 2025 federal election, beaten up by police, her face smashed into the bitumen, with her left eye bloodied and possibly beyond saving.

On this night in late June, scores of aggressive and angry police officers arrived, radios crackling with a response that seemed out of proportion to the handful of protesters holding a peaceful protest at a small suburban location. Thomas stepped forward as the police announced a "move-on" order—and when asked under what laws the police were acting on, officers dragged her to the kerb, struck her repeatedly, while dazed onlookers screamed out to "let her go!"—pleas that were ignored and quickly followed by more thumping of boots, arrests and the clatter of riot gear.

The charge sheet cited the newly amended anti-protest laws in New South Wales, the Minns Government's hasty response to Israel lobbyists who earlier this year claimed that anti-war action in Sydney and a "bomb scare" in Dural—that turned out to be a hoax—could result into attacks on synagogues. SEC Plating is located across the road from a youth-oriented church hall: there's no stained-glass windows, there's no sermons—it's just an old brick shell which is an annexe of the main church site in Punchbowl several suburbs away, and it's a hall that hosts workshops on Saturdays, with little indication that it might be a "place of worship". Yet the Act's wide definition of "religious precinct" gives the police a broad enough scope to criminalise a protest if someone, somewhere, might one day surreptitiously murmur a prayer nearby.

In the aftermath of this incident, NSW Premier Chris Minns regurgitated those same old talking points about "operational independence" and the "paramount importance of community harmony", but we all know what this is: it's the incremental drift towards state authoritarianism, one that the old NSW Liberal Party curmudgeon and former NSW Premier, Robert Askin, would have been proud of.

This law was always going to be political theatre—a concession to the Israel lobby rattled by large pro-Palestine crowds and a coalition of conservative clerics warning of sectarian spill-over—but it is *a law*. The Dural "caravan bomb" scare earlier this year provided convenient ammunition: outrage headlines about homemade explosives, later shown to be false when forensics found nothing but fertiliser and rust. But the truth didn't seem to matter to Premier Minns;

by then the narrative of imminent terror had been lodged into the public consciousness: laws were enacted quickly, even when it became known to the government the Dural incident was a fabrication.

HOW THE DURAL HOAX BECAME LAW

It took just six weeks for a bomb scare hoax in the outskirts of Sydney to evolve into a legal assault on civil liberties. In January, NSW police were tipped off about a caravan parked behind a weatherboard cottage in Dural, and the vehicle supposedly contained mining gel detonators, a tangle of wires and a note naming the Great Synagogue as a target. Premier Minns called it "a terror plot against the Jewish community" and News Corporation tabloids splashed the headlines "Caravan of hate" across their front pages. Yet seasoned counter-terror detectives were sceptical from day one and, by March, the Australian Federal Police confirmed the whole thing was a criminal confidence trick designed to frighten Sydney—or to use the words of the AFP, a "fake terrorism" plot.

However, the official debunking came too late. On 11 February the Minns Government had already introduced the Places of Worship Bill, pitching it as a shield for synagogues, mosques and churches "under siege". The legislation sailed through both houses in nine days, granting police power to issue move-on orders, arrests without warrant and impose $22,000 fines on anyone protesting "in or near" a place of worship—a phrase so loose that it could cover half a suburb.

Civil-liberties lawyers did warn at that time that a prayer room above a convenience store, or even an *ad-hoc* Buddhist shrine in someone's loungeroom, now created an invisible and undefined zone where dissent could be criminalised. When the Human Rights Law Centre tallied the potential reach, they found virtually every major shopping strip in

THE SHADOW OVER PALESTINE

metropolitan Sydney contained at least one designated sacred site.

The political calculation behind this rush was pretty obvious. Although this legislation was developed within the jurisdiction of New South Wales, polling for the upcoming federal election suggested that Labor was losing votes in sections of Sydney amid a moral panic over anti-Semitic vandalism; these laws were drafted as much for optics as for public safety. Tony Burke, the federal Minister for Home Affairs—and member for the neighbouring seat of Watson— weighed in on breakfast television, applauding "urgent action to reassure faith communities," even though he had not read the final bill before endorsing it.

What the bill actually did was create a legal pretext ready-made for selective enforcement. Police command quickly circulated briefing notes describing pro-Palestine rallies as "events of heightened sensitivity", a euphemism that paved the way for heavy-handed police tactics. The government was quick to act: climate activists leafleting outside St Mary's Cathedral in Sydney were "moved-on" by police, while Palestine Action Group members holding candles across the road from a Lakemba mosque were monitored and threatened with arrest.

The biggest question is: who is all of this police power supposed to serve? In practice it insulates three constituencies: the property class, whose factories and showrooms are rebranded as "critical infrastructure"; the well-connected lobbyists who frame Palestine solidarity as a threat to Jewish safety; and a government anxious to look decisive every time a right-wing commentator on talk-back radio or Sky News claims that national security is "out of control". For everyone else, the message is unambiguous: speak against the war on Gaza in the wrong postcode—or *any* postcode, according to these laws—and the state will meet you with cuffs, fines and, just like an Orwellian dystopia, provide you with a future of "a boot stamping on a human face—forever".

HOW NSW'S VAGUE WORSHIP LAWS ENABLE POLICE ABUSE

The protest in Belmore was more than one of the first test cases for the places of worship legislation—it was a warning about how a vague, discretionary law can morph into a blunt instrument of oppression when the government disagrees with certain political opinions. On the surface, the premise might seem reasonable enough: people of faith should be able to gather and worship *in peace*. But the legislation passed by the NSW Government offers no clarity on what constitutes a "place of worship," nor how "near" such a place is. And that ambiguity is the main reason that makes the law so dangerous.

There are over 4,000 officially recognised churches in New South Wales but that doesn't include the many other prayer spaces, meditation rooms, informal temples, suburban mosques, and *ad-hoc* faith centres that exist across the state. Under the law, any one of these can effectively create a protest exclusion zone with a radius known only to the officer enforcing it. "Near" can be interpreted as a few metres, a few blocks away or even in the next suburb.

This is the absurdity: the state can now declare your presence illegal if you're standing within earshot of a room that once might have held a Bible study session. If tomorrow someone holds a silent vigil on the footpath outside a warehouse used last month by a faith-based charity, police could conceivably declare the space sacred and the protest unlawful. That's not *law enforcement*; that's theocratic authoritarianism dressed up in legal niceties.

If this much force can be exercised at a protest near an empty workshop in a church annexe, what happens when the protest is actually about the religious institution itself? What happens when the issue is child sexual abuse perpetrated by the church, synagogues hiding paedophile teachers like Malka Leifer, or bigotry preached under the guise of doctrine? Are those forms of public criticism now to be silenced under the pretence of "protecting worship"? At what point do we acknowledge that the real aim isn't to protect faith communities from harassment—but to shield specific political, economic, and ideological interests from scrutiny?

The fallout from the Belmore protest shows just how quickly the public discourse can be manipulated. In the hours after the assault on Hannah Thomas, social media churned out the predictable accusations—she was anti-Semitic, she provoked the police, she somehow faked the injury, even though the bruising, swelling, torn skin and the real risk of permanent damage or the loss of the eye was obvious.

There needs to be protections for peaceful protest in a democracy, otherwise, it's *not* a democracy. A pluralist society can't be maintained if the right to dissent is confined only to "safe" targets approved by the state. Religious organisations, like governments and other corporations, operate in the public domain, benefit from public funding and rely on public trust and legal protections. Like everyone else, they must be subject to public criticism and scrutiny. After all, as Burke said when he criticised the protest actions of Hannah Thomas, rather than the police officer who inflicted the damage to her, "no one is above the law".

Yet the current New South Wales framework allows any officer to end a protest with force, without a warrant, based on nothing more than proximity to a poorly defined "place of worship". It's not a law for protecting prayer or religious beliefs—it's a law for criminalising opposition. And in that respect, it's already succeeded. The law created the *pretext*, and the police delivered the *violence*. It's a farce.

AUSTRALIA'S COMPLICITY: THE BILLION-DOLLAR PIPELINE THAT LEADS TO ISRAEL

What unfolded in Belmore becomes clear once you start following the money—and the links between bits of aluminium, carbon-fibre clips, micro-processors and spray-cured polymers that flow from suburban Sydney factories into the F-35 fighter jets that are bombing Gaza. SEC Plating is only one link in this extensive network: there are nearly 20 contractors in Sydney alone, and about seventy nationwide, all feeding the Joint Strike Fighter program the Albanese Government insists has "no operational nexus" with the Israel Defense Forces. Yet Australia's share of that program is valued at roughly $4.1 billion, under 52 export licences with Israel, underwritten by Australia's Global Supply Chain agreements. Every time a F-35 drops bombs over Gaza, Australian labour and tax subsidies are flying onboard with the pilot.

And what a wonderful example of "double-speak": the Labor government lectures protesters on "peaceful engagement" and claiming that "no one is above the law", while tacitly profiting from weapons that are destroying apartment blocks and aid convoys in Gaza. Ministers such as Penny Wong rinse and repeat their slogans about an international "rules-based order" but are outraged at the moment someone asks which rules offer a justification for selling war parts to a state accused of genocide by the International Court of Justice.

A state that would rather have its citizens remain unaware of a conflict and be complicit in that conflict—rather than be critics of that state—will always force violence upon those citizens who start connecting up all the dots and try to expose immoral and possibly illegal behaviour.

The footage of Hannah Thomas being slammed to the ground has been far more effective than any government-based denial. It combined two stories into the one that reveals the problem with this legislation: a peaceful protestor bleeding on the ground and possibly losing her eye, juxtaposed against a church annexe that barely looks like a "place of worship", yet used to justify vicious police brutality. A law ostensibly designed to protect worship has become the legal fig-leaf for protecting war profits—and the police who bashed Thomas were, effectively, the bouncers and pimps for a billion-dollar export scheme that Weapons Out of the West banner threatened to expose and embarrass political leaders with.

But the biggest question will always be: where does accountability begin? With the police officer who swung the fist and attacked Hannah Thomas? The commissioner who authorised the police attack? The NSW Government which enacted the places of worship legislation based on a lie? The Israeli lobby in Sydney that is always requesting more and more draconian laws that protect their own interests and silences dissent? Or the federal cabinet that keeps approving export licences to Israel and then denies that military parts are being supplied to F-35 fighter jets and then used to kill civilians in Gaza?

Until that chain is confronted and fully exposed, there'll be more peaceful protestors bludgeoned by the riot police, who are only too happy have laws that protect their thuggery, instead of the public interest, laws that were based on lies and should have never been enacted in the first place.

***

AN ANTI-SEMITISM REPORT AND THE POLITICS OF FEAR

12 July 2025

There's something unsettling about the way political and media attention gathers with such immediacy and intensity whenever an act of anti-Semitism is reported—particularly when that act coincides with moments of increased scrutiny toward Israel's conduct in Gaza or the imminent release of a report concerning anti-Semitism in Australia. The recent incident in Melbourne is a perfect example: Angelo Loras, a 34-year-old man from Sydney, was quickly arrested after allegedly setting fire to the doors of a synagogue, an act Prime Minister Anthony Albanese immediately condemned as "cowardly", a "violent" attack with "no place in Australian society", asserting that those responsible would face the full force of the law.

But something in this case doesn't quite add up. First, the damage was minimal, and the synagogue, as it turns out, is located next to a fire station. No one was hurt, and while the act was unquestionably reprehensible, the media and political response seemed vastly disproportionate. Aside from a handful of photographs on Instagram, Loras has no digital footprint—there's no political activity, no signs of ideological motivation, and no attempt to disguise his actions in Melbourne, all of which were recorded on CCTV. It's reminiscent of a case earlier in the year in the outer Sydney suburb of Dural, where a supposedly politically motivated threat on synagogues was later revealed to be an elaborate hoax, a hoax which resulted in draconian police powers quickly introduced—powers that have already led to documented instances of police brutality, especially against pro-Palestinian demonstrators.

But what do we really know about this incident? It has already disappeared from the headlines, and no new facts have emerged since the arrest. Like other recent provocations— such as the bizarre case where Ofir Birenbaum and journalists from News Corporation entered the Cairo Takeaway in Newtown wearing a Star of David and attempted to bait the kebab shop owners into saying something anti-Semitic and incriminating—this case raises far more questions than it answers. Is there a co-ordinated international effort to generate these flashpoints, as the Australian Federal Police suggested in the Dural hoax? Are these isolated acts by "nobodies" being used to justify a creeping state authoritarianism under the guise of protecting faith communities?

There's also wider issues at stake: the government's reaction to this incident in Melbourne was quick and morally unambiguous. But when Islamophobic attacks occur—hate graffiti on mosques, women wearing hijabs harassed and attacked, or threats made against Palestinian Australians— the response is, at best, muted, or non-existent. There's a dissonance in a political culture that seems more outraged by a burnt door than by the daily incineration of children and aid workers in Gaza—where some communities are granted immediate empathy, while others are met with suspicion, silence and constant surveillance.

No one is excusing violence: *this point has to be made very clear*. But if dissent about Australia's foreign policy—or even basic support for Palestinian human rights—ends up being criminalised under new arbitrary "anti-hate" laws crafted in response to events like this, then the real danger isn't just from rogue arsonists, as bad as that is, it's from a political and media establishment willing to exploit fear on behalf of vested interests.

SELECTIVE OUTRAGE AND THE WEAPONISING IDENTITY

While the double standards are pretty obvious, it's no longer possible to ignore and do nothing about them. When acts of anti-Semitism occur—even those of uncertain origin or limited impact—governments at both state and federal levels move instantly, whether it's lighting up the Sydney Opera House with the flag of Israel, or implementing draconian new laws and police powers. Strike Force Pearl in New South Wales, Operation Anti-Hate in Victoria: these responses came with full media conferences, high-level political engagement, and sweeping new policies. The messaging is clear and consistent—there is zero tolerance for anti-Semitism, *as it should be.*

But when the hate is directed against other communities— Islamic, African Australians, Indigenous people or pro-Palestine people—there's no urgent media conferences, no task forces, and certainly no legislation rammed through parliament in late-night sittings. And this is not to minimise the very real threats that Jewish Australians do face—those should never be dismissed. But the inconsistency in response reveals something much deeper, and far more dangerous, about how political power in this country is being used—and misused—to benefit special groups with vested interests.

This pattern of selective justice doesn't just affect those directly targeted by hate crimes, it distorts the entire legislative and cultural framework of the country. As we saw in the wake of the Dural hoax earlier this year, bad laws are being rushed through parliaments in a panic, drafted poorly and with sweeping powers that end up hurting the very democratic principles they claim to defend. With the federal government now considering a sweeping national plan to combat anti-Semitism—one that appears to have been written less with justice in mind than appeasing powerful lobby groups—Australians are once again being asked to accept a framework of "protection" that is not based on universal rights, but on political expediency.

And it's reaching a point where even asking questions about these legislations and ambit claims—legitimate questions that need answers and transparency—risks the immediate accusation of anti-Semitism. It's now an accusation that has become a political weapon, and one that is used to shut down inquiry and criminalise dissent.

This is not how free societies are supposed to work. Justice can't depend on identity or specific religions—hate crimes against any community should be met with the same level of seriousness, the same legal scrutiny, and the same moral clarity. But a dangerous trend is emerging where criticism of Israel's government—no matter how valid or fact-based—is automatically recast as racial or religious hate, which stifles public discourse and actually undermines the fight against real anti-Semitism. And it becomes a case where if *everything* is labelled anti-Semitism, then *nothing* is.

PROTEST, GENOCIDE, AND THE POLITICS OF MANUFACTURED OFFENCE

There was another incident in Melbourne which provided the mainstream media and the political class another moment in their ongoing campaign to conflate anti-Zionism with anti-Semitism. However, this one was not a mysterious act of arson by an unknown individual from another city; it was a public protest involving around 20 demonstrators who stood outside Miznon, an Israeli-owned restaurant in the Melbourne CBD. The protest wasn't directed at Jewish people, or Judaism, or the existence of Israel—it was a protest directed at the restaurant's owner, Shahar Segal. Segal isn't just a private citizen running a hospitality business; he has also been publicly linked to a private humanitarian organisation accused of corralling starving Palestinians in Gaza with promises of food, only for those areas to be targeted in subsequent bombings and shootings, with over 600 Palestinians reportedly killed in these so-called "safe zones". These are the facts the media—in its breathless reporting—conveniently ignored.

This was a protest about complicity in war crimes. The protestors were not targeting a religious group—they were opposing acts of state violence, and the individuals allegedly involved in supporting or facilitating it. But the media repeatedly described it as an "anti-Semitic attack," and conflated its reporting with the synagogue arson, and then going on further to claim that multiculturalism in Australia is collapsing under the weight of racial hatred.

This isn't just bad journalism—it's political propaganda disguised as reporting on behalf of the Zionist movement, and the conflation of legitimate political protest with racial or religious hatred was such a dishonest act. It removes any space for dissent, silences criticism of Israel's government, and equates protestors with bigots. But as Federal Court Justice Angus Stewart made very clear in the recent *Wertheim v Haddad* case, it is *not* anti-Semitic to criticise the Israeli government, or to protest against Zionism, or to oppose the policies that are causing a genocide in Gaza. These are not some made-up leftist or radical opinions—these are points of law, specifically made by Justice Stewart in a Federal Court.

The selective reporting, however, presented a different story. The ABC—once a public broadcaster with a reputation for independent public journalism—parroted the same lines as the Murdoch press: a "hate-filled protest," "anti-Jewish targeting," "a worrying escalation". But nowhere in the coverage was there serious engagement with what the protest was *actually* about. There was no mention of the accusations against the private humanitarian organisation in Gaza. No reporting on the Federal Court decision, and certainly no context: just the usual lazy, establishment journalism echoing the political class and shielding those in power.

In 2024, the former Attorney-General Mark Dreyfus, claimed that criticism of Zionism or Israel amounts to anti-Semitism. But that position is not only legally incorrect—it was an attempt to remove specific political opinion from public debate, one that is held by millions of people around the world, including many Jewish people themselves. Zionism is an *ideology* based on bigoted supremacy, it's not a race or a religion and must be open to criticism like any other political philosophy.

None of this is to deny that genuine anti-Semitism exists. And to be sure, there are individuals who will weaponise criticism of Israel as a smokescreen for their prejudices. But if we allow those individuals to define the boundaries of public debate, we surrender the entire field to the authoritarians and allow the Netanyahus of the world claim that every act of dissent is hatred, and that all criticism is an act of anti-Semitic violence. It's not just wrong—it's dangerous—it undermines the legitimacy of real work against racism, and allows actual hate to hide behind the very legal and rhetorical protections that are meant to oppose it.

What's happening in Gaza is not some kind of ethereal abstraction. It's not just about ideology. It is about people dying—massacred, starved, displaced—under the watch of the international community. And it's not a secret: every day we see the live-streamed massacres and daily reports of more killings in Gaza, and more settler violence in the West Bank. Israel has even publicly announced its intentions to create concentration camps in Rafah—as if Gaza hadn't already been an open-air concentration camp—yet, the world watches on, allowing this to happen with indifference and complicity.

Nearly every major scholar of genocide has declared that what Israel is doing in Gaza is a genocide. When that is the scale of the crime, we need to speak up more, not be silenced by the apparatus of the state. The way in which we hold power to account must be fearless—to protest against genocide is not an act of *hate*, it's an act of *humanity*. And in any just society, if that's what we really live in, that distinction should be absolutely obvious to everyone.

SEGAL IS TRYING TO SILENCE DISSENT AGAINST ISRAEL

The release of the federal government's anti-Semitism report—prepared by Jillian Segal, the Prime Minister Anthony Albanese's handpicked Special Envoy—didn't seem to be a coincidence. Its timing, dropped into a news cycle already inflamed by the Melbourne synagogue arson and the protest outside an Israeli-owned restaurant, was a nice little political calculation. These two incidents, exploited by political and media elites as examples of Australia's supposed descent into hate-fuelled chaos, provided the perfect emotional backdrop for a document that seems to be less about combating anti-Semitism and more about redefining dissent as hate speech.

Segal's report, heavily leaned upon by Australia's most powerful pro-Israel lobby groups, such as the conservative Executive Council of Australian Jewry—Segal being the Immediate Past President—and enthusiastically amplified by outlets like *The Australian* and *Sky News*, has reignited the public debate over the boundaries between anti-Jewish bigotry and political criticism of Israel. But there's a massive contradiction within this report: it claims to be a shield for vulnerable communities, but in practice—if any of Segal outrageous recommendations are implemented—it will become an instrument used to punish critics of state violence.

Segal is not a neutral figure. As a former head of a pro-Israel lobby organisation and the partner of John Roth, a man who donated $50,000 to Advance Australia—a far-right group that campaigned aggressively against the Voice to Parliament referendum in 2023—her appointment as a supposedly impartial envoy on anti-Semitism raises questions about conflicts of interest, and the intent behind the report were compromised from the outset.

The central part of Segal's report is its push for the formal adoption of the International Holocaust Remembrance Alliance definition of anti-Semitism, which has been used across multiple jurisdictions to blur the lines between anti-Jewish hate and legitimate political opposition to the Israeli state. The joining of criticisms of Israel and Zionism with anti-Semitism have made the IHRA definition a tool of repression in those jurisdictions—used not just against protestors and academics, but against the very idea of open public debate.

Segal's recommendations would roll in a new era of censorship: where questioning military occupation, apartheid policies, or genocide in Gaza would be treated as hate speech, and where institutions would face funding cuts or public censure for hosting controversial speakers or events or not doing enough to stop anti-Semitism in an undefined way—it's already happening on a *de facto* basis as we've seen in recent months, but to enshrine this in law would be a disaster.

Once again, we have to point out that genuine anti-Semitic abuse and violence must be condemned and combatted. But if we are constantly forced to condemn Hamas, we must also be forced to condemn Israel for its actions in Gaza and West Bank. What the Segal report proposes, however, is a shutdown of public debate where publicly condemning Israel would be considered a crime.

In the Australian context, this concern is heightened by the reality that recent tensions have not emerged in a vacuum.

They are linked to Israel's relentless assault and genocide on Gaza—attacks that have killed well over 55,000 and more than likely, a significantly higher number, displaced millions, and shocked much of the world. To release an anti-Semitism strategy that ignores this context is not only dishonest—it's politically dangerous.

There are so many blind spots in Segal's report. There's no mention of Gaza or Palestine. There is no space for solidarity with the suffering of *all* peoples, no room for justified outrage. Instead, the Segal report channels the conversation through a single, ideologically loaded perspective: protecting one community by silencing many others.

This approach won't create harmony, and why Albanese has allowed this process to go this far is difficult to comprehend. Sure, he only had a slim majority in Parliament and with an election to win, offered as much support as possible to appease the Israel lobby groups—and got nothing in return politically—but what's the excuse now? Labor now has 94 seats in Parliament after its crushing win at the 2025 federal election, and is facing a feckless Coalition as the opposition.

Albanese should take this report and, as diplomatically as possible, tell Segal that it represents an outrageous overreach and an implausible, excessive demand—and clearly let her know that all it will do is deepen suspicion, polarise debate, and undermine faith in democratic institutions. That's what Albanese *should* do but we know that he won't: his previous support for the cause of Palestine—as recently as 2019 but before he became the leader of the Labor Party—has been shown to be a charade and a convenient façade. Albanese now exists in the space of power and privilege, and he's unprepared to cede any of this power to support truth, justice, and the right to speak out against oppression, even when supporting one particular group of privilege might be detrimental to his political standing. He's become the Keir Starmer of the South.

But he does need to understand that if we are to live in a truly pluralist society, we must reject anything that weaponises one group's plan to erase the existence of another. And we must insist that the fight against hate includes *everyone*—or it will end up protecting no one.

***

ALBANESE AND WONG ON THE WRONG SIDE OF HISTORY

26 July 2025

The first day of a new parliamentary term always contains the ceremonial pantomime of speeches, pageantry, and the carefully staged managed political of *business as usual*. But outside the walls of Parliament, there is a façade that is starting to break—ever so slowly—but *it is* starting to break. Thousands of protestors converged on Canberra not to celebrate the opening of the Parliamentary term but to demand that Australia end its silence and complicity—in the face of what many consider to be a genocide inflicted by the state of Israel upon the people of Gaza, and to take substantial action against the Israel government's systematic and obvious destruction of Palestine.

The Australian government's position on the conflict in Gaza has been untenable for some time, with Israel continuing to blockade Gaza's borders, preventing adequate food and medical aid from reaching the population, and enforcing mass starvation. International agencies have been forced out of Gaza and replaced with much-criticised Israeli-controlled entity—the so-called Gaza Humanitarian Foundation—the Orwellian name that has become a symbol of the obscene and brutal failure to meet even the most basic humanitarian standards: over a thousand Palestinians have been killed since May, either gunned down at food distribution points or crushed in stampedes after being corralled into cages, just like cattle in a slaughterhouse. And yet, the international response still remains weak and putrid, unable to respond to the stench of Israel's acts of genocide. The Australian government, while it did join a list of 28 countries condemning Israel's actions, has offered little else besides sterile diplomatic language.

Foreign Minister Penny Wong still continues with this sterilisation—delivering statements stifled by caution, and carefully crafted to avoid upsetting Australia's domestic Israel lobby or distort the broader Zionist narrative. Her performative concern is *less* directed at the lives being lost in Gaza and *more* at the political optics of dissent within the Parliament itself. If it wasn't evident before, it was made pretty obvious when Wong moved a rare and severe censure motion against the Australian Greens Senator Mehreen Faruqi, for the grand offence of holding up a sign that said "Gaza is starving. Words won't feed them. Sanction Israel" during the Governor–General's address in the joint parliamentary sitting.

Rather than engage with the message and the uncomfortable truth it represents, Senator Wong punished the messenger, describing Faruqi's actions as a breach of "decorum," accusing her of disrespecting Parliament and denigrating those who disagree with her. The Senate's censure went far beyond a symbolic reprimand; it includes an extraordinary punishment that strips Faruqi of any right to represent the Senate on delegations for the remainder of the term—effectively sidelining her for next three years.

A Senator censured and silenced, not for inciting violence or spreading disinformation, but for calling for sanctions against a foreign government accused of war crimes. It was a clear indication of how far Australia's political establishment is willing to go to preserve its diplomatic and ideological alliances—supporting a genocide even at the cost of democratic dissent. Again, this was a performative and over-the-top action that ultimately wasn't even directed towards Faruqi, or even the Australian electorate: it was directed towards the Israel lobby in Australia, to make it clear which side of the genocide Senator Wong is siding with.

Senator Faruqi, in her response, drew on Martin Luther King's 'Letter from a Birmingham Jail', and criticised the "white moderates", more concerned about procedures and protocols, rather than justice, setting their standards to cover over the truth and not wanting to do anything about the genocide in Gaza. And as the bombs continue to fall on Gaza, as children continue to starve, as neighbourhoods are reduced to rubble, the Australian government will find that the most enduring legacy won't be anything else it does this term, but its silence and failure to act on a genocide that everyone else in the world can see in plain sight.

SILENCE IS COMPLIANCE

The speed at which this censure motion against Senator Faruqi was introduced, debated, and passed was also a sign of how desperate the Labor government is to appease the Israel lobby and Zionists in Australia. Within just an hour of the Senate's commencement, Senator Wong negotiated a censure—not against the state of Israel, whose military actions, according to independent reports, have led to the deaths of well over 80,000 Palestinians—but against a fellow Senator who was simply protesting in silence. All over a cardboard sign—and on a type of cardboard that Palestinians are currently eating, just to fill their stomachs and force away the pangs of hunger, because they have *nothing else* to eat—there were no threats, no incitement, just a plea to acknowledge the starvation of a people under siege.

It wasn't wearing a burqa into the Senate—as Pauline Hanson did in 2017 to make a racist point—or turning the back on a Welcome to Country event—Hanson, again to make a racist point, this time in front of the Governor-General—or wearing a fluro vest, brandishing a large salmon, or wearing a wig—all of these events have taken place in Parliament, yet only Faruqi's actions have received a censure.

Faruqi's act was moral statement, and the nature of her punishment—above and beyond anyone else—reveals the deep capture of Australia's political establishment by the Israel lobby and aligned Zionist organisations, and provides the clearest example of how lopsided the political landscape has become and how pathetically weak our governments are.

Faruqi didn't call for violence or deny Israel's right to exist; she just demanded that Israel be held accountable for its actions and crimes against humanity—had the same sign expressed solidarity with Israel, there's little doubt that it would have gone unnoticed, and even applauded by Wong. And this is the grand act of hypocrisy: the rules of so-called "decorum" are only enforced when they challenge the dominant narrative from vested and racist interests, and the dominant narrative within this Labor government remains solidly pro-Israel, no matter how severe the atrocities become. Senator Faruqi was punished not for disrupting Parliament— she didn't do any disruption anyway—but for daring to tell the truth and speaking out against Israel.

But things are shifting—slowly but surely and, as usual, the political class is lagging far behind public sentiment. The barbarity of Israel's actions is now too obvious, too public and too cruel to ignore. What once existed in the shadows—carpet bombing and "lawn mowing" of refugee camps, deliberate starvation of children, shooting at aid queues—now floods social media feeds, news broadcasts, and diplomatic circles. Protests are growing. The Australian public is beginning to understand what's being done in its name, and many are rejecting it. Eventually, the political class will get it, despite its psychopathic desires to ignore it.

The language used by Prime Minister Anthony Albanese over the weekend has become *marginally* more critical of Israel, where at least he acknowledged that the actions in Gaza breach international law, before self-censoring himself and adding that he's not a lawyer and couldn't be too sure about that. But these sterner words have been said before, yet never matched up with action. The Albanese government refuses to take the next obvious steps—recalling the Israeli ambassador, cutting military co-operation, halting arms exports, suspending trade, or issuing meaningful diplomatic condemnation.

If the Australian government does not change course soon—if it continues to mumble platitudes while Gaza is turned to rubble and its population is massacred—it won't be remembered very kindly at all on this issue, irrespective of how large its parliamentary majority is at the moment. History won't be looking back and admiring Albanese's caution; it will remember the silence and the moral cowardice. It will remember a government that had a choice but chose not to offend a lobby group and stood idly by as tens of thousands of people were slaughtered.

This should be a turning point—not just for Palestine, but for Australia. A nation that claims to champion democracy, human rights, and a rules-based international order can't stand by while those very principles are obliterated in the same way that the Palestinian tent cities have been. To avoid acting isn't neutrality, it's cowardly complicity. And complicity, no matter how softly spoken or politely phrased, will always be on the wrong side of history.

WHAT AUSTRALIA CAN DO TO END THE GENOCIDE

Many Australians claim that the geographic distance from the Middle East limits our ability to intervene, and that includes Senator Wong, who claimed it was "always very difficult from over here to make judgements". But it's a weak and pathetic argument that makes no sense at all. We made a judgement to sanction Russia, which is even further away—there are many other sanctions in place on countries such as Syria, Libya, Yemen, South Sudan, North Korea, Lebanon, Iran—and a quick look at a map will show that all of these countries are far away and not within Australia's usual sphere of influence.

In contrast, Australia actively opposed the apartheid regime in South Africa in the 1980s—another country half a world away with white supremacy beliefs and policies at the time that are not too dissimilar to Israel—and used a great deal of pressure to bring about change, a change that finally arrived in 1990 with the release of Nelson Mandela. And, at the time, there was bipartisan support within Australia to act against South Africa, despite the efforts of the U.S. and British governments to cease and desist.

Many of the same actions could be taken today against Israel to help bring an end to its occupation of Palestinian territories and the genocide it has inflicted on Gaza. Australia could formally recognise the state of Palestine—as France has promised to do in September—and a move already made by over 140 United Nations member states. It could expel Israeli diplomats, suspend military co-operation, and more forcefully condemn Israel's violations of international law. The government could support Palestinian efforts to join global institutions such as the International Criminal Court and the International Court of Justice, and it could endorse South Africa's genocide case against Israel.

Trade restriction is another option. Australia could ban imports produced in illegal Israeli settlements in the West Bank and impose targeted Magnitsky-style sanctions on Israeli military leaders involved in the bombing campaigns and siege of Gaza. It could stop exporting weapons components to Israel's defence industry and cut defence co-operation agreements. Public funds could be divested from companies that support or profit from the occupation and war.

Cultural and academic boycotts would also have impact. During the apartheid era, Australia refused to host South African athletes and artists, and encouraged international bodies to boycott South Africa from global events. What Australia did then, can be applied to Israel today, alongside an increase in humanitarian aid and support for Palestine.

But the reality is that Australia has done almost none of this. Despite the growing body of evidence of human rights abuses and collective punishment in Gaza—and the evidence can be seen almost every single moment on social media and international news broadcasts—the Albanese government has behaved in morally bankrupt way and supported the oppressors.

Within federal Parliament, there seems to be very little appetite for change. While the Greens have consistently called for sanctions and recognition of Palestine, and some Labor MPs have expressed concern—this week, Victoria Labor Party members have pushed for the immediate recognition of Palestine, as has the federal Labor member Ed Husic— the leadership has opted for cautious, ambiguous language. Statements from Senator Wong and Prime Minister Albanese have largely reflected those from the United States, reflexively condemning Hamas because they haven't got anything else to say, and going out of their way to avoid any direct critique of Israel's military campaign or its decades-long occupation of Palestinian territories. And while they actively condemn

Hamas, they fail to explain the ongoing terrorism and settler violence in the West Bank, where Hamas doesn't even exist.

Today's pro-Palestine campaign in Australia is still gaining traction—it's frustratingly slow, but it's moving at a pace that might soon be impossible to stop, and that's what the government fears the most. The trade unions, churches, and student groups were instrumental in the 1980s in building the political momentum needed for action against South Africa are going through a similar mobilisation now and will ultimately force the government to abandon its passive stance.

Public opinion is shifting in Australia, with the continuing mass protests in many cities, more pressure from human rights organisations, and a greater awareness of these issues within the electorate, especially among younger people. But without bold political leadership, Australia risks remaining on the sidelines of history—condemning atrocities in words, but not in deeds.

Australia didn't let distance stop it from acting against apartheid in South Africa. It shouldn't let it be an excuse now. Palestine can't wait, and it really time for Australia to act right now.

***

A WITNESS TO GENOCIDE: THE CALLS TO RECOGNISE PALESTINE

2 August 2025

There was more movement on Palestine this week, driven by the complete humanitarian disaster and unfolding genocide in Gaza. In what is seen primarily as a symbolic gesture at this stage, Australia signed a joint statement with fifteen other foreign ministers—including those from France and Canada—reaffirming their "unwavering commitment" to a two-state solution. But the meaning of this is becoming unclear and shrouded in double-speak and obfuscation: if a two-state solution is the consensus for many countries, then logically, that means a state of Palestine and a state of Israel.

Yet the practical commitment to a state of Palestine remains far away, especially from nations such as Australia, where Prime Minister Anthony Albanese was quick to clarify that there is no move on the table to recognise the state of Palestine, despite his constant rhetoric about a "commitment" and "long-held desire" for a two-state solution. Treasurer Jim Chalmers also chimed in, saying that it was "a matter of when, not if" Palestine will achieve statehood, but without a clear timeline, "when" could be a matter of decades, or well into the next century.

The current pathway for Palestinian statehood is loaded with conditions, caveats and contradictions—all of them are unclear, and seem to be designed to defer action indefinitely. Albanese has insisted that Hamas must be "completely removed" and Palestine must be "completely demilitarised" before any recognition is even considered, a condition that's diplomatically and strategically ambiguous. What does "complete removal" mean? How will a state of Palestine defend itself from likely Israeli attacks if it has no military to speak of? Or guard itself against the settler violence in the West Bank? And who decides when that threshold is met?

More recently, Albanese has introduced another stipulation: that other Middle Eastern countries must recognise Israel before Palestine can be granted statehood. This raises another question—why is the fate of Palestine now tied to the diplomatic positions of other sovereign nations? It's an endless *cul-de-sac* designed to appease Israeli interests, and one that further delays justice for the Palestinians.

Meanwhile, the United Kingdom has taken a different approach, suggesting it will recognise a Palestinian state *only* if Israel fails to implement a ceasefire—a "stick-and-carrot" approach that, like the Australian position, still links recognition of Palestine with Israel's behaviour, rather than applying the inherent rights of the Palestinian people. Other countries have tied recognition to the release of all hostages, despite Israel's repeated violations of ceasefires even after previous hostage releases, and even their refusal to accept the release of hostages as a condition of ceasefires. The double standards are obvious and sickening.

But despite the diplomatic stonewalling from Albanese and Foreign Minister Penny Wong, there is a growing momentum, and much of it has been fuelled by the harrowing images that have shaken the global conscience. One such image—of the emaciated 18-month-old boy, Mohammad Zakaria, clinging to life in Gaza City—has begun to cut through the geopolitical pantomime act. His fragile skeletal body, held in the arms of his grieving mother, has horrified even those who were previously unmoved, and it's this singular photograph that has jolted leaders into at least *sounding* more serious about ending the crisis.

Albanese responded emotionally, saying that "a one-year-old boy is not a Hamas fighter. Clearly, it is a breach of international law to stop food being delivered... but it's also a breach of decent humanity and morality". But as if to cancel out this small slither of support of a starving Palestinian child, within the same breath, he reiterated Israel's right to defend itself. And, as clearly as Albanese could see a breach of international law, he had to defend the right of this rogue state of Israel to make these breaches. Once again, it's all so *sickening*.

The question remains: if this level of suffering and visible starvation is what it takes to trigger rhetorical shifts, what does it say about the world's moral compass? And what does it mean for the thousands of Gazans who have already died—starved, bombed, gunned down—without a photograph to tell their story?

Israel, predictably, pushed back, as it always does—using its team of propaganda journalists to publish false medical records of Mohammad Zakaria that he had other underlying health conditions—remembering that *this is Israel*, who will stoop to unknown depths to justify its obscene actions—going on to accuse Albanese of lying, denying that there is any famine in Gaza, despite overwhelming independent evidence to the contrary.

But this ongoing denialism is losing any small level of credibility that Israel might have once had. This genocide has exposed the horrific logic of the West: that footage of starving children, flattened neighbourhoods, and mass graves are required before the world even begins to acknowledge atrocity, let alone take action. And that speaks to a deeper failure—not just of policy, but of the human values within the decrepit state of international diplomacy.

It should never have reached this point. From the earliest days of this war/massacre/genocide, the evidence of ethnic cleansing, expulsions, war crimes, and mass killing was there. And yet, the global response has been weak, fragmented, and geopolitically caution; Albanese being the best example of this. But now, the horror has become too widespread for political leaders to ignore: the world has arrived at a historical sliding doors moment, and it's one that will determine the moral fortitude of the international community for generations to come.

If this moment is lost, it risks normalising a genocide that we've all been witnessing. It risks sending a message to authoritarian, fascist and militarised states everywhere, including Israel, that mass murder, if done slowly and bureaucratically, will go unpunished, and create the space for more genocides in the future, just because the global community looked away when it mattered the most.

THE GLOBAL TIPPING POINT

We've reached a tipping point that is becoming impossible for politicians to ignore. The outrage is no longer coming from fringe voices or isolated activists that the political class usually dismisses—it's coming from different parliaments, political spectrums, and different jurisdictions. From national assemblies in Europe to local councils in Australia, from global south leaders to civil groups in the West, the calls are getting much louder: something has fundamentally shifted, and the world can no longer look away from what is happening in Gaza.

In Australia, the signs of change are becoming increasingly visible: Senator David Pocock, long known for his independent stance on humanitarian issues, has now joined the call for the formal recognition of a Palestinian state. Independents such as Sophie Scamps and Kate Chaney—representing highly conservative seats in Sydney and Perth—have added their voices, along with Labor MPs such as Ed Husic, one of the few federal politicians to speak forcefully against Israel's actions during this crisis. The Labor Friends of Palestine in Victoria have also become more vocal, demanding urgent diplomatic recognition of Palestine. And it's not just politicians—unions, churches, community leaders are all arriving at the same message: recognise Palestine now.

For decades, the international conversation has been framed in absolutes—*condemn* Hamas, *defend* Israel. But this logic is quickly falling apart, and the world is now saying: *enough is enough*.

This understanding from the public doesn't require expertise in Middle Eastern history or deep familiarity with the arcane nature of UN resolutions and geopolitics: the absolute horrors has become obvious to everyone, except for Israel and its supporters. Families buried under rubble, food convoys blocked or bombed by Israel, a generation of children left traumatised or starved. These aren't just statistics or strategic mistakes—these are *war crimes*. And the global public, weary of the many excuses provided by their leaders, is beginning to demand not just recognition of Palestine as a state, but accountability for Israel as a brutal occupying power.

Yet, despite these calls, recognition can't just be the end—it will be the beginning of a long and uncertain process. Borders will need to be redrawn, with the fundamental basics of stopping the killings and suffering. The rights of millions of Palestinians who have lived under occupation for decades will need to be acknowledged, respected, and restored. And what of the more than 700,000 Israeli settlers who have been encouraged to live illegally in the West Bank? Many of them are radicalised vandals, many are armed, many of them are determined to stay and unlikely to vacate the occupied territory without resistance. Any peace will require not just recognition and good intentions, but international and multilateral enforcement—and is almost likely to be controversial.

The fundamental problem in Palestine isn't just about land or politics: it's about the abandonment of international law in favour of military force, Israeli religious nationalism, and double standards. Since 1948, the conflicts in this region have been interpreted through a distortion of historical European guilt, superpower political games, and biblical claims that should have been dispensed with many centuries ago. The only viable path forward is one grounded in international law—clear, consistent, and enforceable—not through myths of a bible, military supremacy, or the rules of great power diplomacy that seem to change depending on who the victim is.

There's no question that the genocide must stop. The collective punishment, the blockades by Israel, the targeting of hospitals and aid workers by the Israel Defense Forces and their affiliated mercenaries—it all needs to stop *now*. It's a catastrophe that history will remember with shame, unless the world acts now, and even then, it still might be too late.

Israel's Prime Minister, Benjamin Netanyahu must be held accountable—not only in Israel, where he faces charges of corruption and abuse of power—but also by the international community. These crimes against humanity can't be buried under politics, and the pursuit of real justice needs to be uncompromising.

But Netanyahu is not the only one with questions to answer. What about the other world leaders who have enabled and supported Israel's campaign: Anthony Albanese; Penny Wong; Keir Starmer; Ursula von der Leyen? Joe Biden and Donald Trump in the U.S.? These are the names not just being thrown around by punters in the streets or the socialist clubs of Sydney or Europe, but by legal scholars and political ethicists who are now suggesting that complicity during a mass atrocity—even if it does only involve just looking the other way and turning a blind eye—must have legal consequences.

A MARCH FOR HUMANITY: THE CITY THAT SAID ENOUGH IS ENOUGH

It's becoming increasingly clear all around the world, that many people have just had enough of the silence and complicity of governments who have the power to act, but do nothing. They've had enough of the daily images of civilian carnage, of children starving, of families trapped beneath rubble. And as frustration with government inaction grows, that anger and grief is now being translated into mass mobilisation, including one of the most powerful protests in recent Australian history.

Well over 100,000 people marched across the Sydney Harbour Bridge in a torrential downpour, a dramatic act of civil resistance demanding an end to Israel's genocide in Gaza and the immediate recognition of Palestine, becoming a symbol of grief, rage, and solidarity. Following the banner of the "March for Humanity", this was also a symbol of moral defiance.

The demands at this march were clear: sanction Netanyahu, halt all military co-operation with Israel, and formally recognise the state of Palestine. The protest didn't just defy apathy and expectations from the political class that it was just going to be the riff-raff of extremism designed to inconvenience Sydneysiders—it defied that political power. NSW Premier Chris Minns—who has become far more right-wing and more conservative than many Labor supporters would have hoped for—opposed the demonstration from the outset, after his government recently introduced harsh anti-protest laws threatening fines and prison sentences for those disrupting major roads. But despite the intimidation and fear Minns wanted to instil, at least five NSW Labor MPs attended the rally in open defiance of their leader. And over 100,000 protestors.

This wasn't a niche protest attended by rabble-rousers, it was a massive success in diversity. Young Palestinians draped in keffiyehs marched alongside Jewish peace activists in yarmulkes; teachers, nurses, students, and retirees alongside a broad range of people from different age groups—young, old, and everyone in between. Trade unionists stood with climate activists and religious figures. The message was clear: this isn't about geopolitics, it's about *humanity*.

Such a groundswell in popular opinion and perception made one thing very clear: support for Gaza is not a marginal issue in Australia—it has become mainstream. And as government officials continue to couch their language in "balanced diplomacy" at a time when more decisive action against Israel needs to be taken, this protest revealed a public that has moved far beyond the political class that has been left floundering behind, trying to create more excuses to justify their lack of action.

More than anything else, this march wasn't a confrontation with just the government, but a pricking of Australia's conscience, and a question to the nation in the simple terms: when children are being deliberately starved, where do we stand? When a people are being bombed into oblivion, what do we do? Do we speak up? Or do we look away—which is exactly what our political leaders want us to do.

This wasn't a march for votes, or political reform, or even about national pride—it was a march for *humanity*. And in that moment, as the rain poured over the harbour and the echoes of the voices bounced off the steel bridge structures on the bridge above, it became impossible to deny that Australia is changing its perspective on Gaza and the future of Palestine.

That silence that had been enforced by our political class is breaking down, and many more people are refusing to back down—in our streets, in our homes, in our conscience and now, quite literally, on our bridge. Things need to change, *now*.

***

KILLING JOURNALISTS WON'T STOP
THE TRUTH COMING OUT

9 August 2025

The conflict in Gaza has continued to bring of death and destruction to the people of Palestine, with more than 60,000 people killed and 145,000 injured, including a disproportionate number of women and children. It's very clear now—if there was ever *any doubt*—that this is an act of genocide—and there's a heavy weight of evidence, coming in from UN experts, human rights groups all around the world, including from within Israel. The deaths, the ethnic cleansing, lack of medical care, a lack of food, forced and continuous displacement, the destruction of homes, businesses, schools and hospitals—these are the internationally agreed conditions of genocide, whether Israel accepts this or not.

And in the midst of this genocide, the very voices that are documenting the suffering—journalists—are being deliberately murdered and silenced by the state of Israel. Gaza has become the deadliest place for media workers, where fatalities among journalists and media personnel ranges from at least 178 confirmed by Committee to Protect Journalists to well over 237, according to the local Gaza Media Office.

The most recent murders were of Al Jazeera's Anas Al-Sharif and four of his colleagues—Mohammed Qreiqeh, Ibrahim Zaher, Mohammed Noufal and Moamen Aliwa—

in a co-ordinated strike on their press tent outside Al-Shifa Hospital in Gaza City, where the Israeli Defense Forces allege Al-Sharif was a "Hamas cell leader", despite the lack of any evidence at all to support their claim.

And this is the *modus operandi* of the state of Israel—besmirch the reputation of a journalist through a total fabrication, and then use that fabrication to justify the killing—Hossam Shabat was killed in the same manner in March, with a wave of unverified accusations followed up with an Israeli airstrike. Reporters Without Borders, the CPJ, and other press freedom advocates have denounced these acts as "intentional" and "unprecedented", warning that the systematic murder of journalists in Gaza is an assault on global press freedoms and humanity. However, there is usually a comradery amongst international journalists when one of their own is killed in a conflict zone, but nearly every journalist in the mainstream media in Australia has been quiet over the past two years, even though there have been at least 178 occasions when they could have raised their voices. So why the silence?

SILENCING THE NEWSROOM: GAZA'S JOURNALISTS ARE BEING KILLED TWICE

Israel's consistent practice of branding journalists as *militants*, without presenting any evidence that could be independently verified, is a debasement of international law, the key tenets of press freedom and the free flow of information. Journalists are protected civilians under the Geneva Conventions, yet in Gaza they've become routine target practice for the IDF. This continuous blurring of that distinction between combatant and correspondent—even though most of the people that Israel has killed in Gaza have been civilians—not only endangers journalists but undermines the key element of independent reporting in a conflict zone.

The killing of these five journalists came after weeks of public vilification by Israel, making claim after claim about a supposed relationship with Hamas—again, no evidence was provided—to build up a narrative that would justify these killings in retrospect. It's clearly a tactic used by Israel to kill journalists and, just before their deaths, Al Jazeera Media, the United Nations, and the CPJ each issued separate statements calling for the protection of these journalists. These appeals, however, did nothing to stop these killings by Israel.

The death toll in Gaza exceeds the number of journalists killed in any other conflict over the past century—150 journalists were killed during the Iraq War, over an eight-year period, and 81 during the first four years of the war in Syria, and now, 237 journalists in Palestine in less than two years. Despite this, the reaction from Australia's mainstream journalists has been close to invisible. The Media, Entertainment and Arts Alliance—the union representing journalists—has issued sporadic statements, condemning the Australian government's support for Israel's "genocide assault on Gaza", a handful of media releases calling for the safety of journalists, and the creation of a solidarity fund in 2024. But that's it.

From within the ABC—the *unpublic* public broadcaster—there has been some level of *concern*, with News Director Justin Stevens publicly *urging* Israel to allow international journalists—especially the Palestinian freelancers the ABC relies upon—to move freely in and out of Gaza. The ABC's Middle East correspondent, Matthew Doran, recently described the physical toll on these freelancers, including one who lost 34 kilograms and was too weak to hold a camera or even speak. Yet even within these acknowledgements, there was the obvious omission: no explicit reference to the killings of journalists, and no attribution to Israel for being responsible for this. Whether this silence stems from editorial disinterest, fear of political backlash, or direct pressure from media executives, the result is pretty much the same—the most dangerous campaign against journalists in living memory—possibly ever—and Australia's mainstream media journalists, for most part, just want to pretend that it's *just not happening.*

THE LAST WORD WILL BELONG TO PALESTINE

The history of modern war reporting shows a slow but steady tightening of state control over the media. For many journalists, the Vietnam War was the high-water mark for reporting from a conflict zone—reporters moved freely between sides, spoke directly with civilians and soldiers alike, and were rarely targeted—although, clearly, journalists did die while reporting on the conflict.

Of course, this openness proved to be catastrophe for the public image of the United States, as the uncensored coverage eroded domestic support for the war in the U.S. and, ultimately, helped to end the presidency of Lyndon Johnson, who decided not to run again for office in the 1968 U.S. election campaign. In the decades since, governments have learned from those experiences of the Vietnam War that information and soft power can be more destructive than the *actual* firepower. Since that time, media access to conflict zones has been increasingly restricted, from the Pentagon's "embedding" program during the 1991 Gulf War to more recent policies warning that the safety of journalists could not "be guaranteed", effectively excluding them from these zones.

Israel has taken these measures to an extreme. Since October 2023, all foreign journalists have been banned from entering Gaza, leaving coverage to the internal Palestinian reporters already on the inside—journalists who then became direct targets for the Israeli military. At the same time, Israel maintains some of the most restrictive media control laws in the world; its High Court upheld the government's right to limit press activity in Gaza on the grounds of "operational security" and broader "strategic goals"—provisions so broad they allow for the removal of any outlet that Israel chooses, and for any reason, whether it be a factual or fabricated reason. These legal frameworks reinforce near-total control of the narrative: preventing coverage of their war crimes, enforcing pre-approved footage, and silencing dissenting voices.

The killing of journalists in Gaza is more than a tragic by-product of war—it's a direct attack on the important principle of bearing witness. The leaders of the wars in Bosnia in the early 1990s—Slobodan Milošević, Ratko Mladić and Radovan Karadžić—were found guilty of crimes against humanity largely because of the massive weight of evidence that was documented by the actions of many brave independent journalists who upheld those key principles of journalism: *speak truth to power* and make people in positions of this power accountable for their actions.

It's unacceptable conduct for any state, let alone one that presents itself as the "sole" democracy in the Middle East (even though it's not) with a supposedly free press. If Israel considers its actions in Gaza to be defensible, why not allow unrestricted media access and then we can see for ourselves? If its accusations linking reporters such as al-Sharif to Hamas leadership are true, why not present credible evidence? For a state celebrated for its intelligence capabilities and surveillance reach, especially the draconian control over the Palestinian people in Gaza and West Bank, the absence of any proof at all is quite telling.

These repeated claims, unsupported by verifiable evidence, function as propaganda designed to justify otherwise indefensible actions. But despite the suppression, the intimidation and the killings, Israel's control over the narrative is fraying and falling apart quite quickly, with Israeli

Prime Minister Benjamin Netanyahu now facing a global shift in political will.

The Prime Minister, Anthony Albanese, recently announced that Australia will recognise the state of Palestine at the United Nations meeting of the General Assembly in September and said that it's a step towards a long-overdue recognition that is needed to end the violence in Gaza and the West Bank.

Predictably, Netanyahu has condemned such moves from Australia and European nations as "shameful", insisting they won't alter Israel's stance in Gaza. But that's what he always says, and we've come to expect this from a leader who shouldn't be speaking as the Prime Minister of Israel but speaking at the dock at the International Criminal Court in The Hague, and taking up his place in the hall of infamy, alongside all the other war criminals who have been indicted by the Court.

Palestine has been disappointed by the international community many times before, ever since the disaster of the Balfour Declaration was released in 1917, the document that gave rise to the misguided colonialist Zionist project of Israel and set itself on a path of continuous genocide. There's no guarantee that this disappointment won't continue.

But the point is that the symbolism of Albanese's announcement can't be ignored: the weight of numbers is there, and Australia will join the other 147 countries around the world that have decided to be on the right side of history, even if it has taken some of these countries some time to work this out. It also indicates that despite Israel continuing to silence and kill many Palestinian journalists who have been reporting from Gaza, the truth will find a way to come to the surface, as it always does. Their efforts haven't been in vain.

***

AUSTRALIA TO RECOGNISE PALESTINE: WILL ANYTHING CHANGE?

16 August 2025

The Prime Minister Anthony Albanese has announced that Australia will formally recognise the state of Palestine at the upcoming United Nations General Assembly in September, framing the decision as an overdue and humane step toward advancing a two-state solution—"humanity's best hope to break the cycle of violence in the Middle East" as he put it—alleviating the humanitarian catastrophe and ending the genocide in Gaza.

However, his announcement wasn't without conditions: Albanese made it clear that Australia's recognition is "predicated on commitments Australia has received from the Palestinian Authority"—specifically, that Hamas is excluded from any future role in government, a demilitarised Gaza, and holding democratic elections as soon as practically possible, as well as implementing a range of other reforms.

Foreign Minister Penny Wong also suggested that recognition is dependent on pledges made in the past by the Palestinian Authority and other Arab nations in the region, and stated that it's Australia's intention to work with other international partners to hold *them* to account. It's important to acknowledge that within this "two-state" solution, there are *no conditions* being placed upon Israel to accept a state of Palestine, or to demilitarise, or any other reforms: as usual, everyone else is asked to accommodate the desires of the international community, but Israel isn't required to do anything at all.

And, as if to provide himself with cover, Albanese stressed that although Australia's decision is an independent act of a country acting in its own national interest, the decision also aligns with similar moves by other countries such as France, the U.K., and Canada, also adding that Australia wouldn't be dictated to by its allies—including the United States—although he did recognise the influential role of the U.S. in Middle East diplomacy.

This recognition, albeit long overdue, marks a significant shift in Australia's foreign policy in the Middle East, leaving behind the decades of delay on this issue and placing Australia alongside the 148 UN member states that have already acknowledged Palestinian statehood, despite the fact that full UN membership remains blocked due to the U.S. vetoing these decisions at the Security Council.

Of course, domestic and international reactions have been divided. Critics—including Israel's Prime Minister Benjamin Netanyahu and influential U.S. figures such as the Secretary of State, Marco Rubio—denounced the move as premature, claiming it rewards Hamas and undermines peace efforts. Right-wing Jewish groups within Australia such as the Executive Council of Australian Jewry and the extremist Australian Jewish Association have warned of potential ramifications for the Jewish community within Australia, while sections of the Liberal Party have already promised to reverse this recognition if re-elected at future elections, although based on their current electoral standing, this is unlikely to happen for some time to come.

Conversely, the progressive Jewish Council of Australia, human rights advocates and Palestinian solidarity organisations have applauded the decision, although many have suggested that it's only a symbolic gesture unless followed up with stronger action—including sanctions, arms embargoes, and accountability for war crimes and human rights abuses committed by the state of Israel and the Israel Defence Forces.

THE PROMISED LAND: THE LONG ROAD TO PALESTINIAN STATEHOOD

Australia is now scheduled to recognise the state of Palestinian but this is the latest turn in a decades-long saga that can be traced back to the unfulfilled promise when the United Nations was first created. In 1947, the UN General Assembly adopted Resolution 181—commonly known as the "Partition Plan"—specifically proposing the creation of two independent Arab and Jewish states in the British Mandate territory, with Jerusalem placed under international administration.

This is the international fact that many in the Western world—and within Israel—choose to ignore. Yet, despite the adoption of this resolution, the plan—as unjust as it was for Palestinian interests anyway—was never realised: Palestinian statehood of any kind has remained elusive since 1947, replaced with conflict and Israel's forever wars, and blocking the two-state structure that was envisioned by the international community.

Australia, as a UN member and active participant during those deliberations, supported the Partition resolution and, in doing this, played a big role in the establishment of Israel while backing the idea of a Palestinian state at the same time. Why did this plan never materialise? Why did the international community deliver the promised lands for Israel—which now far exceeds what was decided in 1947—but not for Palestine?

Albanese's announcement, historically, isn't an anomaly, but a continuation of what commenced in 1947. Certainly, even implementing what was agreed to by the international community almost 80 years ago isn't a just solution for Palestine, but it has to be a start in resolving this ongoing conflict and crimes against humanity perpetrated by Israel— as well as the many unresolved structural and political challenges that were initially created by the British empire, going back all the way to the Balfour Declaration of 1917.

Of course, there must be an accountable government— free elections in Palestine, remembering that the last free election in Palestine in 2006 resulted in a victory for Hamas— there also needs to be the reconstruction of Gaza, the removal of settlers from the West Bank, and meaningful international mechanisms that can be enforced by the United Nations. Israel, along with the leadership of Benjamin Netanyahu, must face accountability—whether through reparations, criminal courts, sanctions, or other means to force a shift in behaviour, because Israel is going to be the biggest road blockage in the pathway to a permanent peace.

Is it a case of being careful for what we wish for? Recent international history suggests that recognition alone won't stop this conflict—in fact, it could *escalate* it. For instance, the recognition of Croatia in 1991 didn't end hostilities immediately; war persisted for many months. Similarly, international moves toward the recognition of Bosnia– Herzegovina in 1992 resulted in a brutal three-year conflict and genocide. As was the case in Cyprus in the 1960s and in East Timor in the late 1990s, the recognition of peoples or a state needs to be supported with strong international support, otherwise there's no point.

Looking beyond this step by Albanese, it also provides Australia with an opportunity to play a more active role within international diplomacy, and influence the next phase through a commitment to peacekeeping solutions. Despite what the electorate might think about our political leaders, Australia has one of the best democratic systems of government in the world, and it's only right that it attempts to export this to other parts of the globe. One plausible model would be the sustained deployment of UN peacekeepers in the territories, as suggested by Senator Jacqui Lambie—similar to the long-term missions in Cyprus and Kosovo—to maintain security, monitor borders, and support civil administrations.

Whatever the case is, Israel's system of apartheid has to be *dismantled*. The civilian casualty rates are appalling: since the creation of Israel in 1948, the ratio of Palestinians killed through political and military action is around 10:1, and since October 2023, the ratio might now be as high as 500:1, perhaps even higher, when taking into account the unknown number of people in Gaza who have never been found, and are probably covered under rubble.

While acknowledging Hamas's 7 October attack (and yes, we do have to keep acknowledging this to avoid being accused of ignoring the pain of Israel) there is absolutely no justification that exists for Israel's actions to apply a disproportionate force and continued civilian suffering that many around the world have correctly labelled as a genocide. *None whatsoever.*

THE COALITION KEEPS DIGGING A DEEP HOLE FOR ITSELF

As to be expected, the recognition of Palestine has quickly become political theatre and an issue there to be exploited by the Liberal Party for base political purposes. As demonstrated by Peter Dutton in the lead up to the 2025 federal election, this is what the Liberal Party do, and have not much else to offer. *Division and chaos*, that's about it: the wallflowers of Australian politics that the electorate no longer wants to engage with.

Opposition Leader Sussan Ley and her colleagues in the Liberal Party—including Angus Taylor, Michaelia Cash and Dave Sharma—have launched vocal opposition to the government's decision to recognise Palestine. Ley has gone so far to pledge that, if elected, the Coalition would revoke this recognition—rhetoric that's been relayed straight from the mouths of the Israel and Zionist lobby in Australia, and is more about political posturing rather than credible policy, given the complexities around reversing such a decision.

It's important to note that Ley was once a co-convenor of the bipartisan Parliamentary Friends of Palestine group—a position she shared with Albanese over two decades ago—but she has now reversed her opinions, aligning herself with a pro-Israel stance and, based on current political opinions within the electorate, will continue the downward spiral of the Liberal Party towards political oblivion.

The March for Humanity across Sydney Harbour Bridge a few weeks ago attracted up to 300,000 *pro-humanity* supporters, a powerful signal that suggests that the issue of Palestine has broken free from the levels of fringe activism and entered the mainstream, despite the attempts by the media to still portray this as a marginal issue that not too many people care about.

And this suggestion isn't hearsay; it's backed up by polling. A recent Demos survey conducted in July found that 45 per cent of Australians now support formal recognition of Palestinian statehood, and that's twice as many as those opposed (just 23 per cent). YouGov polling has found similar levels of support and, even among Liberal voters, support for Israel is waning.

While Albanese's latest diplomatic announcement might be too late in this process—by about 78 years—at least it aligns with a strong and shifting sentiment within the Australian public increasingly sympathetic to Palestinian statehood. Meanwhile, the Liberal Party, led by Sussan Ley, wants to remain firmly stuck to their positions of the past, even as the electorate—and history—moves ahead at a rapid pace. It's their loss.

***

WHEN JOURNALISM BECOMES PUBLIC RELATIONS

16 August 2025

The Australian mainstream media continues its descent into irrelevancy and complete compromise, especially when it comes to its coverage of Israel and Palestine. Once seen as important check on the excesses of political and corporate power, much of media press is now less concerned about the truth and more about siding up with and protecting those vested interests. The *Sydney Morning Herald*, for example, has been running many stories that align almost perfectly with the messaging from pro-Israel lobby groups, and when the inaccuracies or distortions are exposed—as occurred last week—they've been quick to retreat or quietly amend these articles without any accountability at all. This pattern isn't just a bit of casual sloppiness: it's an insidious link between media organisations, powerful lobby groups, and the political class.

Journalists who report in a way that expresses even the smallest and tokenistic support for Palestine, are punished, sidelined or sacked, as journalist Antoinette Lattouf found out in 2023, when she lost her job for social media comments that were made *outside of her actual job* that were deemed to be too sympathetic towards Palestine. In a similar incident, cricket journalist Peter Lalor was sacked for offering comments about the acts of genocide committed by Israel, even though—again—his comments were made far away from the confines of a broadcast studio. These experiences show how, in Australia, press freedom is conditional and transactional: a robust interrogation and discussion of almost every other issue that we can think of, but non-existent when the subject of Palestine is brought up.

This selective application raises a deeper question about the industry itself. Journalism is meant to be *fearless*, reporting *without favour* and prepared to *confront* the powerful—speaking *truth to power*; that's the main game. When reporters are forced out for telling uncomfortable truths, even when they're speaking these truths in some distant parts of social media, the profession risks collapsing into little more than a public relations scheme for those in authority—Orwell's suggestion that "journalism is printing what someone else does not want printed" still remains relevant: when journalists fail in that duty, they are no longer journalists at all, but *propagandists*, and we're seeing a lot of that within Australia's mainstream media.

The contrast with the experience of Palestinian journalists could not be more different. In Australia, those who speak up risk losing their careers. That's bad enough but in Palestine, they risk *losing their lives*. Hundreds of reporters, photographers, and media workers have been killed in Gaza and the West Bank while performing the craft of journalism.

Conversely, any unwavering support for Israel carries no professional penalty in Australian newsrooms—in fact, it's actually encouraged—while the slightest micromillimetre of deviation away from Israel and in support of Palestinian rights is career-ending. If such standards were applied evenly, there would be very few journalists left in mainstream Australian media at all—while that might be a good thing, it just means that at the moment, there's not much difference between a journalist and a propagandist.

MANUFACTURED LIES AND COMMERCIAL CONSIDERATIONS

The tension between the ethics of journalism and commercial reality has always shaped the media landscape—we did see a lot this after Indonesia annexed East Timor in 1975, where reports by the Fairfax journalist David Jenkins were frequently filed but rarely published—but nowhere is it more extreme than the reporting on Israel and Palestine.

News executives know that advertisers can be quick to withdraw their campaigns if their coverage begins to question Israel's actions or show sympathy for Palestinian civilians—or be dealing with yet another Zionist lobbyist from the wealth class screaming down the barrel of the phone to demand the sacking of a journalist who might have written something mildly critical of the state of Israel.

This commercial pressure shouldn't override the fundamental obligation to truth, yet too often it does. For most news executives and journalists, *it's just a job*: just do as you're told, reduce the paths of resistance, and everyone can just go home at the end of the day, safe in the knowledge that the entire editorial team will still be on the invitation list for Christmas drinks in Bellevue Hill. The result is a media culture where maintaining relationships with powerful lobby groups and protecting advertising revenue takes precedence over accuracy, fairness, and integrity.

This pressure sometimes manifests itself in subtle editorial choices, but at other times it crosses into outright fabrication. The episode involving the *Herald*'s recent report on Hamas is an excellent example of how propaganda becomes the news. The outlet published a story claiming that Sheik Hassan Yousef, a founding member of Hamas, had praised Prime Minister Anthony Albanese for recognising the state of Palestine. The problem was that the claim was obviously false: Yousef has been imprisoned in Israel for many years, with no ability to communicate freely with the media, let alone deliver their commentary to a gormless and compromised journalist in Australia, chewing their lunch looking out over the splendid views of Sydney's Pyrmont Harbour. Yet the story ran in the *Herald* in loud headlines and was soon amplified across the country by News Corporation (of course), the ABC, *The Guardian* and SBS.

It took little more than a basic search to establish that the story was fabricated—no Arabic or English source material existed, and no credible journalist had made such contact. Yet the piece was framed as though direct contact had been made with the journalist in question, Matthew Knott. When the fabrication was exposed, primarily through independent commentators on social media and independent journalists who know how to use basic search engines on the internet, the *Herald* quietly rewrote the article without acknowledgement of the error. Instead of a transparent correction, the story doubled down and was reshaped to obscure their failures.

This continued on the ABC's *Insiders*, where Nine Media's James Massola—a colleague of Knott's—attempted to smooth over the debacle by suggesting it was a "cock-up" rather than deliberate propaganda, just reworked as a minor mistake and *no big deal*: it was better to offer lame excuses than admit to an obvious failure. In contrast to this feckless behaviour, journalists in Gaza and conflict zones all around the world put their lives on the line to hold power to account.

What do Australian journalists do? Too many are in the role of stenographers for state power, presenting propaganda as fact and happy to be part of the very structures they should be interrogating ruthlessly. The cost of their inaction isn't only to individual careers and reputations—there won't be any problems for these mainstream journalists; they'll be able to retire in a life of comfort and be able to regale to each other about all the times they managed to trick the public— but the true cost is to public trust in journalism itself.

If it wasn't for independent media, these falsehoods and fabrications would have gone unnoticed, and recorded as fact. And many Australians still rely on mainstream media as a record of fact at face value, even though it's a reputation that is totally undeserved. This grip on the so-called "truth" means that propaganda—if repeated often enough—becomes indistinguishable from reality and an accepted part of the truth, even though it's not.

A story about Hamas allegedly praising Albanese just fell apart after a simple inspection by social media and citizen journalists, but the damage had already been done: the *Herald*'s actions left an impression that the recognition of Palestine is linked to terrorism, and that supporting Palestinian statehood is also supporting extremists. That was the goal of the *Sydney Morning Herald*, and they achieved this in spades.

It's not just misleading but it's also destructive of the body politic—even if Hamas were to welcome international recognition of Palestine, it shouldn't invalidate the decision of the Albanese government. But the story was framed to discredit Albanese's move by association with terrorism, and not to inform the public: it was propaganda, pure and simple, dressed in journalism.

By stripping away any subtlety, the mainstream media ensures that audiences are offered little more than binary choices between black and white, or of *good* versus *evil*: there are no shades of grey in this discussion—to quote George W. Bush, "you are with us, or you are with the terrorists". This is not journalism, but the construction of a narrative that serves political power. And unless independent voices continue to question and contest these distortions, Australia will be left with little more than manufactured lies masquerading as the truth.

SILENCING PALESTINE BEYOND THE NEWSROOM

As we have seen many times, the reach of the conservative pro-Israel lobby in Australia reaches far beyond the newsroom and, because control over media narratives is never going to be enough, cultural spaces have to become the battleground. Universities, writer's festivals, and literary gatherings—institutions traditionally dedicated to free expression and a contest of ideas—are increasingly being pressured into silence, with the aim of not just stifling criticism of Israel, but to erase Palestine from the public conversation altogether.

The Bendigo Writers Festival was established in 2012 and celebrates writing and storytelling by "bringing together writers, readers, and creative thinkers from diverse backgrounds and genres". It's a successful regional event and over the past thirteen years, it has invited many authors and intellectuals from Australia and all around the globe to discuss the contemporary cultural issues in this complex world we live in. But no event is too small or too far away for the belligerent and chauvinist Israel lobby to shut down any discussion about Palestine.

Perhaps thinking that they were in the back streets of Gaza City and ready to launch yet another rocket attack on innocent civilians, a pro-Israel academic group known as "the 5A" mounted an aggressive campaign against the participation of Palestinian–Australian author Randa Abdel-Fattah. Just days before the festival, 5A accused her of anti-Semitism and extremism, branding her "a racist" and "a direct threat to the Jewish community in Australia". 5A has long lobbied universities to suppress pro-Palestinian activism, and after their pressure in Bendigo was successful, Abdel-Fattah withdrew from the event in protest—how could she not?—

and more than 50 other writers followed suit, objecting to a new code of conduct that banned "inflammatory" or "divisive" topics.

The boycott left the festival in ruins due to the last-minute intervention by 5A, and the cowardly acceptance of this pressure from La Trobe University. What should have been three days of debate and celebration of ideas, descended into chaos, with panels removed and programs cancelled.

Universities should be a place of intellectual inquiry, not rolling over at the first sign of external pressure. Worse still, many Australian institutions have become complicit in their quest to save face with these Zionist tyrants, sacrificing their own principles to avoid controversy. And while conservative groups dominate the discourse, the voices of progressive Jewish Australians—many of whom oppose the occupation and support Palestinian rights—are routinely ignored.

But a democracy that silences writers, punishes journalists, and rewrites news to appease lobbyists is a democracy that has lost confidence in its own values. The 5A group claimed that the Bendigo Writers Festival was not "a safe space" for Jewish people, but where was the safety for everyone else who was subjected to this imperious and bigoted assault on their freedoms to listen to perspectives from Palestinian people? Why is their safety—or the safety of Palestinian people—never up for consideration?

This intellectual dishonesty breeds resentment, mistrust, and fear, while wiping out the possibility of honest engagement. It's a disturbing development in Australian public life: one where power dictates what can be said, who can speak, and what stories can be told, whether it's within the mainstream media, or a literary festival in a regional city.

If there is to be any hope of reversing this development, Australians needs courage from their institutions and honesty from their media; that universities foster debate rather than suppress it, and that journalism return to its core duty of holding power to account. Otherwise, what is the point? For too long, these Zionist lobbyists have dictated the limits of acceptable conversation. To defend free expression is not to endorse every idea, but to protect the space in which ideas can be contested in. The alternative is *silence*—preferred, of course, by the Zionist lobby—but as history has always shown us, silence is the ally of the oppressor.

***

NETANYAHU'S INSTABILITY AS AUSTRALIA START TO ACT

23 August 2025

The endless devastation and genocide in Gaza has finally started to cause unrest within Israel—sure, it's not a popular movement yet but they're belatedly seeing what the rest of the world has been seeing for almost two years—and the alarm bells are ringing all across the world, leaving the Prime Minister of Israel Benjamin Netanyahu increasingly isolated.

For two years, Netanyahu has aggressively sought international support for his actions in Gaza and has fended off most criticisms, but it's reached a point now where it's impossible for any country to defend the actions of Israel, especially after the Integrated Food Security Phase Classification was made by the United Nations that Israel is causing a famine in Gaza, "a man-made disaster" according to UN Secretary-General António Guterres, and "a failure of humanity itself".

Allies who had long stood firmly behind Israel are stepping away—bar the United States and a few other compromised nations—and Australia has become one of the more visible examples of this shift. Prime Minister Anthony Albanese recently announced that Australia will formally recognise Palestine at the UN general assembly meeting in September, and this marked a significant departure from decades of cautious diplomacy—very predictably—Netanyahu reacted with fury, lashing out at Albanese by calling him a "weak politician" who had "betrayed Israel" and abandoned Australia's Jewish community. This outburst came after Australia also refused entry to Simcha Rothman, a member of Israel's far right and ultranationalist political party Mafdal-Religious Zionism—surely, Australia has the right to refuse entry to unacceptable miscreants, especially if their sole purpose to create mischief and promote Netanyahu's political agenda overseas.

For Netanyahu, his reaction wasn't just about Australia's decision but about domestic politics back home. Facing escalating protests, corruption charges, and an increasingly fragile grip on power, he has sought to paint Albanese as an enemy of Israel so he can rally his own supporters—as well as some Australian citizens who are eligible to vote in Israeli elections. It's a familiar right-wing tactic: amplify external threats to shore up fragile authority at home, and while that might work in Israel, the strategy has backfired locally and encouraged even more people to support Australia's actions.

On the weekend, an estimated 350,000 people participated in nationwide marches demanding Palestinian recognition and accountability for Israel's actions in Gaza, one of the largest co-ordinated protests in recent Australian history, and a major shift in public sentiment that can't be ignored by the political establishment. Certainly, Australia has been highly and mysteriously uncritical of the Israel government over the past two years, but surely that has its limits—governments that ignore these types of national actions ignore them at their own peril. And far from isolating Albanese, Netanyahu's attacks seemed only to strengthen the resolve of the government.

Home Affairs Minister Tony Burke captured the mood last week, when he said that "strength is not measured by how many people you can blow up or how many children you can leave hungry", but in the courage to take principled decisions even when they are unpopular with powerful allies—and he went on to offer a clear message to Palestinians: "you are not invisible, we see you"—an odd comment, considering it's almost been two years of the Australian government mostly ignoring the suffering of the people of Gaza and *not* seeing them, and doing everything possible to overlook the crimes against humanity and genocide being carried out by the state of Israel.

The nation-wide marches—as well as the recent Sydney Harbour Bridge March for Humanity, where around 300,000 people attended—shows that protest and public pressure do matter. The massive marches, disturbing images of starving children in Gaza, and the increasingly unreasonable and authoritative demands from the defenders of Zionism—such as the special envoy on anti-Semitism, Jillian Segal—have sent a clear signal to the Albanese government that the public wants more decisive action against Israel and more moral clarity on what everyone else can see with their own eyes.

The irony is that Netanyahu's attempt to cast Albanese as weak has only highlighted his own weaknesses. It's too early to claim that Australia will now act more decisively on Palestine but, at least where it might have previously offered stubborn hesitation, it is now starting to take on more tangible actions, instead of the bluff and blustering, or claiming that it's all too 'difficult to see from afar to judge'—as Foreign Minister Penny Wong suggested in 2023—or mindlessly suggesting Israel has a 'right to defend itself' while implementing starvation as a weapon of war and a genocide against the people of Palestine.

A DISCREDITED LEADER AND THE QUESTION OF SANCTIONS

Albanese now has the political cover to act more stridently on Palestine and against Israel. Netanyahu's political fortunes are in freefall: his authority is crumbling, with waves of mass protests across Tel Aviv and other Israeli cities reflecting deep public anger at his leadership. Internationally, his standing is even weaker. His reputation among European leaders has become toxic, and the International Criminal Court has issued an arrest warrant against him for alleged war crimes— hardly the type of international leader that Albanese would want to be supportive of.

If it wasn't half obvious before, every act by Netanyahu is designed to deflect attention away from Israel's domestic and economic turmoil, from his own charges of corruption, and the genocide in Gaza. Even in Australia, he's become so toxic that conservative Jewish lobby groups are distancing themselves from him, because they've realised that supporting such a discredited leader will damage their own credibility.

Labor backbencher Ed Husic has been one of the most consistent and outspoken advocates for stronger measures— at least since he became a backbencher—that Australia mustn't just "express concern" but needs to hold Israel to account and implement sanctions. This week, he repeated this call, referring directly at the suffering in Gaza.

"We need to work with our trusted friends and allies internationally in terms of sanctions," Husic said. "A lot of our sanctions so far are focused on activity in the West Bank but looking at what's happening in Gaza, we do need to hold decision makers to account. We should remain open minded about sanctions ... people are still suffering from starvation and the Netanyahu government doesn't seem to want to take a change of approach."

This momentum around sanctions is significant. For years, they were dismissed as unrealistic, a fringe suggestion from a radical Greens–BDS movement, and too extreme for an Australian government to consider against Israel. Yet with little sign of a policy change from Netanyahu, sanctions are increasingly being seen as the only international instrument that will influence his behaviour, because it seems that nothing else is working. Certainly, sanctions are a slow-moving instrument, but they do work eventually—and at the least, the discussion itself shows how a fringe idea from just a few years ago has moved into mainstream thinking.

While Netanyahu is the classic and stubborn right-wing 'do-whatever-it-takes' survivor of Israeli politics, there is a realisation that he's not going to survive politically for too much longer. Observers who have tracked his career since the 1990s, and who long warned of his authoritarian tendencies and overreach, can now see his demise quickly approaching. And within politics, when the end arrives, it arrives *very quickly*.

Whether his departure comes through legal prosecution, political overthrow, or internal party revolt, it's uncertain how much longer Netanyahu will remain as Israel's leader, with a splintering and fragmented coalition, and elections due before October 2026. His carefully constructed image as a strongman has crumbled to the point where even long-standing supporters no longer see him as an asset.

PUBLIC OPINION IS SURGING AHEAD OF POLITICAL LEADERS

Australia's shift—albeit a slow shift—is symbolic of a wider reassessment of the politics in the Arab World and a better understanding of the toxicity of Netanyahu's leadership and policies, and the recognition of Palestine is part of a broader shift where many longstanding allies of Israel are beginning to question their unequivocal support.

Some of this reflects the slow but unmistakable movement of a changing international order, where incompetent leaders who thrive on conflict are no longer given a free pass. Australia has been good at moving on these types of leaders—Tony Abbott, Scott Morrison and, more recently, Peter Dutton—Brazil too—but other political systems such as the United States, who reinstalled a clearly incompetent, unstable and divisive President Trump, have not yet worked this out.

While diplomatic processes move slowly—often frustratingly so—the cultural and political undercurrents are moving quickly. People in many countries, including Australia, are just refusing to accept the narratives that have been dished out in the past: they're demanding accountability, justice and a different way of solving problems, not the top-down practices of the past where governments take on the 'here are our policies, sit down, shut up, and just accept them' approach. Those days are over.

The Nationwide March for Palestine was one of these moments. While the media downplayed the numbers as "tens of thousands" (the *Herald Sun* in Melbourne suggested even less, reporting just "hundreds" of protesters), the reality was undeniable: hundreds of thousands of Australians from diverse backgrounds, took to the streets to support the recognition of Palestine, immediate sanctions on Israel, and an end to the famine and destruction in Gaza. *The public has had enough*.

This mobilisation also suggests a deeper frustration within the Australian community: that successive governments—Liberal–National and Labor—have too often acceded to the demands of small but powerful right-wing lobby groups who are determined to shield Israel from criticism, primarily because any critique of Israel undermines their belief that Palestine doesn't exist, and undermines the ethos of Israel as *a land without a people for a people without a land*, surely the most extreme definition of *terra nullius* ever, and the underlying logic that's created the pathway for the genocide currently underway in Gaza.

The public has also had enough of the continuous calls for new laws to silence dissent on behalf of Israel, of equating criticism of Israel with anti-Semitism, and the suppression of any discussion of war crimes and apartheid, which they can clearly see occurring on a daily basis. In a democratic country, the public sees such attempts as unacceptable, and these mass protests are a result of this. If Australia claims to uphold universal human rights, then it cannot apply them selectively at the behest of powerful interests. Palestinians, too, must be entitled to those rights: *that's what the Australia public is saying*.

The public can also see the footage of famine and starving children, cities blown to smithereens, the double and triple standards of international diplomacy. They want action; that much is clear. For Albanese and his government, the decision to recognise Palestine might just be the first step in a much broader process of matching up policy with principle but governments acting without principle, even if they do have a massive majority—won't hold public support for too much longer, as we are seeing with Keir Starmer's Labour government in the U.K., who are now lagging behind in opinion polls to a tinpot Reform UK and an unnamed and a not-yet-formed political party that could be led by Jeremy Corbyn and Zarah Sultana. And this is after the Labour Party secured their largest ever victory in the 2024 general election, just over a year ago.

While there are many other factors in Starmer's diabolical drop in opinion ratings—there are lessons for the Albanese government. Denying a just cause that has popular support and siding with the oppressor does have political ramifications, especially when the leadership of that oppressive and genocidal force has become so toxic.

Netanyahu's political collapse, both here and internationally, shows the limits of politics built on fear and manipulation: it might take a while for that limit to be reached, but it always gets there. As his influence wanes, the responsibility will shift to those who can shape what comes next. The pressure from the public—in Australia, in Europe, in the United States, and in Israel itself—has to be the constant reminder that leaders can no longer afford to ignore the demands for justice. History is moving quickly, and those who hold on to the politics of the past will be left far behind and will pay the political price.

***

THE TELEVISED GENOCIDE: WHAT WILL IT TAKE TO STOP IT?

26 August 2025

At least 20 people were killed in southern Gaza after Israel bombed the Nasser Hospital twice within the space of fifteen minutes, in a deliberate "double tap" strike, and this number includes five journalists and several rescue workers who rushed to help those wounded in the initial blast. This attack on yet another hospital and yet more journalists—broadcast on live television—has shocked audiences worldwide and has set off another wave of international condemnation against Israel.

The first missile struck the top floor of the hospital, killing Reuters journalist Hussam al-Masri, and as civil defence workers—clearly shown in bright orange vests—and fellow journalists scrambled to the site, a second strike hit at the same location. Footage broadcast by AlGhad TV shows rescuers and reporters shielding themselves from debris only seconds before the second explosion, which left their bodies piled together in the rubble, covered in blood and dust.

The journalists killed—who never seem to be mentioned by name in the Western media—were al-Masri; Mariam Abu Dagga from Associated Press; Al Jazeera journalist Mohammed Salam; photojournalist Moaz Abu Taha; and Ahmad Abu Aziz from Quds Feed. And the number of reporters killed by Israel since its military operations and genocide in Gaza began is now over 240, making it the deadliest conflicts for the media in modern history.

Of course, there has been international outrage—not yet from Australia, which still seems be too far away for Foreign Minister Penny Wong to understand what's really going on—but the real actions that can be taken are still missing. U.K. Foreign Secretary David Lammy said that he was "horrified by Israel's attack on Nasser Hospital," emphasising that civilians, health workers, and journalists must be protected under international law and calling (yet again) for an immediate ceasefire. French President Emmanuel Macron called the attack "intolerable," while the U.S. President Donald Trump would only say that he was "not happy about it".

Despite this outrage, the Israeli government just shrugged its shoulders and said the event as a "tragic mishap", with Prime Minister Benjamin Netanyahu expressing "deep regret" and promised a "thorough investigation"—investigations that either never occur or whitewash the evidence—while using the opportunity to claim hospitals in Gaza are used by Hamas for military purposes—a claim regularly made by Netanyahu but never substantiated with any verifiable evidence. Journalistic associations and human rights monitors have dismissed Israel's justifications and have said that the targeting of hospitals and the press points to a deliberate pattern, rather than isolated mistakes.

Legal experts have also suggested that the attack on Nasser Hospital constitutes multiple war crimes, with each element—the bombing of a functioning hospital, the killing of medical workers, the targeting of journalists, and the deliberate repetition of the strike on rescuers—representing a violation of international humanitarian law.

Too many journalists—and civilians—have been killed by Israel without any justification and the broadcast of these crimes should remove any lingering doubts about Israel's criminal intent. For many, the question now is not whether Israel has crossed the line of legality—that line was crossed some time ago and on so many occasions—but how long the international community will allow this genocide to continue without consequences for the rogue and pariah state of Israel.

IS AUSTRALIA'S LINKED TO LINKED TO THESE MASSACRES?

As these images from Gaza continue to shock people all around the world—endless footage showing the deaths of many children and innocent civilians tends to do this—the uncomfortable questions need to be continued to be asked: has Australia, directly or indirectly, supplied the weapons used in these atrocities? Prime Minister Anthony Albanese has repeatedly insisted that Australia does not export arms to Israel but mounting evidence contradicts Albanese's denials and raises serious concerns about Australian complicity.

In July, shipments of Australian-manufactured components for F-35 fighter jets were sent directly from Sydney to Tel Aviv, forming part of the global F-35 supply chain in which Australian defence companies play a significant role. The F-35 is central to Israel's air bombing campaign in Gaza, with precision-guided bombs and missiles launched from these squadrons repeatedly striking civilian infrastructure, including schools and hospitals. The Albanese government maintains that such parts are not weapons themselves but, as described by Minister Wong, "non-lethal components," a weak argument when those components directly enable warplanes responsible for mass civilian casualties.

Beyond the F-35 components, the Canberra-based defence contractor Electro Optic Systems has confirmed that it has sold its R400 remote weapon stations to Israel. Initially provided on loan for demonstration, the systems were later upgrade to "full sales", contradicting official claims that they were only under trial. A media release from Israel's Ministry of Defence located one of these demonstrations in the Negev desert, verifying the presence and testing of the Australian system on Israeli soil. By EOS's own admission, multiple R400 units were delivered before the current genocide commenced, creating a direct commercial link between Australian manufacturers and the Israeli Defence Forces.

Despite this, Albanese continues to deny that any weapons sales exist. Speaking on ABC Radio just yesterday, he downplayed Australia's role and reiterated: "Australia, of course, is not a major power in the Middle East. And in spite of some of the rhetoric which is out there, Australia, for example, does not provide arms to Israel." Yet, official government records reveal that as of August, at least 35 active military export permits to Israel remain in force. Senator Wong has confirmed these exports are being made to Israel, albeit under the guise of "non-lethal components". These permits cover a range of "defence and dual-use goods," and while the precise items remain undisclosed, but this information undermines the government's repeated public reassurances. Why does Albanese keep denying the undeniable facts?

This dissonance between rhetoric and reality has led to accusations that Australia is attempting to conceal the complicity of its defence involvement with Israel and the genocide in Gaza, and that's why it pays lip service to anything to do Palestine and drags its feet along the ground, until it's forced to do *something*. The refusal to acknowledge these exports not only misleads the public but shields Australian companies from future legal action regarding their role in alleged war crimes committed by Israel—Israel has repeatedly targeted hospitals, journalists, and humanitarian workers, and any foreign-supplied equipment enabling those attacks could fall under international legal responsibility.

Of course, there are many aspects of international relationships that need to be taken, including the fact that Australia, like Israel, is a colonial–settler project that performed its own acts of genocide and may find it difficult to condemn the actions of another state, when it was responsible for the same actions against Indigenous people from 1788 onwards.

These might be factors, but they are not excuses. The persistence of military exports in the face of overwhelming evidence of civilian slaughter raises the blunt question: how much more proof is required before Australia stops arming a regime accused of systemic violations of international law? How much of the filthy lucre will Australia accept from Israel? How much more proof does Australia need to force stronger action against Israel? When will Australia finally condemn Israel?

FROM RECOGNITION TO REAL ACTION

Recognition of Palestine at the United Nations in September—if it actually does occur—will be a historic step, but it won't in itself, stop the killing and massacres in Gaza. Israel has a long list of actions that have openly ignored international law and equally ignores any international condemnation that is made against it. But what will make Israel stop and take notice is a binding ceasefire, backed with accountability for everyone who has been responsible for this genocide, economic sanctions and decisive action to cut off the supply of arms and weapons to Israel Defense Forces.

The international community already has the legal tools available to it. The International Court of Justice has issued binding orders requiring Israel to facilitate humanitarian relief and halt operations in Rafah that risk annihilating Gaza's population. These rulings, however, haven't been enforced and the UN Security Council, paralysed by vetoes from the United States, has failed to act.

However, even a modest UN protection presence at Rafah and Kerem Shalom would save lives immediately and would be a start. Certainly, critics will point to events in Bosnia, Rwanda, Somalia and Sudan where the involvement of the UN was a dismal failure, but there have been other successes in East Timor, Cambodia, Mozambique and Cyprus that can be used for guidance. The point is that doing nothing is *not an option*. There are mechanisms that are available to the international community and these mechanisms must be used.

Accountability needs to be a central part of these mechanisms. The International Criminal Court has already confirmed arrest warrants for Netanyahu and Defence Minister Yoav Gallant. Member states are obligated to co-operate with the Court—arrests, evidence-sharing, and protection of judicial independence—yet political interference and the lack of recognition of the Court by the United States has slowed this momentum. Supporting the ICC, rather than undermining it, is the best way to show that international law applies equally to all. Alongside this, aid access must be fixed: many reviews have shown that the highly publicised maritime pier created under the Biden administration moved little food or medicine compared to what could be delivered by opening land crossings. Unlocking ground routes is the fastest, most practical humanitarian measure available.

Meanwhile, Australia needs to face up to its own moral failures. Diplomatic recognition of Palestine has to be linked with concrete actions if it is to carry any credibility. That needs to begin with a *total* cessation of defence exports to Israel, including components and dual-use items, alongside full transparency through publication of the active, suspended, and refused export permits.

The loopholes that currently allow Australian equipment and parts to reach Israel via subsidiaries or third countries have to be closed down. Australia should also broaden its Magnitsky-style sanctions—currently applied to just seven Israeli citizens and one entity in the West Bank—extending them beyond extremist settlers to include Israeli politicians and officials who have been responsible for unlawful attacks, war crimes, crimes against humanity, using starvation as a weapon of war, and incitement against Palestinians.

Australia must also unequivocal co-operate with the ICC and remove the discretion of the Attorney-General to block co-operation with the Court. Australia's own laws can also be applied to dual-Israeli citizens returning to Australia who may be implicated in war crimes.

Humanitarian support can also be properly reinstated for UNRWA, after it was halted by Minister Wong after unfounded claims by Israel that staff were involved in the October 2023 attacks by Hamas. Economic sanctions and refusing goods from Israeli settlements in the West Bank; and suspending companies that have been involved in any violations in Israel from government procurement contracts. These are all actions that Australia can and should take.

The role of the media also needs to be addressed. Within Australia's mainstream media, platforms are handed to Israeli officials under indictment or to propagandists, with little or no challenge from their hosts. Recent interviews with Netanyahu by Sharri Markson on Sky News, and propagandists Israel's Minister for Diaspora Affairs, Amichai Chikli and deputy Minister of Foreign Affairs, Sharren Haskel, on the ABC's *7.30*—despite active arrest warrants and international condemnation, reveal a disturbing willingness of Australia to normalise actual and accused war criminals, a situation that was well documented in Mark Aaron's book published in 2000, *War Criminals Welcome: Australia, a Sanctuary for Fugitive*

War Criminals Since 1945. Holding media accountable for amplifying such voices without scrutiny is an essential part of confronting the broader culture of impunity.

The Foreign Press Association has called the Nasser Hospital killings a "watershed moment," urging governments to act decisively to protect journalists and civilians. Whether that call is listened to will determine not just the future of Palestine, but also the credibility of the entire international legal order. If this international order cannot stop a genocide—one that we've been witnessing for the past two years—then what is the point of it?

The fastest pathway to stopping the killing is clear: enforce the ceasefire, guarantee access to aid, accountability backed by co-ordinated embargoes and sanctions that make it difficult for Israel to bypass. The laws and the precedents that can be applied, already exist: what is missing is the political will from the cowardly international leaders that do have the power act, but do nothing with that power. Australia has a choice: it can choose to continue to hide behind denials and ambiguous diplomatic statements, or step forward with action that matches its words. The world—and Palestine—can't afford to wait any longer.

***

THE SINKING CREDIBILITY OF ASIO

30 August 2025

Australia's decision to expel Iran's ambassador is the most dramatic diplomatic incident in over 80 years, with Prime Minister Anthony Albanese using ASIO assessments —announced by the Director-General of Security, Mike Burgess—to make a link that Iran was behind the arson attacks on the Jewish community in Sydney and Melbourne in late 2024. In Albanese's words, these were "extraordinary and dangerous acts of aggression orchestrated by a foreign nation on Australian soil," claiming that Tehran sought to undermine social cohesion and spread fear among Australian Jews.

On the surface, these allegations are serious, of course they are. The attacks—one at the Adass Israel Synagogue in Melbourne, the other at the Lewis Continental Kitchen in Bondi—were described as part of a broader pattern of hostility directed by Iran. Yet beyond the Prime Minister's carefully chosen words about "credible intelligence", there's many areas that need to be resolved, and much material that just doesn't make any sense. No evidence has been publicly presented to substantiate the broad claims from ASIO and, unlike the usual diplomatic processes, the ambassador was not summoned for consultation or given an opportunity to respond. Instead, Albanese moved directly to remove the ambassador, a rare and provocative action.

There are so many obvious contradictions: Albanese has consistently downplayed Australia's role in Middle Eastern affairs—as recently as last week—often defending his muted response to mass pro-Palestine marches and Israel's genocide in Gaza by insisting that "Australia is not a major player in the region", or in the case of Foreign Minister Penny Wong, her comments that it's difficult to "judge from afar" the grotesque actions of Israel. If that's the case, why suddenly elevate Australia's position by making it the first Western government in decades to expel an Iranian ambassador? And on such flimsy material presented to the public?

There is also the question of just how plausible it would be for Iran to be involved, which would gain nothing at all except for international opprobrium. Of course, Iran, like many authoritarian states, runs surveillance operations on its diaspora communities, including on the 85,000 Iranian Australians, many being dissidents who are hostile to the government of Tehran. But orchestrating crude arson attacks on local synagogues in Australia doesn't have any strategic relevance or importance.

Not only is there no precedent for Iran directing such attacks in Australia, but the incidents themselves were amateurish and clownish—fires that caused limited damage, allegedly carried out by hired bikies whose own text messages reveal incompetence rather than professional co-ordination. As notorious as Iran's Revolutionary Guard is, it's established methods involve large-scale, high-impact operations abroad— lighting fires at minor community sites is not its *modus operandi*, and would probably be insulted at being accused of such an incompetent act.

This narrative coming from ASIO is even more questionable when considering the nature of the targets—at least one synagogue affected was known for its anti-Zionist stance, making it an unlikely target for a regime that is vehemently *opposed to Israel*, rather than the Jewish religion itself.

The attack on the Lewis Continental Kitchen, a small kosher restaurant in Bondi, also raised further doubts—why choose a modest food business when larger, more symbolic Jewish institutions are nearby? The inconsistencies feed a belief that the Australian government is either overreacting, or—more likely—that there are other motives are at play.

Complicating these issues is the credibility of ASIO itself. This is the same intelligence agency that supported the false claims of weapons of mass destruction in Iraq in 2003, a "credible assessment" that justified an invasion and a war which killed over 200,000 people. Over 20 years later, Australians are being asked to "just trust the intelligence" once again, and it's understandable that they might be sceptical, especially when it involves an escalation with Iran, and possible another invasion and a war. Without transparency, ASIO's role looks less like a credible and analytical assessment and more like political theatre, where intelligence is being politicised to fit in with the policy objectives, either of Australia, or other international players.

Against this background, the timing of this expulsion also needs to be taken into account, coming just a week after Israeli Prime Minister Benjamin Netanyahu publicly berated Albanese for his intention to recognise Palestine at the upcoming meeting of the General Assembly at the United Nations. These events suggest the expulsion might be more about appeasing international relationships and managing domestic political pressure that any genuine national security threats.

INTELLIGENCE AND THE PALESTINE CONNECTION

While governments occasionally expel lower-ranking diplomats and declare them *persona non grata*, forcing an ambassador to leave is an extreme measure. Iran has already indicated that it will expel Australia's ambassador from Tehran in retaliation—perhaps a moot point, considering Australia already evacuated the diplomats before the announcement was made—and it has firmly rejected the allegations levelled by Australia.

The timing of this move also opens up more speculation. Albanese's decision to recognise Palestine at the United Nations drew condemnations from Israel and the United States but, in contrast, Iran strongly welcomed the move, as did its ambassador in Canberra. Was his expulsion a convenient way to silence his voice? Or could the situation provide Prime Minister Anthony Albanese with an excuse to backtrack from his promise to recognise Palestine? Albanese had already hedged his position by insisting recognition should proceed only in co-ordination with other states in the region and the acceptance of Israel's right to exist. Iran, of course, refuses to recognise Israel at all, making it an easy scapegoat if Albanese decides to delay or dilute his commitment, providing the Prime Minister with the political cover where he could argue that Iranian "aggression" makes it impossible to advance Palestinian statehood while maintaining Australia's credibility on security matters, however weak that might be.

There's also other inherent contradictions within Iran. Iran has the largest Jewish population in the Middle East outside of Israel, a population of around 10,000 people. While Jewish life within Iran is not free of restrictions, it is worth remembering that after the 1979 Revolution, Ayatollah Khomeini issued a *fatwa* to protect the Jewish communities who live inside Iran. Tehran's hostility has always been directed at Zionism as a political ideology and the Israeli state, not at Judaism as a religion, and this situation makes the claim that Iran would target a non-Zionist synagogue in Melbourne even more illogical.

The deeper concern is the way intelligence is being used here. Professional intelligence work requires solid sourcing, verifiable evidence, and rigorous analysis. But intelligence agencies also exist in a clouded political space—funded through secretive channels, operating through cut-outs and plausibly deniability, sometimes venturing into activities that governments always seem to deny. The record of agencies such as MI6 and the CIA shows how often intelligence has been politicised, manipulated, or simply wrong. But it hasn't stopped that intelligence from being used to justify nefarious ends, as shown through the "weapons of mass destruction" debacle in Iraq.

If this is the basis for expelling the ambassador, then Australia has moved once again into dangerous territory—using intelligence as a political weapon. Whether the target is Iran and a war that Israel and the United States have longed for over many years, or obstructing Palestinian statehood—or both—the consequences will be profound.

THE DOUBLE STANDARDS AND THE POLITICS OF BELIEF

There is also a severe diplomatic imbalance at play that many people in Australia have called out. Iran, accused without clear evidence of sponsoring two arson attacks that caused minimal damage—certainly no damage to human life—has faced the most serious diplomatic sanction Australia can impose, short of severing these relationships altogether. Meanwhile, Israel—accused of war crimes by the International Criminal Court, practicing a brutal form of apartheid, and accused of genocide by many reputable international bodies—faces nothing at all, never faces any condemnation or red lines that cannot be crossed and, if anything, is encouraged to continue its crimes against humanity, supported through yet another shipment of arms from Germany and United States, and F-35 parts provided by Australia.

Israel's bombing campaigns have killed more than 64,000 Palestinians—at the very least—including civilians, doctors, and journalists. The Australian aid worker, Zomi Frankcom, was killed by a deliberately targeted Israeli drone strike in Gaza in 2024, yet the Israeli ambassador is still there in Canberra, rescued by Albanese's infamous political caution, diplomatic inertia and a few words of "concern" from Foreign Minister Wong. In this context, the expulsion of Iran's ambassador is selective, and breathtakingly cynical.

The mainstream media, too, has largely fallen into line, amplifying ASIO's claims with hardly any scrutiny at all. Hard questions about the credibility of the evidence have been rare, and what little scepticism exists has been drowned out by the government's framing of events. This blind acceptance has a familiar ring to it and Australians have been here before: the Hilton Hotel bombing in 1978, where bungled intelligence led to wrongful arrests; the 2003 Iraq war, where false intelligence about weapons of mass destruction paved the way for invasion and mass slaughter; the debacle of Man Haron Monis, the terrorist behind the Lindt Café siege in 2014, who was also an ASIO operative.

Security services, like all human institutions, are imperfect, and there's no question that they will make mistakes. But when their judgments carry consequences as profound as unjustified wars, mass casualties, a siege in the heart of Sydney, or the unprecedented expulsion of an ambassador, there can't be any margin for error.

In practical terms, the fallout from this affair within itself, will be limited. Australia has doesn't have a significant trade with Iran, and the embassy's primary functions concern air travel, tourism, and consular assistance for dual citizens. The closing of the embassy might complicate the lives of the few Australians visiting family or touring Iran, and Iranian Australians dealing with paperwork or cultural exchanges.

But strategically, the expulsion achieves little. It doesn't weaken Iran's regional position, nor does it advance Australian security in any meaningful way. What it does achieve though is symbolic theatre: a show of resolve directed not so much at Tehran, but at domestic audiences and international allies.

The Australian government will claim that it has acted out of security necessity, but in reality it has exposed itself to accusations of hypocrisy, politicisation, and subservience to allies. Expelling an ambassador on the flimsiest of grounds, while excusing far graver offences by Israel, undermines the credibility of both the government and its intelligence services. This is a decision that won't be remembered as a principled defence of Australia's sovereignty, but as another moment when intelligence was used as a political weapon, and the truth was left far behind.

***

FROM KNESSET TO COUNCIL:
THINK GLOBAL, INFLUENCE LOCAL

6 September 2025

The recent Australian Mayors Summit Against Antisemitism was presented as a "community safety initiative" but its agenda was far more political than that. Over several days on the Gold Coast, local mayors and councillors from across the country were given all-expenses-paid trips to hear from speakers carefully chosen by the US-based Combat Antisemitism Movement to push their particular agenda. While the event advertised the idea that it was address anti-Semitism within Australia, in reality, it was a platform designed to discourage criticism of Israel and its ongoing genocide in Gaza.

The Movement, which organised and financed the Summit, is heavily funded by Republican-aligned donors in the United States and has a history of targeting pro-Palestinian academics, attacking human rights organisations, and amplifying political rhetoric and attacks against the United Nations.

Its ultimate goal is to universally implement the International Holocaust Remembrance Alliance's definition of anti-Semitism—a definition that many legal experts and civil liberties groups warn is being used to link critiques of Israel with anti-Semitic hate speech, which would then be used to legally sanction anyone who makes any kind of criticism of Zionism or Israel's genocidal actions in Gaza.

Australia's Special Envoy for Antisemitism, Jillian Segal—who incidentally has been very quiet about the recent spate of neo-Nazi fascist attacks throughout Australia—was a keynote speaker at the event and has been one of the most vocal advocates for embedding this definition into public policy. Former neo-Nazi leader Jeff Schoep also appeared on the program, while one of the conference co-chairs, businessman and political donor Stan Roth—the brother-in-law of Segal—contributed $50,000 to the far-right lobbying group Advance Australia, which has run campaigns against "mass migration", and advocated for the recent right-wing March For Australia event.

The presence of these types of figures just shows how ideological this Summit was, and far from it being a neutral or inclusive forum on community safety, it just reflected the agenda of a narrow, hard-right movement, exporting US-style Zionist culture wars and violence into Australian politics.

What makes the Summit particularly concerning is the expectation that will now be placed on the attendees. As we know, nothing is free in politics: when councillors accept funded trips to glossy conferences and propaganda talk-fests—*all expenses paid*—there is a strong chance that they will return to their councils and communities carrying the ideological baggage of their hosts, with the expectation that they will deliver on their agenda. The message delivered at the Summit was clear—advocacy for Palestinian rights and criticism of Israeli government actions are to be stigmatised and silenced, even at the local council level of Australian politics.

And it has now reached the point of *pure ridicule*. Among the items officially deemed "anti-Semitic" are watermelons displayed in solidarity with Palestinians; the simple slogan "Free Palestine" (of course); wearing a *keffiyeh*; the phrase "All

Eyes on Rafah"; or referring to Israel as a "settler colonial state" and Gaza as an "open-air prison". It's the politics of the preschool playground and it's as absurd as the Bundestag in the 1930s outlawing pretzels or accordions as symbols of resistance and foreign influence—although, given the mindset of that era, it's quite possible that it would have been considered.

But we have already arrived at—or even surpassed—that point where the absurdity or extremity of these measures no longer matters. The image of the innocuous watermelon is now treated as a *threat*, all because this stubborn fruit— through the process of evolution—landed on the colours of green and red, and dotted itself with black seeds: *anti-Semitic, guilty as charged* and to be *hanged from the neck until dead*.

And yet, despite their ridiculous and infantile demands, there is no shortage of local councillors and politicians eager to enforce the dictates of the Zionist agenda and accept their political proctology, fearful of jeopardising funding or support from the Israel lobby. As we have seen with the proscription of Palestine Action in Britain—where pensioners and even people in wheelchairs have been arrested for simply holding up a sign—political leaders of all persuasions are increasingly choosing to make *themselves* the object of ridicule rather than risk the opprobrium of the Israel lobby. That's how bad this has all become.

None of this should distract from the fact that anti-Semitism itself is abhorrent and must always be condemned. We always need to point this out as a ballast of any commentary about Palestine, because it always opens the unreasonable "what-about-ism" and accusations of anti-Semitism. Of course, *we will condemn anti-Semitism*, but we will also condemn the actions of Israel and Zionist supremacy.

The Holocaust revealed the consequences of state-sanctioned anti-Semitic hatred. Yet, matching up legitimate criticism of the political project of Zionism with that same hatred does a disservice both to Jewish communities and to democratic freedoms in Australia. Zionism, after all, is a political ideology—one shaped as much by English evangelical Christianity and European colonial interests as by Jewish nationalism, and historically influenced by currents of anti-Semitism that sought to remove Jewish populations from Europe rather than embrace them as equal citizens.

By aligning with organisations that push for this conflation, political leaders in Australia continue to narrow the space that exists for open and democratic debate. Councillors who attended the summit should now be pressed to explain not only what they learned, but whose interests they now serve and allow voters to decide at the next election whether a practice that prioritises excusing Israel from its genocidal actions over addressing the genuine threats posed by rising far-right extremism is acceptable or not.

COMMUNITIES ARE REJECTING THE AGENDA OF THIS SUMMIT

Many unions, grassroots community organisations, and even Jewish groups themselves, have called out this Summit—the Jewish Council of Australia, for example, was one of the most prominent voices urging councillors to boycott the event. Their position was clear and unambiguous: this was not a summit to combat anti-Semitism, but rather a carefully packaged exercise in pro-Israel propaganda, advancing the right-wing political ideology of Zionism under the guise of community safety.

And the criticisms have gone far beyond "the fringe" which usually the terminology used to dismiss these voices. The Australian Services Union, Democracy in Colour, Jewish Voices for Peace, councillors from the Inner Sydney Greens, and a range of other civil society groups have all warned that these events compromise accountability. The message is clear:

anti-Semitism is real and must be condemned, but political junkets financed by foreign-linked organisations with explicit ideological agendas must also be condemned and have no place in Australian public life.

Transparency International and other governance watchdogs have long argued that while accepting travel and hospitality from lobby groups might not technically breach the law, it erodes public trust in local decision-making, irrespective of which level of government it occurs. Ratepayers don't elect local representatives so that they can accept paid trips from overseas interest groups and return with a pre-packaged political program, ready to be foisted upon them. Councillors are meant to be accountable to *their* communities, not to donors in Washington or Tel Aviv.

At the heart of this is also a deeper philosophical point: to suggest that opposing Zionism—or Israel—is inherently anti-Semitic is not only intellectually dishonest but actively harmful to democratic institutions. Zionism is not synonymous with Judaism, nor is it universally embraced by Jewish people. Indeed, some of the loudest critics of Zionism today are Jewish organisations and individuals—as we saw on the weekend in Bondi at the event organised by Jews Against the Occupation '48 to show their support for Gaza and the Sumud flotilla—and includes conservative religious communities who reject the idea of a nation-state on theological grounds.

To label these critics as "not real Jews" or the offensive "Kapos" and dismiss their arguments as *anti-Semitism,* is to deny the diversity of Jewish voices and to reduce centuries of debate into a single, state-sanctioned right-wing extremist narrative. This process punishes pro-Palestine advocacy, it stifles dissent and silences people. It's also a process that undermines democratic principles and restricts what people in Australia can say about foreign governments and their actions.

There's no question that the work against anti-Semitism needs to continue—but it can't be hijacked by bad ideas requested by small minority of ideologically-driven zealots. Zionism, as an ideology, should be open to the same scrutiny and criticism as any other political project. To shut down that conversation is to confuse faith with politics, and to make the mistake of blind allegiance to a state, over solidarity against racism.

WHY THE SUMMIT WILL FUEL THE ANTI-SEMITISM IT CLAIMS TO FIGHT

The 250 local council representatives who attended the Summit will now have to return to their communities and justify why they were there. One councillor in particular—the mayor of Sydney's Inner West Council, Darcy Byrne—took part despite opposition from his fellow councillors. The Council had been on the verge of adopting a Boycott, Divestment and Sanctions resolution against Israel, but this was blocked after Byrne's intervention—a move that left many people in the Inner West community bewildered and disillusioned.

The astroturf Better Council group, backed by the Zionist movement to campaign against pro-Palestine initiatives at the local government level, threw its weight behind Byrne and the Labor Party during the 2024 council elections, rewarding his role in shutting down the BDS resolution. His prize was a junket to the Gold Coast and the promise of political support in future elections, provided he continues to *do the right thing*. This is how the process works. Why support action against the state of Israel—even if that's what fellow councillors and the local community are demanding—when there's an election to be won?

However, this issue goes far beyond the one mayor. This Summit was bankrolled by some of Australia's wealthiest pro-

Zionist organisations and corporations, including entities in heavy industry and peak Jewish lobby groups. Their ability to provide unlimited funding for such events is precisely what should raise many red flags about influence and integrity but all it's doing is raising the flags for more political interference and opening up the gates for more donations.

When elected representatives accept hospitality and travel from lobbyists with clear political agendas, the line between independent governance and corporate capture becomes dangerously blurred. This is a problem that has long been associated with the federal and state levels of politics and needs to be stamped out. But to now see it more obviously entrenched at the local government level—where transparency and accountability should be at their strongest—is really concerning.

If the stated aim was to counter anti-Semitism, it has already failed. In the week leading up to the Summit, neo-Nazi groups marched openly through Australian streets, presenting—at least on the surface—the most immediate threat to Jewish communities. Yet the Summit gave no meaningful reaction to these movements: not a single word against the neo-Nazis and fascists visible in our cities, as though it went out of its way to accommodate ideological bedfellows, a trilogy of Nazism, fascism, and Zionism.

Instead, the Summit focused almost entirely on redefining anti-Semitism to shield Israel from criticism, targeting symbols such as watermelons and keffiyehs. *The important parts of anti-Semitism.* Paradoxically, this approach will probably add to anti-Semitism rather than diminish it. When people witness elected officials attending lavish junkets—bankrolled by foreign-linked lobby groups—to defend the policies of a corrupt, hard-right genocidal Israeli government, resentment and cynicism will only get worse.

At its core, the Summit was not about protecting Jewish Australians from harm—if it was, Jillian Segal would have condemned the shameful actions of the Zionists against the Jews Against the Occupation '48 at Bondi Beach on the weekend. Instead, the Summit was about shielding Israel's current government from accountability, exporting American-style lobby politics into Australia, and embedding a culture of silence around one of the most pressing human rights crises of our time. When this ugly edifice eventually crumbles—and it inevitably will—local political leaders who attended will have to explain why they sided with influence peddlers and propaganda merchants instead of defending free speech, democratic principles, and the fight against genuine anti-Semitism.

***

WHEN WILL WE START TO CONDEMN ISRAEL?

10 September 2025

Israel has launched a missile strike on the Qatari city of Doha, claiming that it was targeting Hamas leaders meeting in a residential compound to discuss a ceasefire deal to stop the genocide in Gaza. Six people were killed, although the main part of the Hamas leadership has survived. This is the first known Israeli strike on Qatar, an irresponsible act that shattered long-standing diplomatic protocols and raised alarm across the region. The compound was located within a district recognised as a peaceful diplomatic enclave— making the attack not only militarily jarring but symbolically devastating.

The United States, which maintains extensive military and diplomatic ties with Qatar, was informed only moments before the strike began. President Donald Trump later said he "felt very badly" about the location of the attack and instructed his envoy to warn Qatari officials—though the warning reportedly came too late to intervene. Qatar, however, emphatically rejected any prior notice, asserting that the notification arrived only as explosions were already underway.

Germany has condemned the attack as "unacceptable" and a violation of sovereignty; the U.K.'s Prime Minister Keir

Starmer has called it a threat to regional stability; and the Arab League, the UN, and many other world leaders voiced outrage, warning that this strike will destroy work towards a ceasefire and negotiations to release hostages, which Israel has no intention of agreeing to.

American officials suggested the strike "does not advance Israel or America's goals"—even though that's exactly what it does—undermining U.S. efforts to broker peace. Critics argue the attack deliberately targeted the heart of diplomatic efforts, disrupting ongoing ceasefire-for-hostage talks and signaling a hardening of Israel's posture toward Gaza's remaining strongholds.

In striking inside a nation serving as mediator, the assault conveyed a clear message: Israel is prepared to act at will, indifferent to international norms or the diplomatic roles of its neighbors. The implications extend beyond Qatar—they reverberate across the broader peace architecture of the Middle East.

BEYOND DOHA: A REGION UNDER FIRE

Israel's assault on Doha was not an isolated incident; it highlights a far broader campaign of transnational military engagements that has redrawn the contours of conflict in the Middle East. Since October 2023, Israel has pursued a strategy characterized by audacity and impunity, striking across at least eight countries and pressuring traditional notions of international law and state sovereignty.

An Al Jazeera mapping of Israeli operations from late 2023 to mid-2025 reveals strikes deep inside Syria (approximately 550 km from Israel), as well as in Iran and Yemen at distances nearing 1,500–2,000 km—demonstrating the operational reach of its advanced air force and drone fleet. Armed Conflict Location and Event Data (ACLED) documents nearly 35,000 separate attacks in just five countries—Israel-occupied territories, Lebanon, Syria, Yemen and Iran—before June 2025.

Lebanon has borne the brunt of near-daily violations of the fragile 2024 ceasefire, with Israel frequently targeting southern suburbs of Beirut, including Hezbollah infrastructure and depots. In past months, a rare escalation even saw airstrikes in northeastern Lebanon's Hermel and Bekaa regions, killing Hezbollah fighters and signaling that no part of the country lies beyond Israel's reach.

Meanwhile, Yemen has emerged as a second front. Following a Houthi ballistic missile strike near Tel Aviv's airport in May 2025, Israel launched a series of sweeping air and naval operations against Houthi-controlled areas—striking Sanaa's international airport, the port of Hodeidah, and related infrastructure, resulting in widespread destruction and dozens of casualties.

Naval confrontations have extended even further: two Global Sumud Flotilla vessels attempting to deliver humanitarian aid to Gaza from Tunisian ports were reportedly hit by drone strikes—one in Tunisian waters near Sidi Bou Said, and another docked in port—despite flashing footage contradicting Tunisia's official denials. These incidents represented Israel's boldness in targeting ships under the banner of international activism and solidarity.

Together, these operations trace a disturbing arc of escalation. Whether through airstrikes, drone attacks, or naval strikes, Israel has repeatedly flouted international conventions by targeting sovereign territories and non-combatant vessels. Yet global responses have remained muted: investigations are announced, resolutions softly worded, and arms sales continue unabated. Governments frame violations as criminal ambiguities or necessary security actions rather than illegal aggression. Diplomatic backlash remains scattered, often tepid, uncertain.

As regional tension mounts and borders blur, one question becomes impossible to ignore: how long will the world tolerate this de facto normalization of cross-border violence?

A DEAFENING SILENCE WHERE URGENT CONDEMNATION IS NEEDED

The global response to Israel's transnational offensive has been glaringly inadequate. Although echoes of concern ripple through statements from several governments and international bodies, they fall far short of the unified condemnation we've historically seen in the face of authoritarian overreach.

In the aftermath of the recent assault on Doha, Turkey's President Erdoğan denounced the strike as a blatant violation of international law and Qatari sovereignty, accusing Israel of adopting "terrorism as state policy" and intentionally igniting regional conflict. Germany's leadership labeled the attack "unacceptable," warning it jeopardized ongoing efforts toward a Gaza ceasefire and hostage release, while U.K. Prime Minister Keir Starmer publicly condemned it as a threat to regional stability during a call with Qatar's Emir.

Beyond these voices, responses remain fragmented and restrained. When Israeli strikes hit targets inside Iran—ranging from nuclear facilities to residential areas—the United Nations human rights experts issued sharp condemnation, and countries including Japan, Russia, China, Egypt, and various Gulf states expressed alarm and called for urgent de-escalation.

Yet despite these moments of public outcry, the broader international posture leans toward caution and inaction. European Union member states remain divided—Spain and others push for sanctions and strategic re-evaluation, while others resist escalation of policy measures. This contrasts sharply with the decisive stance once taken against fascism and totalitarian governance—and lays bare a frustrating hypocrisy: when states perceive threats from China, they issue pointed warnings; when violations come from Israel—an established ally—they issue carefully calibrated statements.

Leading Western powers continue to publicly express sorrow or concern, while continuing military and diplomatic support almost uninterrupted. This two-faced diplomacy reflects political paralysis in the face of mounting humanitarian catastrophe and blatant breaches of global norms.

Public frustration is rippling across societies worldwide, yet political leaders remain hesitant. As Spain's Prime Minister Pedro Sánchez lambasted European inertia and lobbied for tangible actions such as arms embargoes and recognition of Palestine—only to face resistance within the EU— frustration grows louder. Meanwhile, United Nations bodies, though vocally concerned, lack the enforcement mechanisms to compel meaningful change.

Amid mounting impatience, the world now faces a critical question: Will political convenience outweigh moral clarity forever? History teaches that ideological threats demand timely, resolute unity. If global leaders delay meaningful condemnation and deprioritise enforcement of international norms, they risk undermining the very foundations of international law and peace.

***

THE LINE IN THE SAND AT DOHA

16 September 2025

It was interesting to see the responses and reactions to Israel's recent strikes on Qatar, when dozens of Arab and Islamic leaders arrived in Doha for an emergency meeting in a rare show of unity—their meeting intended as an act of solidarity with the Palestinians and to develop a strategy of curtailing the aggressive actions of Israel in the region. This was more than a routine diplomatic summit—there was anger, frustration and a show of defiance, aimed not only at the state of Israel but also at the United States, Europe and the broader international community that has long shielded Israel from any form of meaningful consequence.

Ultimately, this might end up being Benjamin Netanyahu's greatest success story (unintended, of course): uniting a diverse and disparate pan-Islamic world into a strong voice that is starting to work collectively against Israel's belligerence, overreach and destructive hegemonic ambitions.

For decades, major powers—with the United States leading the pack—have enabled Israel's policies: the genocidal devastation of Gaza; the steady expansion of illegal settlements in the West Bank; and military operations and incursions across the Middle East/Western Asia. Israel's strikes in recent months in *seven* neighbouring states and capital cities, have reinforced the perception that it acts with impunity and encouragement from the West, despite the weasel words of denial that usually come out of the mouths of international leaders and foreign ministers. According to the leaders in Doha, that impunity has crossed a threshold. The message from this meeting is clear: *enough is enough*.

Western governments, especially in Washington, Paris, London, and Berlin, continue to release statements of "concern" from one side of the mouth, while the other side more quietly agrees to supply weapons and intelligence, and provides diplomatic immunity for the Israeli leadership. The language is always carefully measured, but the effect is the same—whatever Israel does, it faces no consequence or cost. This duplicity has become intolerable for those leaders in Doha, who argue that such an indulgence has only emboldened Israel to further escalate its campaign of violence and to make a Palestinian state all but unattainable.

And there's a massive contrast between rhetoric and action from the West: France, Germany and Britain have all issued condemnations, but then go on to resume military co-operation and trade the following week, not even caring if anyone notices this brazen duplicity. The United States remains Israel's strongest backer, and its veto power at the United Nations serves as the ultimate protector.

For the leaders in Qatar, this hypocrisy is no longer sustainable. If Western governments truly believe in the principles of international law, then the same tools applied to other aggressor states—sanctions, arms embargoes, travel bans, suspensions of intelligence and military co-operation— needs to apply to Israel as well. Yet Israel remains an exception, protected by a force field created in Washington and reinforced in European capitals.

THE TARNISHED GLOBAL IMAGE OF ISRAEL

For Israel, keeping up appearances is all that seems to matter. Prime Minister Netanyahu and his government might thrive on domestic belligerence and the rhetoric of defiance, but internationally they are acutely aware of the costs of being seen as a pariah state. Israel's self-image is built on its claim to be a supposed "advanced" nation—despite its dark-ages barbarism, psychopathy and acts of genocide in Gaza—and wants to be seen indispensable partner in technology, trade, and security. Measures such as restrictions on travel, the suspension of research and technology agreements or the imposition of targeted sanctions threaten not only the economy of Israel but also its carefully cultivated reputation as a modern and globally integrated state, even if it behaves differently and contravenes international law. If it wasn't obvious before, this appearance is on the verge of collapsing: this is what tends to happen to pariah states.

The leaders at the meeting were unanimous: these vulnerabilities of Israel need to be exploited. If Israel is to be confronted—and it will be—it must be done through sustained pressure that forces it to reassess the costs of its actions in Gaza and beyond.

There are precedents for this: in 1997, Israel's plans to assassinate a leader of Hamas—Netanyahu's preferred *modus operandi* ever since he become Prime Minister—provoked a furious response from Jordan's King Abdullah, who threatened to suspend the peace treaty with Israel. The United States, aware of the potential collapse of one of its most valuable regional accords, placed intense pressure on Netanyahu and within days, Israel was forced to back down. The lesson was in this case was clear: Israel might ignore words from the entire world community, but it can't ignore *clear consequences*, especially when they are specifically directed from the United States.

The collective power of the Arab and Islamic bloc is immense. Fifty-seven nations, representing a quarter of the world's population, hold leverage across many key sectors—technology markets, financial networks, energy resources, security and regional co-operation. If co-ordinated more effectively than they have been in the past—given their many regional and political differences—these states could disrupt Israel's access to capital, restrict its economic lifelines, and undermine its diplomatic privileges. Such measures would go beyond the symbolic, making it clear that there can't be any *business as usual* while Israel continues its campaign of genocide in Gaza and its persistent violation of international law.

THE CRACKS APPEARING IN WESTERN SUPPORT

The United States remains Israel's ultimate guarantor—as it always has been—yet even this relationship is showing the signs of strain. President Donald Trump might continue to present himself as Israel's most reliable ally, loudly proclaiming his unconditional support—Secretary of State Marco Rubio is currently in Jerusalem partaking in that bizarre ritual of U.S. leaders inserting their fingers into the Western Wall in the presence of Netanyahu—but beneath the surface, there's a growing frustration.

Netanyahu's intransigence and freelancing belligerence is undermining Trump's own ambitions to implement *the art of the deal* in the Middle East, sabotaged any chance of renewed engagement with Iran, and engaging the United States in even more reputational damage across the region than it already has. Even within the MAGA movement—Trump's biggest supporter base—many voices are beginning to question the logic of sending billions of dollars in aid to a government that openly disregards American interests, even to the point of humiliation.

Republican hardliners such as Rubio and Lindsey Graham maintain their ritualistic loyalty—both in the United States and in Israel—but there are different conversations taking place behind the scenes. Trump is a politician driven more by ego than ideology, and is being angered by appearing weak, and Netanyahu's maniacal defiance and intransigence increasingly makes him look exactly like that. For all the rhetoric of "unshakable bonds" and allegiance that almost every U.S. politician has to provide, the reality is that Israel is quickly becoming an unpredictable and strategic liability for Washington.

The questions raised in Doha are no longer confined to the Arab and Islamic world. Western countries now need to confront their own inherent contradictions: do they genuinely want stability in the region—and within *their own* countries, as the recent riots in Spain have shown—or will they continue to support Israel's descent into a pariah and its rogue-state behaviour? Do they seek peace and security or are they happy to see a perpetual conflict? Every shipment of arms, every veto at the United Nations, every muted statement of "concern" just exposes the widening gap between Western rhetoric and reality. And that's going to cause many problems for political leaders, whether it's in Britain, the United States, Spain or in Australia.

The gathering in Doha was more than symbolic—it was a warning aimed directly at Washington, London, Paris, and Berlin: platitudes and empty condemnations will no longer be enough. If Islamic and Arab states can maintain unity, their co-ordinated action—through sanctions, suspensions of co-operation and economic pressure—there will be consequences for Israel of the like that it has never seen before. Israel won't end its campaign of destruction out of conscience; it will do so only when the costs become unbearable and it's in a position where it's forced to act.

The genocide in Gaza won't end by its own volition. And nor will Israel stop its territorial ambitions, even if it kills every remaining Palestinian man, woman, child and baby in Gaza and the West Bank. This will end only when those who enable it—Israel and the West through silence, weapons, or diplomatic diffusion and indifference—are forced to confront their complicity, and when Israel is made to understand that its brutality and genocide carries consequences that it won't be able to escape for too much longer.

***

HOW A CHILDREN'S HOSPITAL FOLDED TO EXTREMISM

20 September 2025

The controversy began when the Royal Children's Hospital in Melbourne hastily cancelled a panel discussion on the effects of war on children's health. The event was scheduled as part of the hospital's professional development program and had been only promoted internally but just a few days before it was due to take place, the hospital withdrew its support. Why? Because of one complaint from Sydney psychiatrist Dr Doron Samuel, who claimed the event would cause "moral injury" and "vicarious trauma" for Jewish staff and patients.

No evidence was provided to support these claims, nor was there any explanation of how a broad discussion about war's impact on children could trigger such harm. Despite this, the hospital capitulated without any further investigation, and decided that it was easier to shut down the event than to risk controversy—yet another example of an institution surrendering to the endless pressure from the Zionist lobby in Australia, at the expense of open debate and academic freedom that we'd normally expect to see in an open democracy.

Also, Dr Samuel isn't some kind of neutral observer— he campaigned for the Liberal Party during the last federal election, where he was active in the inner-west seat of Reid, and gained notoriety by calling the Australian Greens "Nazis" while urging the Liberal Party to adopt the same rhetoric (incidentally, the Liberal Party suffered a swing of 6.8 per cent against them in the seat of Reid, undoubtedly due to this kind of behaviour). That someone with such a record could derail a medical seminar with a single letter raises serious questions about the independence of Australia's leading public institutions.

The panel was to examine how war traumatises children and how to redress these issues, and many children that have lived through recent wars in Syria, Sudan, Afghanistan, Gaza and other conflict zones around the world—now reside in Australia. Insights from this type of forum would have been invaluable in helping clinicians in hospitals better support traumatised children in Australia. Instead, the event was silenced, not because of its content, but because of a political fear of offending—real or imagined—a powerful right-wing and ultranationalist lobby.

The irony is that the discussion wasn't designed to single out Israel. It was to cover conflicts globally—yet the assumption that Israel's actions would inevitably form part of the conversation was enough to prompt its cancellation. This raises a fundamental question: can open and honest debate about global conflicts—and their impact on vulnerable populations and children—survive in Australia when institutions cave in so quickly to political intimidation and innuendo?

Hospital executives, like too many CEOs of public institutions, are ill-equipped to deal with this type of political pressure, where they take the path of least resistance than defend the principle of open discussion. Similar patterns have played out elsewhere—at the ABC, in schools and in universities—where complaints from politically motivated groups, often with no real relationship or stake in the institution, have resulted in dismissals, censorship or unwarranted public apologies. The trend is clear: a campaign from the Zionist lobby exists to eliminate dissenting voices, and too many Australian institutions are unwilling to resist it.

A PATTERN OF SILENCING DIFFERENCE OF OPINION

The cancellation at the Royal Children's Hospital wasn't just a one-off incident. It fits into a broader and disturbing pattern that has taken hold across Australia's cultural and academic life. Of course, this has been an issue in Australia for some time—and it is even more pronounced in the United States and Britain—but since 2023, the climate of fear, silencing and self-censorship has escalated.

What happened in Melbourne shows how absurd the situation has become: a psychiatrist in Sydney, with no professional relationship to the hospital, was able to derail an educational seminar on children and war, simply because there was a chance that Israel's actions in Gaza might be mentioned.

This climate of fear goes beyond hospitals: literary magazines have been pressured into closure, cultural festivals have cancelled events, and community forums have been silenced through intimidation. The message is clear: any initiative that might allow discussion of Israel's conduct, irrespective of how remote that discussion might be, is vulnerable to attack. Public institutions, which should be strongholds of open inquiry, instead find themselves paralysed, more concerned with appeasing lobby groups than fulfilling their responsibilities to the public. The obvious question is: what exactly do they fear?

The answer seems to lie in the way fringe actors on the right have successfully positioned themselves at the centre of the debate. Those aligned with the most extreme Zionist positions insist that any criticism of Israel amounts to anti-Semitism—

which is currently being lobbied for implementation by the Special Envoy to Combat Antisemitism Jillian Segal—and too often, institutions accept that framing, *without question.*

The Royal Children's Hospital seminar was not designed to attack Jewish people; it was meant to discuss the psychological and medical consequences of war on children. The fact that it was cancelled reveals the extent to which institutions now bend to political pressure.

This unreasonable behaviour has reached into other community spaces as well. At a small gathering in Marrickville, cardiologist Peter MacDonald raised a provocative question as a member of the audience—not in any official capacity—where he referred to recent reports that Iran was behind alleged anti-Semitic attacks in Sydney, and suggested that these could have been Mossad-engineered incidents.

"Am I being totally naïve," he asked, "or has the Zionist lobby infiltrated ASIO as well?" The comment made no reference to Jewish people, nor did it disparage the state of Israel directly. It was framed as a question about intelligence agencies and security affairs, and his full question lasted for less than 20 seconds.

Yet the fallout was immediate: St Vincent's Health Australia placed MacDonald on forced leave, issuing a statement that it "does not tolerate anti-Semitism, racism, bigotry or hate," even though no explanation was provided as to how MacDonald's remarks fit those categories. No procedural fairness was given to him and no transparent inquiry was undertaken. This action came after a letter from Alex Ryvchin, co-CEO of the Executive Council of Australian Jewry, accused MacDonald of causing "great harm" by indulging in "wild fantasies" and demanded that he be disciplined. And of course, St Vincent's acted as requested, *no questions asked.* What other group of people in society have this kind of power?

It's extraordinary: a cardiologist who saves lives through surgery was pushed out of his workplace on the basis of a lobbyist's complaint, without evidence of misconduct and without debate. That this could occur at a time when Israel, through its intelligence agencies and military, has been accused by the United Nations of committing genocide in Gaza makes the response even more illogical. Instead of open discussion, Australia now sees the automatic silencing of those who ask uncomfortable questions, and has bureaucracies siding with those bad actors who are causing a genocide in Gaza.

A GENOCIDE CONFIRMED

The silencing of debate in Australia comes at the same moment the international community has reached its most damning conclusion yet: *Israel has committed crimes against humanity* in Gaza, including *genocide*. The findings of the United Nations Commission of Inquiry are clear: after almost two years of investigation, the commission determined that Israel has committed four of the five acts defined as genocide under the 1948 Genocide Convention, including targeting civilians, mass killings and the obstruction of food, water and medicine to create life-threatening conditions for an entire population.

The UN has gone further, warning that *silence* on this issue is *complicity*, and governments that fail to act risk not only their credibility but their own moral and legal standing under international law. For Australia, Prime Minister Anthony Albanese and Foreign Minister Penny Wong cannot claim ignorance anymore and the choice before them is clear: uphold international law or become enablers of genocide.

Chris Sidoti, one of the UN commissioners, put the reality in clear terms: "We are told that the number of children who have had one or both legs or arms amputated is greater than in any other conflict this century," he said. "We know the number of children who have lost one or both parents. The psychological trauma will last their whole lives."

These are not accidental deaths, not the tragic "mishaps" Israel insists upon. They are the predictable and direct consequence of a military strategy built on saturation bombing, scorched earth—the so-called "mowing the lawn"—and the deliberate destruction of Gaza's civilian infrastructure: homes, hospitals, schools, universities, roads, farms, fishing fleets, churches, mosques, even cultural and archaeological sites.

When such overwhelming evidence is presented, the implications extend far beyond the killing fields of Gaza. Every public institution that caves in to the pressure from lobbyists by cancelling events, forums, or academic discussions needs to ask itself: what exactly are you supporting?

By silencing debate on Gaza—whether it's at a hospital, a university or a small community hall—institutions become complicit in concealing a genocide that the UN has now formally recognised. While no one is suggesting hospital executives or university administrators will face trial at The Hague, their actions contribute to a wider culture of denial and silence that allows atrocities to continue unchecked.

For governments, the stakes for them are much higher. Complicity is not an abstract concept: they are the decision makers. It can mean military exports, intelligence sharing, or simply "looking the other way", all of which the Australian government has been doing since October 2023, despite their many denials.

But it now has a clear choice: align Australia with international law, take meaningful action, and call out Israel's policies of genocide and mass destruction—or continue enabling Israel's campaign and be remembered as a state that chose to stand on the wrong side of history. The choice could not be clearer and it should be a *lay down misère*.

RECOGNITION AND IS THE POWER OF THE LOBBY WANING?

Australia has now taken a small but significant step—it's not the *end*, but it should be the *beginning* of the end of Israel's disastrous and genocidal actions in Gaza and Palestine. At the United Nations General Assembly in New York, Prime Minister Anthony Albanese announced that Australia formally recognises Palestine as a sovereign state, joining more than 150 nations worldwide. "The cycle of violence must end," Albanese said, framing recognition as part of building momentum toward a two-state solution, although what kind of *two-state solution* is anyone's guess, and will still probably take many more years to achieve.

Canada, United Kingdom France, Belgium and Portugal have made similar declarations, but the shift that is starting to take place is clear: Western governments that had long resisted acknowledging Palestinian statehood are now moving towards the global consensus. For Australia, this recognition means that Mahmoud Abbas, President of the Palestinian Authority, will be formally acknowledged as head of state, and official government documents will now refer to the "State of Palestine".

This recognition though isn't enough, and it *will never be enough*: far from it. Acknowledging the State of Palestine today won't bring back the countless men, women and children who have been slaughtered by Israel Defense Forces, or undo the collective punishment, racism and apartheid inflicted by Israel upon the Palestine people since 1948.

However, symbolism in international relations *does matter*, and this action is not just symbolic. Recognition is part of a co-ordinated effort to break the deadlock, end the bloodshed in Gaza, secure the release of the remaining hostages, and deliver on the Palestinians' long-held aspiration for statehood. For decades, Palestine has been recognised by much of the world, yet blocked by a handful of powerful nations unwilling to defy

Israel and its supporters. Now, that blockage is beginning to break down.

The question remains: will this recognition diminish the influence of the Zionist lobby in Australia? For years, they have worked to shut down debate, suppress discussion, and label critics as anti-Semitic, no matter how tenuous the link. Their tactics are the signs of an absolutist and extreme ideology—and the determination to silence all opposition. Yet their efforts failed to stop Australia's recognition of Palestine.

This doesn't mean their influence has disappeared: powerful people in these positions rarely throw away their power and, just like the white extremists in South Africa during the last days of apartheid in the 1990s, relinquishing this control will be a slow drawn-out process.

However, the more extreme and unreasonable the demands from these lobby groups become, the more they alienate the mainstream public. When institutions cancel forums on child safety, sack doctors and heart surgeons or silence academic panels at the whim of a small but powerful lobby acting behind the scenes, more questions will be asked by the public about why a democratic country like Australian should accept such interference from such groups, which is more akin to the behaviour of the infamous Stasi police or KGB in the former Soviet bloc countries.

Recognition of Palestine is only one step—far more will be required to end the siege of Gaza, secure justice for Palestinians, and ensure Israel is held accountable for its actions. But it is also a sign that the political ground is shifting. The Zionist lobby will fight hard to preserve its influence, but for the first time in decades, its power shows small signs of decline. And in that space, a new conversation about justice, sovereignty, and accountability will finally begin to emerge.

**

THE GRAND ILLUSION OF A PEACE PLAN

30 September 2025

The Trump–Netanyahu proposal for Gaza is the 21st century "peace in our time" moment where if the parties agree—even though no one from Palestine or the Arab world has been involved in the proposal—the genocide will stop immediately, the Israel Defense Forces will retreat, and a phased withdrawal will proceed concurrently with a "demilitarisation" of Gaza. Within 72 hours of Israel's acceptance of the deal, all hostages held by Hamas will be returned, and only then will Israel release 250 Palestinians serving life sentences and a further 1,700 detained since 7 October 2023, alongside a remains-for-remains exchange formula which, of course, heavily favours Israel.

Hamas and other factions must "decommission" all weapons, not have any role in any future government, and accept amnesty or safe passage abroad—measures that would be verified by independent monitors and underwritten by an "International Stabilisation Force", which will then secure the Gaza Strip, train suitably-vetted Palestinian police, help seal the borders with Israel and Egypt, and enable a progressive Israeli drawdown. Israel, apparently (if anyone can believe it), will not annex or formally occupy Gaza, though a security perimeter may persist until Gaza is certified "properly secure," a measure which the proposal does not define.

In other details, governance would pass to an unelected technocratic Palestinian committee handling day-to-day services, but under the supervision of a new international oversight body, the "Board of Peace", which is almost as Orwellian as the Gaza Humanitarian Fund, which has so far killed over 2,500 Palestinians while they were seeking food. This interim structure is supposed to act as a bridge to the eventual control by the Palestinian Authority, contingent on reforms and "deradicalisation," after which the pathway towards Palestinian self-determination *might be* discussed. *Might be.*

Under this proposal, a state of Palestine will be deferred, it's fully conditional, and discretionary; there's the *possibility* of a *pathway*—a half-hearted promise of a promise—not the recognition of an inherent right.

On reconstruction, the proposal promises immediate aid, such as restoration of power, water, hospitals, bakeries, rubble clearance—delivered via UN agencies and the Red Crescent and rebuilding what Israel has comprehensively destroyed— in conjunction with a "Trump-branded" development drive and a special economic zone to supposedly energise Gaza's economy, while also stipulating that no one will be forced to leave and those who have left Gaza, can return.

This, however, is all *political theatre*, and it's hard to call it a "deal" if it's coming from one side alone: Israel has "approved" the plan; Hamas has not—they weren't even a part of the process, nor was anyone else from Palestine or the Arab world, and first saw it when it was released through the media. It's a one-sided *fait accompli* offered on a take-it-or-leave-it basis: Trump has publicly warned that refusal would bring full U.S. backing for Israel to "finish the job"—code for completing the genocide, which Israel will probably do anyway—while Netanyahu has suggested the proposal will achieve Israel's war aims.

The top-down nature of the proposal raises basic questions about consent, enforcement, and legitimacy, and continues that process of making Palestinians as invisible as possible: how can a supposed peace plan that doesn't include the victims of Israel's brutality and is at the behest of the two instigators of the genocide—Israel and the US—be regarded as a just outcome?

THE MASSIVE CONTRADICTIONS AND DUPLICITY

If the Trump–Netanyahu proposal is presenting itself as a neat little roadmap to peace, its inherent contradictions and omissions reveal a dismal and depressing reality. The proposal calls for Gaza to be administered by a technocratic Palestinian committee, the supposedly neutral and apolitical "Board of Peace" which will be chaired by Trump himself and divisive figures such as former British Prime Minister, Tony Blair. The document fails to explain how this committee would be formed, who would choose its members, or how day-to-day decisions would be made. The division of authority between the committee and the board is left completely undefined, leaving open the risk of paralysis—or worse, a domination imposed by the United States—and Israel—purporting to be a neutral and benevolent entity, when in reality, it's nothing of the kind.

The role of the Palestinian Authority is also ambiguous. The proposal suggests that once the Authority "completes its reforms"—whatever that is—it could reassume control of Gaza. It's almost like *Alice In Wonderland*: there's no timelines, there's no schedules, and no indication of who would certify that the Authority has achieved these undefined reforms—it will just mean whatever the Board of Peace wants it to mean.

Netanyahu, meanwhile, has explicitly rejected the return of the Palestinian Authority to Gaza, contradicting the very framework he has agreed to. This contradiction exposes the worthless nature of the document, which promises a working political landscape—but can't reconcile Israel's categorical opposition to Palestinian statehood with the U.S. commitment to keep that option alive, however conditional. In this scenario, every country in the world is expected to recognise the right of Israel to exist, but Israel refuses the right for Palestine to exist and, under Netanyahu, this right will *never* exist.

Security is another unresolved issue: the International Stabilisation Force is described as the guarantor of Gaza's demilitarisation, training Palestinian police, securing borders and replacing Israeli troops. But the plan doesn't identify which countries would provide the troops, under what rules of engagement they would operate or how they would interact with Israeli forces still maintaining a "security perimeter". Would it act in the role of peacekeepers, a police force, or a parallel army? What would happen if they clash with Israeli troops and would they be asked to take on Hamas directly?

For Palestine, any aspirations they have, *might be* considered—*might be*—if after an unspecified number of years, they comply with an unspecified number of undefined measures, in undefined circumstances and in an undefined manner. And even if they achieve this undefined and impossible task, there's absolutely no guarantee of anything. For Israel, it's a lot easier and very *specific*, as it always has been: Hamas must be destroyed, the Palestinian Authority must be excluded, and security and state apparatus of apartheid must remain firmly in its own control.

The credibility of the mediators also adds another layer of controversy. Trump as the chair is incredible, but Blair's name is highly toxic in the Western Asia/Middle East region, after his role in the false claims of "weapons of mass destruction" in 2003, which led to an invasion of Iraq, and the violent deaths of over 655,000 people, possibly up to 1 million. Why then is

Blair being proposed for this so-called "Board of Peace"? It would be like appointing Adolf Hitler to head the task force for creating the state of Israel after the Second World War.

Jared Kushner's return as Trump's informal adviser also raises the alarm bells, given his financial relationships with Arab monarchies in the Gulf and his openly stated view of Gaza as "valuable waterfront property" that's ripe for redevelopment. Taking this into account, the plan looks less like a peace agreement and more like another imperialist intervention, where outside powers impose structures that serve their strategic and economic interests while sidelining Palestine: it's a repeat of the brutal imperial behaviour from the nineteenth and twentieth centuries.

Ultimately, the contradictions within the Trump–Netanyahu plan are not just drafting oversights; it's a deliberate attempt to give Israel exactly what it wants and permanently subjugate Palestinians to an eternal state of servitude and slavehood. Instead of peace, it's likely to be yet another blueprint for failure and will collapse under the weight of its own ineptitude. And, perhaps, that was always in the intention.

A SHIFTING DIPLOMATIC GROUND

The regional response has been more varied, however. Saudi Arabia, Jordan, the United Arab Emirates, Qatar and Egypt have welcomed the announcement, although these states are politically compromised: their own survival is built on U.S. military, financial and diplomatic leverage, and blackmail. This makes them structurally unable—and often unwilling—to take strong pro-Palestinian action beyond aid convoys, carefully managed mediation roles and issuing diplomatically supportive statements—which is what they have dutifully done on this occasion.

The Palestinian Authority have also given a cautious backing, characterising the plan as part of ongoing international efforts to end the war. Others, such as Palestinian Islamic Jihad, have rejected the proposal outright, calling it a recipe for further destabilisation and an erosion of Palestinian sovereignty, which it more than likely will be.

Netanyahu has apologised for the Israeli strike in Qatar that killed a serviceman in early September, promising not to repeat such actions. But this is classic behaviour from Netanyahu and Israel: commit an egregious act that kills many, promise not to do it again, and then repeat the action soon after. While this admission of an error revealed just how critical Qatari mediation remains to even the possibility of a move towards peace, it does raise serious doubts about how much Israel—and Netanyahu—can be trusted.

In the background of this is the broader diplomatic shift underway at the United Nations and beyond. A growing number of states have moved to formally recognise Palestine as a sovereign state, with Australia, Canada, the United Kingdom, France, Belgium and Portugal last week among the latest to link themselves up with more than 150 other UN members who have done the same.

These recognitions are largely symbolic—at this stage—and are not changing the realities on the ground at all, but at least they signal the mounting frustration with Israel's conduct of the war and a willingness to assert Palestinian rights in international forums. In theory, they increase pressure for a genuine political solution; in practice however, they highlight the massive gap between the empty rhetoric and the deeply conditional, indefinite and undefined promises embedded within the Trump–Netanyahu proposal.

THE RHETORIC OF EMPTINESS

Netanyahu appeared in the U.S. Congress last week—yet again—and was given multiple standing ovations and the type of long-standing applause that might be reserved for leaders of *real* substance, such as the ovation that was granted to Nelson Mandela in 1994, the anti-apartheid activist and politician who served as the first president of South Africa from 1994 to 1999, globally recognised as an icon of democracy and social justice, and a recipient of the Nobel Peace Prize.

How can it be that Congress provides an even greater ovation for Netanyahu, who is a wanted war criminal, accused of crimes against humanity and genocide, and has been a maniacal stain on the politics the Middle East region since the 1990s, and done everything possible to avoid peace for Palestine? What does this say about America?

For Netanyahu, who was grinning like the Cheshire cat during the announce, this alignment with the U.S. is essential: he can't afford to have any daylight between him and Trump, Israel's last dependable and most profitable ally. Yet even still, there are inherent contradictions. Netanyahu has convinced Trump that he's "committed to peace", yet he's also committed to his far-right coalition partners in government that the war won't end until Hamas is destroyed and Palestinians are removed from Gaza and the West Bank.

It's classic Netanyahu double-speak—a promise of different things to different audiences. He's always had the duplicitous stench about him and, whatever he might have to say—or agrees to—he simply cannot be believed. A ceasefire agreed in January this year collapsed within weeks when Israel resumed military operations, and the U.S. raised no objections. Even now, he is already disputing the proposal that has been announced, saying that Israel Defense Forces "will remain in most of the territory", and that Israel will "absolutely not" agree to a Palestinian state. The deeper question is not whether Netanyahu will comply with any agreement but whether Trump will enforce it, as past experiences suggest the United States will always allow Israel to breach commitments without consequence.

Palestinian groups have already suggested the proposal is essentially the terms of a surrender, a belief reinforced by the fact that the plan was drafted without Palestinian participation and is—more than likely—in defiance of international law. Previous negotiations for Palestinian envoys in Qatar were met with Israeli strikes, for which Netanyahu apologised—not for targeting negotiators but for failing to hit them. Netanyahu is *never* about peace: he is an extremely violent man and will use any violent tactic to achieve his political goals.

The timing of this Trump–Netanyahu proposal is also suspicious. Just as international momentum was building for initiatives such as Colombia's "Uniting for Peace" resolution at the UN—which would impose sanctions on Israel and create a protection force in Palestine—along comes Israel and the U.S. to pre-empt them and drown out all viable alternatives. This has happened before: in May 2024, when the International Court of Justice ordered Israel to stop its assault on Rafah, U.S. President Joe Biden announced a phoney ceasefire to defuse any pressure on Israel, pushing away Algeria's draft resolution to enforce the Court of Justice ruling. This plan functions in the same way: a distraction, buying more time for Netanyahu, and acting as a shield against accountability under international law.

Many reputable organisations—the United Nations, B'Tselem, Physicians for Human Rights, the International Association of Genocide Scholars, Amnesty International, Palestinian Centre for Human Rights, and Human Rights Watch—have recognised that Israel is committing genocide in Gaza. The Trump–Netanyahu plan isn't a peace settlement that recognises this but, instead, it's a managed capitulation that brushes over the killings and human rights abuses: the terms and conditions have been dictated by outsiders and the perpetrators of war crimes and crimes against humanity, is designed to preserve Israel's impunity, and packaged as diplomacy for domestic and international audiences to keep up the appearances of doing something when, in fact, it's a self-serving document that rewards the aggressor. *Peace in our time*.

It's a plan which offers political cover for its architects—and for Trump too—while ignoring both the humanitarian crisis and the root causes of conflict. Like so many initiatives before it, it's likely collapse because it was never about a real peace—bold declarations and high ceremony giving way to broken promises, a continued violence, and the ongoing reality of occupation.

***

THE NATIONAL PRESS CLUB SHOOTS THE MESSENGER

5 October 2025

The National Press Club has cancelled an upcoming address by Pulitzer Prize-winning journalist Chris Hedges, who had been tentatively scheduled to speak in Canberra on October 20. "The Betrayal of Palestinian Journalists" was to examine how the mainstream media has failed in the ethical duty to report truth and ignored solidarity with colleagues working and dying in Gaza.

Hedges' lecture was to highlight how Western media outlets, including many in Australia, have repeated Israeli disinformation despite clear evidence of atrocities, censorship and the routine targeting of Palestinian journalists, with over 278 killed since the start of Israel's assault on Gaza in 2023. The proposed lecture was removed from the schedule, and CEO Maurice Reilly relayed to Hedges that "in the interest of balancing out our program, we will withdraw our offer," despite the Club's public commitment to being a "vigorous champion of media freedom".

Of course, Reilly's explanation has provoked widespread criticism from journalists, academics and supporters of free speech in Australia, who have accused the Club of hypocrisy and political cowardice. Reilly later justified the cancellation by noting that the Club was hosting several speakers on the issue Palestine, including Chris Sidoti, Ben Saul, UNICEF spokesperson James Elder, and Judge Navi Pillay, who had served on the UN inquiry that found Israel is committing genocide, arguing that the Club needs to "balance" its speaker lineup.

But this is disingenuous: Hedges' address concerned journalistic ethics and accountability, not geopolitics, and cancelling such a figure undermined the very principles the Club claims to uphold. And surely, a club that purports to be an organisation representing the intellectual interests of journalists *should* be presenting the type of address Hedges was going to provide.

Reilly has denied any external pressure, insisting that the decision was made solely by the Press Club's board. Yet, there's many questions about the relationships between some Australian journalists and pro-Israel advocacy groups, many of whom have attended "Journalists' Mission to Israel"—a media "study tour" sponsored by the NSW Jewish Board of Deputies. The program, according to its organisers, is designed to "demonstrate the complexity of the situation in the Middle East," but such trips often serve to frame narratives in Israel's favour and shape sympathetic media coverage back home.

The cancellation of Hedges is a direct affront to press freedoms in Australia—and shows that one of the nation's elite media institutions has become more concerned with political optics and donor sensitivities when it comes to Gaza—like so many other institutions—rather than with defending the right to speak truth to power.

A MORAL WITNESS

Chris Hedges is an acclaimed war correspondent who built his reputation by reporting from the world's most brutal conflicts for well over thirty years, including from Central America, the Balkans and the Middle East/Western Asia. He was the Middle East and Balkans bureau chief for the *New York Times*, and was a member of the team that received the Pulitzer Price in 2002.

Hedges' approach to journalism is based on what he refers to as the "moral witness"—the belief that a reporter's duty is not just to relay information but to confront power and expose injustice, even at personal risk, and suggests a clear delineation between two types of war correspondents: the few who risk their lives to document the realities of war—such as the ones in Gaza—and the many who "play at war," relying on official briefings and producing narratives shaped by military and political handlers.

It's a distinction that has never been more important than in the coverage of Gaza, where "official" accounts from Israel are routinely presented as fact while the testimony of Palestinian journalists and civilians is marginalised or dismissed. By their actions, it's clear which side of this ledger the National Press Club stands on.

During his years reporting from Gaza, Hedges witnessed first-hand the destruction and terror inflicted on its population. He's seen children shot by Israeli soldiers, families buried under bombed homes and entire neighbourhoods reduced to rubble under what Israel claimed were "surgical strikes". For Hedges, the language of state-sanctioned reporting—"collateral damage," "security operations," or "being caught in crossfire"—is an example of the moral blind spot within modern journalism.

Since the Israeli assault on Gaza in late 2023, Hedges has turned his attention to the "betrayal of journalism" itself, suggesting that Israel's military campaign amounts to genocide and ethnic cleansing—now confirmed by many reputable human rights organisations—carried out with the backing of the United States and Europe and justified through a compliant global media that reproduces official lies. According to Hedges, this is not just a political failure but an ethical one—a symptom of a profession that has surrendered its moral authority to the interests of power, profit and propaganda. The action of the National Press Club is symptomatic of that.

The highest obligation for a journalist in the field of war should be to veer towards truth, not neutrality, and Hedges said that we "cannot stand by while one people is exterminated and call it balance". His address at the National Press Club was expected to explore this collapse of journalistic integrity—how the media's complicity in Gaza reflects a broader decay in Western journalism, driven by corporate consolidation, political fear, the loss of moral courage, and a failure to hold power to account.

The silencing of Hedges isn't just about the one event—it's about the crisis he has spent his career warning about: a media culture so compromised by power that it no longer tolerates those who insist on telling the inconvenient truth.

THE HYPOCRISY AT THE HEART OF THIS DECISION

This decision by the National Press Club has tarnished its credibility, as well as raising many questions about its commitment to media freedom, as it's now engaging in the kind of censorship that it has frequently challenged in the past.

In 2019, the Club hosted "Press Freedom: On the Line," a forum that was held after a spate of police raids on journalists' homes, unions and news organisations during the time of Morrison government. That event became a key part of the #YourRightToKnow campaign—a co-ordinated effort by Australian media to push back against government secrecy and defend the public's right to information. The Club's own publicity at the time offered a direct question: *When government keeps the truth from you, what are they covering up?*

THE SHADOW OVER PALESTINE

While the Club wasn't officially a part of that campaign, it was a strong supporter of the notion that journalism's core duty is to confront the powerful, not to appease them.

Six years later, it's apparent that for the Club, there are certain issues that *can* indeed be swept away. By cancelling Hedges—a lecture that was to be dedicated to the betrayal of journalists in Gaza—the Club has answered its own question about *your right to know*. The Club has aligned itself with the same forces of suppression it claims to oppose, trading moral conviction for comfort and conformity, and engaging in its own betrayal of the principles of journalism.

The Club was a signatory to the International Association of Press Clubs statement in September 2024 that condemned Israel's killing of journalists in Gaza, and called for independent investigations into the deaths of reporters, denounced attacks on hospitals and medical staff, and reaffirmed the protection of journalists as an essential part of international law. But that was just lip service: when the opportunity arose for a journalist of the calibre of Hedges to discuss these crimes from first-hand experience, the National Press Club chose silence.

Reilly has also claimed that "when the details of the address were made available, we made a decision to pursue other speakers on the matter". What exactly were those details? It's not as though Chris Hedges is an unknown journalist who just appeared out of nowhere: the National Press Club would have known exactly who they were working with. Who were the details of the address made available to? What were these deliberations? Who made the decision?

The claims of "no external pressure"—as far as we can tell—might be plausible, but what about pressure from within the National Press Club or from the other 86 journalists who have been on the Israel-sponsored "study missions" designed to shape media narratives that are favourable to the policies of Israel? How many of these are also members of the National

Press Club? Of course, a claim of "no external pressure" can always be made when compromised club members know exactly what needs to be done *internally*, when the moment arises.

These connections explain why an event that exposed media complicity in Gaza and those sailing too close to the government of Israel was deemed to be too uncomfortable to host. And, of course, who would want to be reminded of their complicity and failures to act or listening to Hedges' talk about a blood-soaked Gaza while enjoying Merimbula rock oysters, Daintree barramundi, Chantilly crème or the many other fine dining choices available for members during these addresses? It's hard to enjoy the Four Pillars gin or Drambuie—or Hawke's Legend Ale—in the after-lunch bar when reminded of the many journalists in Gaza who died in their choice to tell the truth, when the main choice Club members need to make is whether they can fork out the $165 for their annual membership, and whether it will be a valid tax deduction or not.

This incident has shown the National Press Club—supposedly a forum for fearless journalism—is just another weak symbol of timidity, a gatekeeper of acceptable speech rather than a defender of free expression. The institution that once championed the public's "right to know" now appears to be deciding what Australians are allowed to hear.

The question that now confronts Australia's media community is much bigger than one cancelled talk: if the National Press Club can't find the courage to host a veteran Pulitzer-prize winning war correspondent speaking about the killing of journalists, what remains of press freedom in a country that once prided itself on it?

***

THE PEACE MIRAGE: WILL ISRAEL FOOL THE WORLD YET AGAIN?

10 October 2025

US President Donald Trump's proclamation that this Gaza ceasefire marks "a great day for the Muslim and Arab world" is typical of his bombastic style of diplomacy: a grand announcement made to create a headline—and a last-gasp effort to gain the Nobel Peace Prize (which turned out to be unsuccessful)—rather than a genuine attempt at ending the conflict and holding Israel to account for its war crimes and acts of genocide.

Trump's plan is a one-sided act where Hamas has been handed a 20-point ultimatum, and a choice between compliance or annihilation. The agreement is based on short-term issues—the exchange of captives and hostages, limited Israeli withdrawal and the delivery of humanitarian aid—while leaving the many questions of reconstruction, future governance and sovereignty mainly unresolved.

Certainly, any agreement that results in a ceasefire has to be welcomed, but what's the cost to a just and lasting peace in the region? The deal seems to be more about the spectacle of negotiation and political convenience: the fact that Israel Prime Minister Benjamin Netanyahu so readily accepted the plan and gained approval in Knesset within days, suggests that it's not really a framework for peace—which effectively would signing his own political death warrant—but more a strategy for him to buy some time and prepare for the upcoming Israeli general elections, due before the end of October 2026.

Looking at Trump, his instincts are based around the "transaction", ego and self-promotion, and his record over two terms shows a pattern of timed announcements that maximise media exposure or opportunities for personal gain and self-promotion. His approach to the Middle East/Western Asia is more about foreign policy stunts engineered for the media, rather than serious reform—from the Abraham Accords to the impromptu recognition of Jerusalem as Israel's capital in 2017—and implementing simple solutions in a region built on historical and political complexity that requires difficult negotiations and clever diplomacy, none of which Trump has the stamina for.

This Gaza deal—and, of course, we'll have to let this latest action play out to see what the exact outcome is—might end up being another act in a long-running political performance played out by Israel and the United States over the past eight decades. Trump's preference for the spectacle, combined with Netanyahu's endless habit of scuppering agreements at whim whenever it suits him politically, suggests this ceasefire is built on self-interest rather than sincerity—a mirage that might collapse and end up continuing the occupation, just like all the other ones that have preceded it.

ANOTHER NETANYAHU GAMBIT FOR POWER AND CONTROL

For Netanyahu, the Gaza ceasefire isn't a peace accord but a *new strategy*—a quickly-agreed-to plan that allows him to recalibrate his campaign for political survival. His leadership over the decades has never been guided by goodwill or the pursuit of reconciliation, but by a relentless focus on his authority and perpetual conflict, irrespective of the cost to Israeli society—Netanyahu would sell out Israel in a heartbeat, if it could be used to save his political skin—and it's becoming more apparent that the electorate is not going to provide him another opportunity to sell them out, irrespective of when the next election is held.

Throughout this war, humanitarian aid was obstructed, ceasefires agreements were broken, and hostage negotiations delayed until the constant public demonstrations made them politically unavoidable. Every decision that Netanyahu has made over the past two years—in fact, during his entire career—has been shaped by his instinct for *preservation* rather than *principle*.

In reality, war is Netanyahu's *only* remaining instrument of governing and a leader in this situation doesn't have too much time remaining in their political career. Each escalation in Gaza and the blaming of Hamas reinforces his narrative of Israel's perpetual victimhood—a state surrounded by enemies and in constant need of his leadership. This is not sustainable. The siege mentality he cultivates legitimises repression at home and aggression abroad but the political costs of this latest war have mounted: international condemnation has intensified, the International Criminal Court is closing in on him, and Israel's once-supportive allies have had enough and their support is falling apart at the edges.

In the aftermath of this ceasefire, Netanyahu is now trying to position himself as the diplomat who ended the war and brought the hostages home, even though he did everything possible to prolong the war and soiled every offer from Hamas to return the hostages. This is the standard process for Netanyahu—continue with the circus act, use every catastrophe as a political opportunity, and somehow claim a victory, even though it's obvious that his strategies over the past two years have failed.

But Netanyahu is shallow and predictable: this is all a calculated move toward the next election—rebranding himself as a pragmatic peacemaker, while quietly maintaining the occupation of Palestine—and this could allow him to distance himself enough from the extremists in his coalition like Itamar Ben-Gvir and Bezalel Smotrich, whose maniacal and barbaric rhetoric is offensive to many foreign governments, and is increasingly alienating the Israeli public.

While we always should remain hopeful, none of this suggests a genuine move toward peace. Netanyahu's ceasefires in the past have always been tactical or non-existent: a pause to deflect criticism, absorb international and domestic pressure, and consolidate control before resuming his approach of *business as usual*. The ambiguity surrounding Gaza's postwar governance in this plan is deliberate: as long as Gaza remains broken, aid-starved, and politically fragmented, Israel can continue to exercise *de facto* control without the burdens of occupation. The reconstruction of Gaza will be delayed or undefined, Palestinian leadership will be divided, and the dependency of Palestine on their erstwhile oppressors will be entrenched, which gives Netanyahu exactly what he wants.

This is at the heart of Netanyahu's "two-option" strategy, where he gets the best of both worlds: either resume military action under the guise of security or tie up the Palestinian leadership in another endless cycle of negotiations—a modern-day extension of the Oslo "agreements", designed to keep onside with international opinion while ensuring nothing changes at all in Palestine. And in either case, Netanyahu wins: Israel retains dominance as an occupying colonialist-settler, settlements in the West Bank continue to expand, and Israel's brand of apartheid becomes further entrenched.

A DISSONANT WORLD BUT ARE THERE ANY GROUNDS FOR HOPE?

While this might seem like an overly pessimistic outlook—and why shouldn't there be a high level of pessimism after the litany of broken promises over the past eight decades—

are there any grounds on which this Gaza plan *could work?* Absolutely nothing has changed since 1948 when Israel was created on the stolen lands of Palestine—*a land without a people for a people without a land*—mainly due to the intransigence led by the United States. Could this plan succeed after all the previous failures? Why would this one be any different?

The key issue *at this point of time* is that the geopolitical world is reacting in a different way in 2025, primarily because of Israel's genocidal overreach. The moral, diplomatic and strategic force shield that protected it for decades—a combination of American immunity, European indulgence and Arab disunity—is no longer as strong as it used to be. A global change seems to be underway and, for the first time in generations, Israel's dominant narrative and *hasbara* is collapsing under the weight of its own contradictions and sheer inhumane brutality. Put simply, *Israel has gone too far.*

The devastation in Gaza—almost 70,000 civilian deaths (although according to UN Special Rapporteur on the Occupied Palestinian Territories, Francesca Albanese, the figure might be closer to 680,000), razed neighbourhoods and systematic targeting of hospitals and infrastructure—has triggered an unprecedented collapse in Israel's international credibility. The imagery of human suffering, transmitted across the world, has pierced through Israel's simplistic propaganda that no-one believes any more, and forced a moral awakening across the world, similar to how the United States war in Vietnam piqued international consciences during the 1960s.

The legal pursuit of Israel at the International Court of Justice and the ICC has stripped away the old rhetoric of "acting in self-defence," reframing Israel's actions as one of deliberate cruelty and oppression. The recognition of Palestine by France, the United Kingdom, Canada and Australia—long seen as Israel's most dependable Western allies—has marked a symbolic but profound shift within the world community, where over 150 countries now formally acknowledge Palestinian statehood, a clear sign that the era of Israeli impunity might be finally coming to an end.

This transformation isn't just confined to international institutions; it is also reshaping the domestic politics of Israel's allies. In the United States, what was once a bipartisan act of faith for Republicans and Democrats is now beginning fracturing—and we can look at the commentary of Marjorie Taylor Greene in the U.S. Congress as an example of this— while these are only small fissures at this stage, the fractures are certainly starting to get bigger.

Even within Trump's populist base, elements of the MAGA movement now view Israel as a liability, its actions morally indefensible and politically toxic—it's hard to be pro-life when Israel is killing a classroom of babies and children every single day of the week—and younger generations of Americans, exposed to unfiltered realities through social media, are rejecting the old Cold War binaries of *democracy versus terrorism*, or to use the words of George W. Bush, " you are with us, or you are with the terrorists". Across Europe, governments are having to deal with the growing public opinion that's opposed to the genocide and the ongoing sale of military equipment to Israel.

In the Arab world, the political deliberations are shifting just as dramatically. States that sought regional stability through quiet normalisation—Saudi Arabia, Egypt, Jordan, Qatar and the UAE—can't ignore the outrage that's appearing on their own streets, where they see the Gaza war not as a regional dispute but as an existential affront to their dignity. Even rival such as Turkey and Saudi Arabia are finding a common cause in the need to contain Israel's extremism and create a different regional balance to deter this expansionist behaviour. What had once been a fragmented bloc of Arab states is now forming partnerships based around the shared goal of ending the war, even if this is more about their own respective political survival than any form of altruism.

Coming into this shifting political dynamic is President Trump, not as a visionary peacemaker but as a manager of a decline, whether he likes it or not. His intervention reflects the reality that even Washington's most transactional leaders now view Israel as a burden. The Gaza war has also exposed the limits of American credibility: a superpower preaching human rights while enabling atrocities and the moral cost of complicity has begun to outweigh the strategic benefits of alliance. For the first time in decades, exhaustion—diplomatic, economic and psychological—has achieved what diplomacy couldn't: a fragile consensus that the war must end, and that some form of Palestinian sovereignty must take shape.

AFTER THE FIRE: GAZA'S STRUGGLE FOR JUSTICE

The early stages of the ceasefire—deals for prisoner exchanges, the influx of humanitarian aid and Israel's limited troop withdrawal—appears to be holding but beneath the surface, there's a long list of unanswered questions. Who will govern Gaza? Certainly not Tony Blair, that is *totally unacceptable*. What happens to Hamas—will it disarm, dissolve or reconstitute itself under another a new name? How can reconstruction proceed under the blockade that has defined Gaza's as an open-air prison for nearly two decades? Will Israel finally release its iron-gripped control over Palestinian borders and resources or just rework the occupation under a new legal entity?

The proposed roadmap—a four-phase plan resulting in a new authority, Hamas's disarmament and a theoretical pathway towards a two-state solution—all sounds familiar because we've heard it so many times before: variations of this theme have been announced, celebrated and then discarded for well over thirty years. And each variation has failed because of the same reason: Israel seeks to continue the subjugation of Palestinians rather than end it. The architecture of these plans have always been based on a denial—a denial of sovereignty, denial of justice and the denial of the right for Palestinians to resist an occupation.

Meanwhile, the displaced people of Gaza are currently walking north through the scorched remains of their cities, and this, despite all the devastation and despair, represents an act of *profound defiance*. It mirrors the cyclical tragedy of Palestinian history—from the Nakba of 1948 through the displacements of every subsequent war—and highlights the truth about Palestine: despite the attempts to erase them, Palestinians continue to return, and *will continue to return*. Their movement back to their homes—even if they are just rubble—is a moral declaration that Palestine exists, and will continue to exist, despite the genocidal intentions of Israel.

This resilience continues despite the cynicism of international diplomacy. For decades, "peace" has been a performative lip-service act, rather than something that has been genuinely pursued—conferences, accords and commitments have recycled the same hollow words of reconciliation without meaning, insisting on more negotiations instead of the pursuit of justice and support for Palestinian rights.

Genuine peace cannot emerge from this endless cycle of violence, especially if the perpetrators of the genocide—the state of Israel and Benjamin Netanyahu—escape punishment for their crimes. It will also require the dismantling of Israel's systems of apartheid, and the recognition of Palestinian nationhood as an inalienable right—not some concession to be negotiated away that wasn't even mentioned in the Trump–Netanyahu 20-point plan.

This ceasefire does present the world with a *big opportunity*—not to impose another formulaic "peace process," but to choose accountability over their collective amnesia. If the international community enforces *real consequences*—sanctions, legal action and political isolation for Israel—it might end up being the beginning of transformation for the region. If it doesn't, the ceasefire will just become a brief stop-gap measure in Netanyahu's forevers wars which, in themselves, have been one long continuum of war against Palestine which commenced in 1948, if not before.

The fate of Gaza, and of Palestine itself, doesn't depend just on American diplomacy or the restraint of Israel but depends on the global conscience forcing political leaders to listen and act, just as they did in the 1960s on Vietnam; just as they did in the 1980s to force an end to apartheid in South Africa. For the first time in decades, the illusion of Israel as the "good-guy" in the region has cracked: peace without justice for Palestine is not peace at all. The world needs to act: otherwise, it will just a brief silence in between the dropping of the bombs, before history repeats itself again.

***

JOURNALISM, FEAR AND THE PRICE OF OBEDIENCE

27 October 2025

The recent treatment of Pulitzer Prize–winning journalist Chris Hedges in Australia has exposed a deep moral and professional failure within the mainstream media. After his scheduled address at the National Press Club was cancelled a few weeks ago—a cowardly and politically compromised decision—the speech he was due to deliver was hosted at independent venues in Sydney and Melbourne, and is available online through Consortium News. Listening to that speech, it's clear why the Press Club cancelled the event—it wasn't convenient, polite or politically safe—they were going to being held to account and, generally, powerful players in Australia's mainstream media *do not* like being held to account.

In his speech, Hedges criticised Western media for its reporting on the events in Palestine, and called out the journalists who have largely ignored the genocide in Gaza, and defaulted to a recycling of Israeli government talking points instead of trying to verify the truth. His argument was simple and clear: Western journalism has abandoned its true purpose and has lost its integrity.

If we needed a reminder of this collapse of integrity in journalism, it was on full display when Hedges had a follow up appearance on the ABC's *Late Night Live*, and was interviewed by David Marr. What should have been an important exchange between two experienced journalists instead became an act of defence in protecting the narratives of power and establishment. Marr insisted that journalists have an obligation to report the "excuses" or explanations offered by the Israel Defense Forces and, in a rebuttal that should be evident to everyone, Hedges replied with a simple statement: "no... our job is to report the *truth*".

This small exchange revealed everything that's wrong with the response of mainstream journalism to Israel's war on Gaza. Rather than interrogating power, many journalists act as an echo chamber for it. Marr's suggesting that this idea of "balance" needs to repeat official propaganda—is exactly the type of moral relativism that Hedges has spent decades railing against. The ABC, once regarded as the pinnacle of independent journalism—not just in Australia but internationally—has increasingly become a platform for rehearsing the official lines of Western governments and their allies. While there might have been strong resistance in the past—such as when Prime Minister Bob Hawke pressured the ABC to give less coverage to anti-war perspectives and more prominence to the government's pro-war position during the 1991 Gulf War—today, it seems to be a case of *just tell us what you want us to say, and we'll say it*.

Meanwhile, journalists continue to die in Gaza—not as incidental casualties of war but as deliberate targets. Israel has bombed homes and offices known to house reporters and, in some cases, the bodies of journalists were found to have been mutilated, in an obvious act to stop the documentation of the genocidal actions of the Israel Defense Forces. This is like no other conflict: more journalists have been killed in Gaza than in both world wars, the Vietnam War, the wars in Yugoslavia, Iraq and Afghanistan combined, according to the Watson Institute for International and Public Affairs'

Costs of War project. In Gaza, the targeting of journalists and aid workers has become a routine hobby of the IDF, and always met with Western indifference and excuses when it happens, as demonstrated by Marr in the safety of his studio environment.

This is what Hedges was trying to expose: a moral corruption so deep that even the murder of journalists provokes barely more than bureaucratic shrugs and a few media releases from foreign ministers wanting to *show concern*. His message is a call for courage and reflection—qualities now largely absent from the institutions that once defined the Australian media, at least at the ABC.

Hedges's insistence that "our job is to report the truth" might sound like an old-fashioned or even a naïve ideal, during an age of managed narratives and ideological posturing, but it's that single statement that cuts through the evasions and reveals the crisis of journalism today: when telling the truth becomes a radically subversive act, it's not the failure of the journalist—it's the failure of the media establishment itself.

THE COLLAPSE OF CREDIBILITY

This confrontation between Hedges and Marr might not make front-page news—and certainly not within Australia's mainstream media—but it says a lot about a deeper and more corrosive problem within Australian journalism: the willingness of respected figures and institutions to protect power rather than challenge it. This is not just a professional failure, but a moral one—the kind that defines the boundaries of acceptable speech in a country that supposedly sees itself as a protector of freedom of expression.

Others in the field have faced the same pressure and chosen a different path. The journalist Antoinette Lattouf— one of the journalists who remembered that *our job is to report the truth*—was dismissed by the ABC for posting factual information about Gaza, and refused to bow to the immense intimidation from the ABC. Her career suffered temporarily, but she kept her credibility—and, in the long run, that's what matters in journalism. She's now rebuilding her platform through independent media and podcasting, proving that holding onto that integrity is critical, even if it ends up taking the journalist to a different field. Marr, by contrast, traded his credibility for favour from the establishment, and this trade has cost him far more than he realises. And once credibility is thrown away so easily, it's very difficult to get it back.

Two of the clearest guiding principles in journalism are often quoted but rarely followed. The first, from the legendary BBC interviewer Jeremy Paxman, suggested that his first preparational thought before interviewing political leaders was *why is this lying bastard lying to me?*

The second one is more readily quoted and comes from the academic Jonathan Foster: "If someone tells you it's raining and another tells you it's dry, it's not your job to quote them both—it's your job to look out the fucking window and find out which is true". Journalism doesn't need to be overly complicated, and we should be able to narrow it down to these basic credos: seek the truth, verify it, and tell it without fear.

This moral inversion—where empathy becomes heresy and truth-telling becomes a risk to one's career—has destroyed more reputations than it has saved. From journalists through to executives, many have chosen to sacrifice integrity to appease political and institutional power. As with Marr or the former ABC chair Ita Buttrose—who was the main instigator of the sacking of Lattouf from the ABC in 2023— the question lingers like a stale smell: was it worth destroying your reputation so comprehensively? Was the defence of the state of Israel and the preservation of corporate relationships associated with the Israel lobby, really worth destroying your own credibility and conscience?

Those who speak truth in times of suppression, like Hedges or Lattouf, will ultimately be remembered for their courage; those like Marr and Buttrose will be consigned to the dustbin of compromise, remembered for their fear of speaking out and holding up the white flag of surrender. This is their legacy.

THE GLOBAL SURRENDER TO ISRAEL'S NARRATIVE

This is part of a much larger pattern that we can see in many Western democracies. The same instinct to protect Israel from criticism has infected entire governments, political parties and public institutions, even when it's to their own cost. From London to Berlin, from Canberra to Washington, politicians and journalists are destroying their credibility to defend a state that's engaged in systematic violence against Palestinian people.

In the United Kingdom, the Metropolitan Police have humiliated themselves by arresting elderly peace protesters, people in wheelchairs and pensioners under vague pretexts linked to pro-Palestinian demonstrations and the proscription of Palestine Action as a terrorist organisation, and public resources are being wasted to criminalise people of conscience.

The U.K. Prime Minister Keir Starmer, recently wanted to overrule Birmingham police after they decided to ban the supporters of Israel's Maccabi Tel Aviv club from attending a football game with Aston Villa, citing public safety concerns over violence by the club's fans, as demonstrated by their violent, destructive and offensive behaviour in Amsterdam during a game against Ajax in November 2024.

Starmer immediately condemned the decision as "antisemitic" and that "no one should be stopped from watching a football game simply because of who they are"—even if the Birmingham police described the Maccabi Tel Aviv supporters as a "toxic combination of hooliganism and anger"—adding that he would do "doing everything in our power" to overturn the ban.

A few days later, Israeli police cancelled a domestic Maccabi match in Tel Aviv for the same reason: the violent behaviour of its supporters. The hypocrisy did the full circle, and the Labour government was made to look foolish: what was regarded as "antisemitic" in the U.K. was the same action taken by police in Israel. At least in this case, the calls by Starmer to do *everything in our power* calmed down: surely by now, he'd realised the stupidity of his actions but even still, we can't be too sure about that.

This willingness to sacrifice dignity and reason for the sake of political support and unison with Israel borders on the pathological, a kind of collective conditioning—like the *Manchurian Candidate* holding up the Queen of Hearts—a reflexive, panicked obedience that overrides any form of moral and political logic. Institutions that should stand for public accountability instead retreat into an absurdist clown show, protecting the Netanyahu government from even the mildest criticism. All throughout the media and within politics, public figures are throwing away their integrity— if they ever had it in the first place—ever so eager to look foolish and prostrate themselves to maintain favour with a malevolent foreign player in Israel, even if they are causing a genocide in Gaza.

These motivations are not a secret: money, influence and the racist imperial history that views Israel as the West's outpost in the Middle East/Western Asia: a friend who is doing the dirty work of the United States and other imperialist partners. But even acknowledging those obvious influences doesn't make the behaviour less disturbing. It's an abdication of moral agency on a mass scale—the surrender of conscience to propaganda. And the cancer has spread far beyond politics, culture and the media: even sport is not immune.

In Melbourne last week, the mascot "Captain Blue" was sacked by the Carlton Football Club after walking out of a Bar Mitzvah when he discovered it was raising money for Israeli soldiers. His comment—"I'm not doing this for fucking Zios"—was quickly framed as an act of antisemitism— apparently the term *Zios* is now deemed to be antisemitic and derogatory—and he was dismissed. In another case earlier this year, Fremantle Dockers captain Alex Pearce was forced into public contrition after reposting a pro-Palestine message from the Irish band Kneecap, and the usual suspects from the pro-Israel lobby came out to demand his suspension from the AFL.

In another issue, the cosmetics retailer Lush closed down its stores and website across Australia on Thursday and installed "Stop Starving Gaza" signage in its shop windows, only for shopping-centre managers at Westfield to issue a directive to cover over these signs—a simple humanitarian message that was deemed to be offensive to Israel. How have we arrived at this point in history, where the brutal, fascist and genocidal operations of the state of Israel, is so openly protected by corporate interests?

When athletes and business are punished for important moral gestures—even a sports mascot—it shows how deeply the fear and coercion from the Israel lobby has filtered through into public life. An Australian culture that once prided itself on fairness, debate, and dissent now polices and clamps down on empathy.

Australia—and every democracy that claims to value liberty—needs to stop criminalising truth and compassion. Free debate, religious equality and the right to dissent won't survive if public discourse is managed by intimidation and the worship of a foreign government, even when it's committing genocide. The silence that's being enforced today in defence of Israel's war in Gaza is not neutrality—it's outrageous *complicity*.

No-one should ever need permission to speak the truth, and it's a question of whether we want to live in a society that's governed by fear from organised power, or one that offers a space for the moral courage to speak out, no matter how uncomfortable that might be.

***

CONCLUSION

THE SEARCH FOR AN ANSWER TO THE PALESTINE QUESTION

The question of Palestine is still one of the world's deepest moral tests—it's not the only one but it is the most significant—and it's the mirror that's constantly held up to check on humanity's conscience. Since 1948, generations of Palestinians have endured dispossession, siege and exile, yet they continue to hold to the most basic of human aspirations that should be afforded to all peoples: the right to live freely in their *own* land.

The long duration of Israel's occupation has produced not only great suffering but a profound resilience—a resilience that resists the desires of the occupier to remove their presence. Every act of Palestinian resistance, whether it be a song, or a tattered flag that's been carefully placed amongst the rubble that once housed a family, is a reminder that there's the one enduring hope that military force can never remove: the hope that justice will not be denied forever. However, the world's silence—aside from the occasional glance from world leaders to show their feigned *concern*—has enabled the ongoing destruction of Gaza and the continued human rights abuses in the West Bank: they've done their best to stifle the hope of the Palestinians, and it's these leaders that we should show our full contempt and outrage for. For sure, Benjamin Netanyahu is a violent and contemptible man but there are many others around the world who have aided and abetted his actions, and they are also the ones who need to face judgement for their complicity.

The events chronicled in this book have exposed the hypocrisy of the so-called rules-based international order. When global leaders look away from the acts of deliberate starvation, mass displacement and the bombing of hospitals—*the genocide*—the structures of international law fall apart: there are no international laws if we fail to observe them. The suspension of UNRWA funding, the manipulation of Israel's "self-defence" as justification for collective punishment, and the suppression and killing of journalists who dare to report truthfully—these are not the foundations of peace; they are symptoms of complicity.

Yet despite this current despair, history suggests that no occupation lasts forever, however brutal or long in its duration, and the political systems that are built on fear and exclusion ultimately collapse under the weight of their own contradictions. The same generation that's now watching Gaza burn on their screens and mobile devices—young people across every continent, sharing stories that are unfiltered by corporate media—are rejecting the narratives that have sustained this injustice. This is a global empathy that transcends borders, and it's a cultural shift might end up being the most lasting legacy of all.

As much as they will try, the future of Palestine won't be determined by the political leaders or the generals painting with the blood of war from the comfort of Tel Aviv or Washington, but in the moral awakening of ordinary people who choose to see what is happening—and are refusing to ignore what they can see with their own eyes. Change might be slow, frustratingly uneven, and come at an immense cost, but it *will* come. This is cold comfort for the people who have suffered immensely since the occupation commenced in 1948—and the new genocide that began in 2023—but the wall between the powerful and those without power eventually crumbles and can't stand forever.

For Palestine, the path ahead is uncertain: for many years it has been promised much, but left with nothing, and the empty rhetoric and natural lies that come from the mouths of the likes of Netanyahu and Donald Trump are a continuation of those failed promises. However, the change that does needs to come, will come, eventually. It requires courage, imagination and the building of new alliances beyond the Western governments that have continuously and deliberately failed.

When the dust finally settles in Gaza—irrespective of how long that takes—what will remain will be the stubborn dignity of a people who never gave up on their right to exist and directed us towards new world structures where Palestine was no longer a *question*, but an *answer*.

***

INDEX OF PEOPLE

ALSO BY EDDY JOKOVICH + DAVID LEWIS

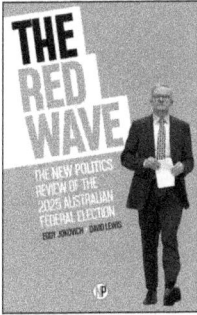

THE RED WAVE: THE NEW POLITICS REVIEW OF THE 2025 AUSTRALIAN FEDERAL ELECTION

The 2025 federal election didn't just redraw the political map: it exposed the cracks in Australia's democracy and demanded the country confront some hard truths. With Labor's historic victory, the Liberal Party's collapse, and the electorate's disillusionment reaching breaking point, *The Red Wave* captures a seismic moment in modern Australian politics. This is not just a postmortem of an election—it's a compelling narrative about the end of one political era and the uncertain birth of another. 254 pages.

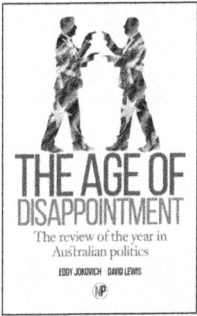

THE AGE OF DISAPPOINTMENT: THE REVIEW OF THE YEAR IN AUSTRALIAN POLITICS

From the timidity of the Labor Party and the crisis facing the Liberals, to the rise of independents and challenges within the Greens, *The Age of Disappointment* explores the shifting sands of Australian politics—the missed opportunities of the Albanese government, the cynicism of Dutton's opposition, and the public's growing disconnection from traditional power structures. Beyond Australia, the book examines the global zeitgeist reshaping Western democracies, the ramifications of Trump's re-election in the U.S. and the controversial support for Israel government, set against the backdrop of an increasingly disillusioned electorate. 404 pages.

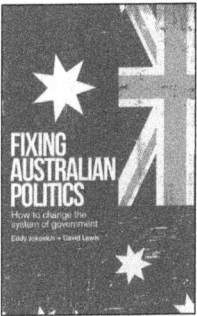

FIXING AUSTRALIAN POLITICS: HOW TO CHANGE THE SYSTEM OF GOVERNMENT

Australia's political landscape stands on the precipice of transformation. The need for reform is palpable, driven by evolving societal values, demands for greater transparency, and a push towards inclusivity. *Fixing Australian Politics: How to change the system of government* outlines a multifaceted strategy to reshape Australian politics across various fronts—electoral systems, campaign finance, governance, media, the Constitution, and diversity in representation. These reforms are critical for the rejuvenation of the nation's political framework and the restoration of public faith in the democratic process. 208 pages.

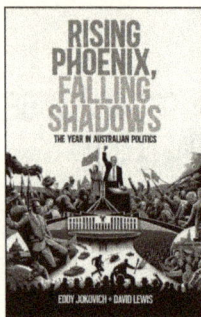

RISING PHOENIX, FALLING SHADOWS: THE YEAR IN AUSTRALIAN POLITICS

This exploration of Australia's political landscape in 2023 uncovers a year that began with high hopes, but marred by a series of unmet expectations and enduring challenges: the Voice to Parliament referendum and its subsequent defeat, the persistent housing crisis, cost of living and environmental concerns, AUKUS and Palestine—going through the intricate web of political and social dynamics that define contemporary Australia. 446 pages.

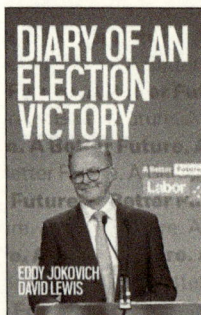

DIARY OF AN ELECTION VICTORY: LABOR'S RISE TO POWER

In early 2020 at the onset of the coronavirus pandemic, Morrison held record high electoral ratings: Albanese was told to not worry about the next election, and focus on 2025. In 2022, Labor saw an opportunity: Morrison had made promises he couldn't deliver and it unravelled quickly. This explores the key political moments of the 2022 election year, Morrison's demise, and Albanese's ascendancy and victory against the odds. 304 pages.

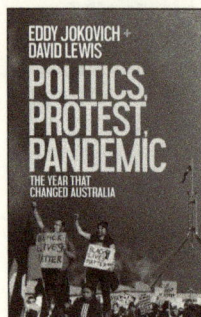

POLITICS, PROTEST, PANDEMIC: THE YEAR THAT CHANGED AUSTRALIA

2020 was one of the most dramatic years in human history, shaped by the coronavirus pandemic that influenced society in so many different ways, combining health, politics, economics, business and education into the one sphere—and that proved to be difficult for many governments around the world to manage. This is the story of the year in federal politics, one of the most dynamic years ever in Australian political history. 414 pages.

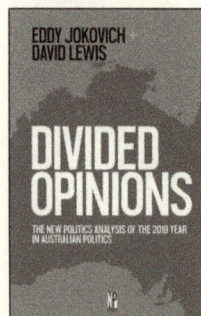

DIVIDED OPINIONS: THE ANALYSIS OF THE 2019 YEAR IN AUSTRALIAN POLITICS

As the mainstream media struggles to retain audiences and survive under new business models and shrinking revenues, independents are filling in the gaps left behind by the older mastheads. *Divided Opinions* presents the best work from the New Politics podcast published in 2019—a must-read analysis of one of the most dynamic years ever in Australian politics. 338 pages.